IF WE DON'T GET IT

ALSO BY STEFAN M. BRADLEY:

Upending the Ivory Tower:
Civil Rights, Black Power, and the Ivy League

Harlem vs. Columbia University:
Black Student Power in the Late 1960s

Alpha Phi Alpha:
A Legacy of Greatness, The Demands of Transcendence

IF WE DON'T GET IT

A People's History of Ferguson

STEFAN M. BRADLEY

NEW YORK
LONDON

© 2025 by Stefan M. Bradley
All rights reserved.

No part of this book may be reproduced, in any form, without written permission from the publisher.
Requests for permission to reproduce selections from this book should be made through our website: https://thenewpress.com/contact.

Published in the United States by The New Press, New York, 2025
Distributed by Two Rivers Distribution

ISBN 978-1-62097-905-1 (hc)
ISBN 978-1-62097-940-2 (ebook)

CIP data is available

The New Press publishes books that promote and enrich public discussion and understanding of the issues vital to our democracy and to a more equitable world. These books are made possible by the enthusiasm of our readers; the support of a committed group of donors, large and small; the collaboration of our many partners in the independent media and the not-for-profit sector; booksellers, who often hand-sell New Press books; librarians; and above all by our authors.

www.thenewpress.com

Composition by Dix Digital Prepress and Design
This book was set in Garmond Premier Pro

Printed in the United States of America

10 9 8 7 6 5 4 3 2 1

This book is respectfully dedicated to my dearly departed father, Alphonso Bradley, who spent his life fighting for the freedom and life chances of young people like those who hit the streets of Ferguson.

Michael "Mike Mike" Brown Jr., high school graduate and American citizen, changed the course of the twenty-first century when a Ferguson police officer shot him to death and allowed his body to lie in the street for four and a half hours. Brown's death reignited the modern Black Freedom Movement. *Photo:* Washington Post.

CONTENTS

FOREWORD by Jonathan Pulphus	ix
AUTHOR'S NOTE	xxi
INTRODUCTION	1
1. Red's Ribz and Racial Capitalism in Ferguson	11
2. Today *Was* a Good Day: Michael Brown Encounters Darren Wilson	19
3. Who Let the Dogs Out?: Repressive Police Action	35
4. Democracy Is in the Streets: Mothers, Thugs, and the Dispossessed	53
5. Moment or a Movement?: Youth Organizing for Freedom	67
6. Bring Toilet Paper: Police Repression and Young Professionals	89
7. Thug Life: Representation of Black Youth in Local and National Media	103
8. Whose Movement and Whose Streets?	113
9. Leadership and Money in Movement Making	127
10. Fun in the Frenzy: Comedy in the Chaos	143
11. Soldiers and Scholars: Ferguson Comes to SLU	159
12. Mizzou and Princeton Too	187

VIII CONTENTS

13. Hope Burned: No Indictment and
Destructive Rebellion 195

14. Life Goes On: Where Are They Now? 207

CONCLUSION: America, You're Welcome 241

ACKNOWLEDGMENTS 249

NOTES 253

INDEX 269

FOREWORD

Perhaps the officer thought that he could beat me into obedience so that I would stay in the house and never come back out. However, that baptism by fire just strengthened my resolve. Today, soldiers are incarcerated, some no longer able to witness the fruits of their labor. A million-dollar business is replaced with a million-dollar nonprofit. These are the results of a battle that was borne out of the frustrations and the righteous rebellion of many who had grown tired of mistreatment. The spilling of blood from a killer cop's bullet sparked a movement.

Looking back, Dr. Stefan Bradley and I could not have imagined the gravity or impact of what a tiny suburb in an almost unimportant space would do to the world. I met Dr. Bradley a year before Mike Brown was murdered and witnessed his devotion to Black people and their history. I was an eighteen-year-old freshman at Saint Louis University (SLU). He was the director of African American Studies at SLU, tasked with recruiting youth like me to take on the academic major as a degree. I took one of his introductory classes and was captivated enough by his charismatic and brilliant teaching to commit not only to the course but also to the cause.

Three months later, Ferguson officer Darren Wilson murdered Michael Brown, and the ensuing police "investigation" left his body on the ground for 4.5 hours as tensions escalated. Being a student of Dr. Bradley's, I had become accustomed to seeing him in glossed Oxford shoes, crisp dress shirts, suits, and business professional attire. When I saw him on West Florissant, the street that became the epicenter of the movement (now respectfully and affectionately designated as Mike Florissant) in August of 2014, he was dressed for a protest in Nike shoes, jogging pants, and a long-sleeved T-shirt. He was dressed and looked casual, like I did. We both knew what time it was. However, neither of us could fathom what the voices of protestors would mean to the world, as we faced police in riot gear, hysterical media (some of them hell bent on painting the protesters as villains), and military-grade vehicles complete with war-ready gear and overly rambunctious authorities.

Street activism has a way of drawing you in, and as it escalates it almost comes with a euphoric high fueled by adrenaline. Before his 1969 death, the great Black Panther Party chairman Fred Hampton, of the Chicago chapter, described revolution as being prepared to "die *high* off the people." [1]

Fighting to demand justice in the face of the unknown was righteously sensational, a way to address centuries of incessant, unceasing brutality—cultural, spiritual, and physical. Organizing to disrupt the business-as-usual culture following injustice was arousing and almost intoxicating. Committing to be a part of something larger than myself and a story longer than my time on Earth was a thrill.

Struggling for change comes with high levels of stress and fear that can lead you to myriad places. Sometimes it will crush you and make you fold, but sometimes, and in particular this time, it will manifest its energy into something powerful. I rode that wave of energy and mobilized thousands to resist. Where I am from, brothers like to say, "If you are not meant to be in the streets, you should stay on the sidewalk or the porch." You cannot have one foot in and one foot out, so you have to make a decision. I chose to be in traffic literally and figuratively. I helped shut down the shopping center the St. Louis Galleria Mall, interrupt business at the St. Louis Lambert Airport, caused traffic jams in wealthier districts like the Delmar Loop, and occupied police headquarters, such as the St. Louis Metropolitan Police Department.[1] Seeing the confusion on the faces of many in public, being warned that I would be arrested if a protest was not called off, getting honked at by angry, impatient drivers who were more concerned with a commute than with our burgeoning revolution, and receiving the middle finger from many passersby caused extreme anxiety in me. However, standing in the streets beside my comrades, successfully interrupting the flow of apathy and outwitting the police, brought unmatched fulfillment.

The first confrontation I had with police in Ferguson was the day after Michael Brown's murder. I was leaving a mentor's (Etefia Umana, chair of the board at Better Family Life) house, walking toward West Florissant Avenue, when these officers, clad in riot gear, were aggressively crowd controlling young people. I approached the group of officers and yelled out, "Leave those babies alone!" One officer with a large weapon in hand turned to me and responded, "Get the hell out of here!" I refused and proceeded to confront the officer. He held up and pointed a large weapon that mirrored an Armalite Rifle (AR) and doused me with nonlethal pepper spray. It was terribly painful. I learned, shortly after getting treatment from my partner and family, that milk was the best solution to the trauma to my body. Since that incident, I have had endless numbers of standoffs and encounters with police. When I was in the streets both in Ferguson and St. Louis, I faced mine-resistant ambush protected military vehicles (MRAPs), combat-ready dressed police, long-range acoustic device sound cannons (LRADs), detainments, flash bangs, checkpoints, rubber bullets, and more pepper spray. While intimidating and risky, it was often the excitement of the danger, putting myself on the line for the prospect of ever-elusive justice, that kept me going.

While movement participants out of Ferguson all agreed that

Mike Brown's murder was a tragedy rooted in racism, organizers against the police brutality faced many internal issues. The social movement was diverse in terms of identities, tactics, and intentions, which naturally led to conflict. Some in Ferguson designated those in the struggle as a protest family. Like any other family, there were disagreements and tension that happened and threatened what we perceived to be our end goal: justice. Pride, ego, greed, lust, and violence fractured the movement. They have plagued social movements historically. While common human flaws, these realities were an annoyance and often angered me.

When Mike Brown was murdered and the community responded, strangers were coming into contact with strangers. Although some people already knew each other, you had people from all over the city, state, region, nation, and world coming into Ferguson and St. Louis in droves with various agendas. The picture of Mike's body being laid out in the street went viral on social media, and his story made it quickly to the news. Outraged by this, people came together in the streets, rubbing elbows with many for the first time, and many of them brought their biases and unhealed trauma. At the same time, millions of dollars came through Ferguson in philanthropy, people with modest platforms gained thousands of social media followers, national to international news correspondents covered the events, celebrities and activists like rapper J. Cole, MC Hammer, Iyanla Vanzant, and actor Omari Hardwick (of the television series *Power*) visited. Ultimately, President Barack Obama had to respond and sent the U.S. attorney general, Eric Holder, to appease the nation, which saw one of its centrally located cities in perceived peril.

Even though attention and resources funneled into St. Louis, there were only a few people and organizations that got access to or were allowed to be gatekeepers to it all. This bred issues and resentment. The "founders" of the #BlackLivesMatter (#BLM; Alicia Garza, Patrisse Cullors, and Opal Tometi) hashtag and their ascension to prominence caused great tension in St. Louis and Ferguson. While the hashtag became prominent in 2013 following Trayvon Martin's murder the previous year, it did not truly get traction and become the notable slogan it is today until after Mike Brown's murder. When donors looked to support the movement in Ferguson, this group positioned itself to receive resources off of the moment, which was being bolstered by the citizens in the St. Louis area who stood up on August 9. The organization gained popularity following its association with Ferguson and benefited from the organic sweat equity of determined everyday citizens who banded together on that day to right a wrong without a thought of compensation. As a result of this, people have called for BLM accountability, which has to this day been unanswered. This upset me greatly, because before August 2014, the BLM founders did not have million-dollar real estate properties, big-ticket speaking engagements, and a wealth of resources behind their organization. Ferguson seemed to be a sweet lick to some, and an opportunity to garner fame and fortune.[2]

DeRay McKesson is probably one of the most familiar people from Ferguson, with his blue vest. He was not from St. Louis but came down to join the protests. He gained a massive following due to his articulate and concise delivery of messaging from those on the ground to news correspondents. He utilized Twitter heavily, which allowed him to further share effective perspectives on strategies from activists and disrupt myths about the movement. Another activist named Darren Seals allegedly assaulted DeRay because he believed DeRay to be no better than the BLM founders (Darren has since been tragically murdered, and we are still looking for those responsible).[3] Like the BLM founders, DeRay gained prominence from the movement and was not a local, which bred distrust for many, including Darren. While people in movement have split opinions about DeRay, I never had issues nor felt like he abused his position. I disagreed with what happened and would have attempted to intervene, de-escalate, and diffuse the situation had I been present when it happened. DeRay helped organize actions such as the Galleria Mall Shut Down and Occupy the Police. He had skin in the game and took the risks that everyone else who was genuinely committed to the movement took. He was not perfect, but I felt like he deserved better, as no one at the time was articulating the sentiments of the protesters as eloquently. That could have been because others were not asked; nonetheless, the movement needed a voice, and he filled the void.

When I hit the ground, I did not have any ties to any community organizations. I had ties with campus organizations, but they were not gatekeepers for resources around Ferguson. My protest group, Tribe X, wasn't founded until almost a month into my being out in the streets resisting for change. I was just going out there with friends and pushing the line. Groups like Organization for Black Struggle (OBS) and Missourians Organizing for Reform and Empowerment (MORE) became stewards of money based on relationships they had built with donors. They positioned themselves to be conveners of organizing spaces and facilitators of jail support. The groups also founded a community organizing seminar for youth activists. Controversy arose because there were protesters with heart and soul for the people who lost their jobs, dropped out of school, got arrested, or otherwise interrupted their lives to be engaged in the streets. Some felt that money coming into Ferguson did not belong to any one organization, but rather it belonged to "the people" or those out there on the ground protesting. Ultimately, this conflict erupted into an occupation at the office of OBS and MORE at the World Community Center (WCC) on May 14, 2015, by people in the movement who had grown tired of the control that the aforementioned organizations had on movement coffers. The name of the direct action was #CutTheCheck, and it led to a disbursement of $50,000 split between participants. I understood the sentiments of the organizers and beneficiaries in terms of calling for serious conversations around resources; however, I felt like the money should have gone toward movement actions. Incidentally, I was offered a check but thought better of it and walked away.

Beyond the different infighting, Tribe X had its own issues. Our entire organization was split following conflict surrounding the role of our mentors as stewards of Tribe X's financial and social media accounts. Again, when money is involved, disagreements on how it is allocated and who is responsible for it happen, naturally. Dhoruba Shakur, one of my fellow Tribe X members, and I were at odds about whether the Tribe X mentors should continue to occupy their role as stewards. He believed that Tribe X members should be in charge of their own resources and that the mentors had too much power. I disagreed and felt that it made sense for them to be involved with the account so that members could focus less on administrative functions and key in on protests alongside events. During the meetings where this was discussed, we had a heated exchange, which led to Dhoruba and I nearly coming to blows. As I reflect on this moment, I want to inform the reader that there is presently no animosity or issues between Dhoruba and myself, as this happened years ago. We have had conversations and come to an understanding since then, realizing that we were young and no one had ever before tried to build a movement. Admittedly, though, I was enraged in that moment.

Throughout the movement, I was with my high school sweetheart, Alisha Sonnier. She was with me at almost every protest from the beginning. When I had my first confrontation with the police the day after Mike Brown was murdered, Alisha rescued me. She was walking with me to confront the officers, but unlike me, stayed at a safe distance when the officer gave a command. Of course, I did not and crossed the line, which ended up being a theme between her and me throughout our actions. At the time, I thought she took risks but always had a limit. I, on the other hand, acted as if I was a No Limit Soldier. Once I got pepper sprayed, she carried me back to Etefia Umana's house and nursed me back to health with the assistance of my mom. We, alongside other brothers and mentors, were co-founders of Tribe X and organized many direct actions.

I was not perfect; I was eighteen. I fell prey to temptations in the movement and had a brief dalliance with a sister in the struggle, which naturally fractured my relationship. I, of course, did not do it with the intention of hurting Alisha, but because I was selfish and let my carnal desires lead me astray. The other sister had similar things going for her that my partner had: beauty, love for her people, intelligence, and drive. I was a child and did not know how to maturely articulate my desires and transparently keep it one hundred. This one decision erased days of time spent protesting, months of dedicated organizing, and years of building together. Tribe X was almost destroyed by this one lapse in judgment. I share this personal detail not as a plea for sympathy or for

Tribe X founders Jonathan Pulphus (with bullhorn) and Alisha Sonnier (with fist raised) lead protesters in a chant. Young leader Damon (formerly Diamond) Latchinson is marching behind them with a cell phone in hand. *Photo: David Carlson,* St. Louis Post Dispatch

FOREWORD XVII

catharsis. I made the mistake when I was a teenager and I have since matured. I share this to warn other young activists of the importance of being honest and truthful with your partner and comrades. Temptation, in all its forms, abounds in movements. I encourage young activists to take their time and not make the mistakes that I made.

By the time Saint Louis University (SLU) responded to the crisis, I had been in the streets for weeks while navigating the early semester of classes. I had a load of 18 credit hours, or 6 classes, which is the maximum amount of allowed courses for a full-time student. SLU is a Jesuit institution and has a tagline of "Men and Women for Others," or "Magis," which means to do more for God. Yet, the university was largely mute on the suffering and military occupation that was happening to the men and women in Ferguson, which was only ten miles from the campus. The silence pained me greatly. When SLU decided to respond, it hosted a vigil praying for peace. University officials did not call out police brutality, plead for justice, or seek accountability for the racist police attack. It raised my ire because after the police had killed one young Black man in Ferguson and another in the Shaw neighborhood of St. Louis, after my peers and I had gone to war each night for human decency, we were long past thoughts and prayers. This enraged me because, as a Jesuit institution, the university's position did not hold true to its professed Jesuit principles.

One night, I got a call from Talal Ahmad, a fellow Tribe X member, who had long voiced his dissatisfaction with the higher-education institution's response. He explained in a heavy breath, "If we are going to do that thing with SLU, we gon' have to make it happen now." I told him I agreed and was ready for whatever. I was working a shift at SLU's Pius XII library but was ready to leave whenever. Dhoruba Shakur ended up calling me shortly after and said, "Be ready, we are coming." I called all the SLU Black students and allies I knew that had sentiments about Mike and Ferguson. I asked them to stand at all four entrances of the university campus because I didn't know which side the march was coming in from. I asked to be excused from my job, and, thankfully, my supervisor was supportive. When I learned where the march was coming from, I ran to West Pine and Grand on campus. There was a sea with thousands of people chanting, "No justice, no peace!" and "If we don't get it, shut it down!" By the time they arrived where I was standing, the campus security, the Department of Public Safety (DPS), had assembled to block the protestors from entering campus. Dhoruba was helping lead the march with Alisha, other Tribe X members, and movement leaders (like Amir Brandy of the Peacekeepers). DPS yelled, "Y'all have to move on, students are here studying!" Dhoruba handed me the megaphone, and I yelled, "I'm a student, I have my ID and a lot of guests to accompany me!" Other students in the march, including Alisha and I, lifted their ID cards and motioned forward. The DPS officers looked puzzled and backed up, eventually allowing thousands into the campus. I led the marchers around the campus clocktower on Spring and West Pine, which is a central place on campus. This night began what came to be known as "#OccupySLU."

A lot of people think the protests were mainly during the first few months after Mike's murder, but they kept going well into a year and beyond. Every year while I was at SLU, I was doing something tied to Ferguson. If it wasn't a protest, it was an event. I had no off button and was ready for anything, whenever. This came with benefits in terms of my being able to advocate, but my undying devotion to this movement drained my health. I remember our Monday mourning actions.[4] We visited the homes of politicians and police chiefs early Monday morning making demands around policing and accountability. I typically worked a night shift at the library on Sunday, got my homework done, showered, woke up at 5–6 a.m. to make it to the protest, returned to campus for a full day of classes, participated in student meetings, led the campus Black student organization, ate, found time for myself, went back to work, and dove back into equally busy days. That was an average day, and I did not take my foot off the pedal.

For pleasure, I began partaking in drugs and alcohol, but it also became an escape. I attended an SLU student event about health and a community organization representative explained the consequences of smoking cigarettes. I disclosed that I just began, and she said I needed to stop. I explained that I would stop whenever, and that it was not a big deal. She looked me dead in the eye and said, "No, you won't." Sadly, her prediction holds true to this day. When dealing with the stress of social movements, being knee deep in it, I regularly navigated heightened emotions of anger, fear, anxiety, and sadness. The dependency was a coping mechanism, a way to release the frustrations, as well as the mental and spiritual trauma I went through when I was not in front of a rally. Putting down the megaphone, I'd pick up a cigarette, hookah hose, or a bottle. The relief from an American Spirit, comfort from a Blueberry tobacco tube from a pipe, and solace from Seagram's liquor was an escape from worries of the risk of arrest from police, expulsion from university officials, termination of employment, and death threats for my activism. To unplug from the danger, I fell in love with distractions from reality.

As I endured trauma and learned self-care tips after interventions from health experts, allies, and family, I got better control of my health. I stopped being hard on myself and began protecting my peace. The possibility of having a legal record as an aspiring attorney frightened me, being permanently removed from the academy alarmed me, and the statements of intimidation intended to produce harm to my person startled me. I worked to deepen my spirituality, took a pause from traditional social movement activities, engaged in therapy, and got to an important place of healing. This helped me refocus myself and understand that the social movement work tied to Ferguson and beyond is going to be there (and has been there). Making sure *I* was going to be here was of paramount importance.

Today, I proudly serve as a director of grant initiatives for a local group. The organization I work for provides grants to nonprofits aimed at addressing intergenerational poverty and trauma in disadvantaged areas. I manage a portfolio worth $1.5 million, ensuring compliance with contracts, reporting, and evaluation. Community organizations that are served by my job include several that have been impacted by the Ferguson Uprising. It is a privilege serving the organization and learning how to deepen my development and administrative capacity in service to our community and as a seasoned advocate at all times.

When Dr. Bradley and I stood side by side with other young people on West Florissant in August 2014, I didn't know that I would still be writing and talking about Ferguson years later. I had no idea that my comrades, like Joshua Williams, would still be locked up. I did not know leaders like Darren Seals would be murdered. While there have indeed been tragedies and disappointments, there has also been transformation. I had no clue that a tiny suburb in the middle of nowhere would touch the world as it did. In the face of death, dread, and despair, the stand that we took against police brutality in the name of Mike Brown was not swept under the rug. As the state tried to hush and suppress our voices, we stood tall and yelled until our lungs gasped for air so the world could hear: "IF WE DON'T GET IT, SHUT IT DOWN!"

Jonathan Pulphus, St. Louis, Missouri

AUTHOR'S NOTE

I have invested nearly everything I have into Black youth. More than sterile scholarship or subjects for teaching, I approach them with respect and relationship in mind. I respect and trust their ideas, instincts, innocence, and even their ignorance. I believe them, but more than that believe in them. I have never been so thick as to think that merely teaching them history and Black studies was my most important function. Caring for them as humans and cultivating them as leaders of this nation and world has always been the ultimate goal and my biggest flex.

I try to relate to them on most levels, but I keep very clear boundaries in that we cannot be friends. I do not drink or smoke or gossip about other young people or professionals with my students. I do, however, laugh with them and at them as I listen to their plans. I let them be angry and feel rage. I help them think through resolutions. Whether they are incarcerated or in medical school, I expect greatness from them. Anyone who knows me understands that I do not play about the young people for whom I care. Without hyperbole, I will fight, kill, and die for them. I have risked, and will continue to risk, it all for them. Everyone in my family feels the same about young people.

In the years leading to the Ferguson Uprising, I spent my time in hospitals visiting young people who nearly died from disease or suicide attempts. I honored those who succumbed to death. I

AUTHOR'S NOTE

bailed young people out of jail (before and during the Uprising) and wrote to them while they were inside, putting money on their books and sending them literature. I testified for them and acted as a character reference when they got in trouble, and I threw parties for them when they achieved victories. When they had mental breakdowns about coming out to their parents or the stresses that came along with not knowing how to "do" college or life in general, they came to stay in my home with my family until they found peace. When they were hungry, my family fed them. I advised their organizations, went to their games, threatened to fight racists with them, cried with them, cussed them out (if necessary), and even tried one or two of their dances to great laughter. I have traveled with them, paid for them to study abroad, and fronted them tuition money or other funds to survive. I knew their families and dreams.

Regularly, I spent my good time, energy, and money on them, knowing that my investment in them would pay off for the world. That sometimes puts me in a tough place professionally because I have always taken the stance that I will never love an institution more than I do Black youth. Because of that I have had to leave a job, but I have never left behind my conscience. Young people know that about me, and they respect and care for me mutually. Being in community with Black youth is not an exercise for me but rather a way of life.

For years, I have been quite timid and reluctant to write a book on the Ferguson Uprising because I did not want to give the impression that I was taking financial advantage of the tragedy that occurred on August 9, 2014, and afterward. I am a scholar and historian of modern African American history, social movements, and higher education. My life's work in the academy has focused on the role of Black youth who used their power to advance goals for freedom. I have attempted to move young Black people from the margins of American history to the center of the narrative as it concerns democracy and progress toward freedom. I have been blessed to publish my written work and speak widely with respect to my findings. Further, I taught and mentored thousands of students about the nuances of the Black Freedom Movement. I am a devoted educator.

With that in mind, I take seriously what Hands Up United co-founder and courageous Ferguson community organizer Tory Russell wrote in a 2019 article for *Essence* magazine: "The clout chasers are all but gone now. Most have bolted for major liberally funded social justice cities or to white institutions to be on the other side of case studies."[1] I am proud of the fact that I spent countless hours, energy, and resources on the movement over the years. It never occurred to me that I was garnering clout from the movement, especially in light of the contentious conversations I have had in my place of work, but I can sympathize with how it must look to those who remain in Ferguson, organizing for justice.

Russell, who came from a family of civil rights activists, added,

Hands Up United co-founder Tory Russell (in black T-shirt and medallion) addresses a crowd of St. Louis activists and Ferguson community residents from all walks of life. Some eventually represented the state in elected office. *Photo: Wiley Price/ St. Louis American.*

"Our so-called movement brothers, sisters, and allies were building their platforms on our backs and redirecting resources to their pockets." Reading the article stung, as I had left St. Louis in 2017 for a better job opportunity at a "white institution" in California and then moved again in 2021 when another "white institution" in a "social justice" town recruited me. I was intentional about making my students, colleagues, and new communities aware of the part that Ferguson Uprising activists and organizers like Russell played in catalyzing democracy on the ground level.

Five years after Brown's death, Russell made the prediction that "the sheer laziness of some of these so-called journalists will equally be to blame when future generations are confused and lacking true historical knowledge about what really happened in and to Ferguson."[2] Furthermore, he lamented, "the word Ferguson in a panel discussion title or in a headline was a sure fire way to gain viewership, sure, but it was rarely from our perspective." The vantage point of those in the vanguard of change is essential to achieving a more accurate narrative of the Black Freedom Movement.

Taking to heart author Chinua Achebe's admonishment, "Until the lions have their own historians, the history of the hunt will always glorify the hunter," it is time to give the lions their glory.[3] By shying away from using my professional skills to contribute to the narrative of the movement, I realize I have been doing a disservice to history. I may not be the best scholar or even a real activist by many standards, but I have seen the lions in action; they were pure, fierce, and bold. At this, the ten-year anniversary of the Uprising, I feel a duty to publicly feature the role of young Black people, who moved beyond apathy to shut down public thoroughfares, businesses, councils, and private institutions in search of justice. They were imperfect leaders with notable flaws. After all, they were healing from their own histories and traumas. Still, they chose to trust each other to create community, which is a primary component of justice work.

AUTHOR'S NOTE

In preparation for this book, I read an August 23, 2014, tweet by St. Louis rapper and Hands Up United co-founder Kareem "Tef Poe" Jackson. He discussed his decision to join (and lead) the movement: "For me to spend as much time as I do rapping about revolution and not contribute to being on the ground w/ the ppl would be a travesty." I am no rapper, but I recognize bars when I see them. This book's purpose is to recenter attention on the place and people that created the greatest cultural shift in the new millennium. They are the inspiration for *If We Don't Get It*.

To be sure, there would have been no "racial reckoning," no Donald Trump or Joe Biden presidency, no Kamala Harris presidential campaign, no Black Lives Matter notoriety, or surge in jobs related to diversity, equity, and inclusion (DEI) if it were not for the nameless and unknown rebels of Ferguson. It started with a few Black mothers and has morphed into millions of people protesting in streets around the world.

I have been teaching about the Black Freedom Movement for more than two decades. One of the hardest things for me to explain to students, however, is how the fires of the movement were stoked in specific cities and towns, without which the flames would never have spread. Places like Montgomery, Birmingham, and Lowndes County, Alabama, had not been hotbeds of activism before the civil rights movement. When driving through and around them, it is not easy for an outsider to envision the chaos that is represented in the history books. Fifty years from now, it may be difficult for people to understand how the sleepy city of Ferguson, Missouri, became "Ground Zero" of the new-millennium Black Freedom Movement. Other than being the venue of what historian Peniel Joseph calls the Third Reconstruction, Ferguson, like many suburbs, is largely unexciting.

I can readily admit that I am not particularly courageous or brave. Well, if courage involves telling the truth about American history, then perhaps I am. If, however, courage involves putting my life in peril, then in most cases, I avoid that at all costs. To say that I was a significant participant in the movement would be untrue. I did, however, bear witness to the most influential young people in America as they fearlessly engaged in a seemingly unwinnable war against poverty, police abuse, racism, and sexism. Some went to prison, others went to law school, and some became artists. Many have kept the ethos of the movement and will readily state: "Mike Brown Forever." All of them—the nonprofit leaders, politicians, scholars, and construction workers—deserve their rightful place in history as freedom fighters, for their roles in organizations like the Lost Voices, Hands Up United, Millennial Activists United (MAU), Organization for Black Struggle (OBS), Tribe X, and Black Student Alliance, among others. Or, they were confidently independent of any particular group but deeply devoted to getting justice for Mike Brown and Black St. Louisans in general. The purpose of this book is to tell the story of the Uprising using their words and from their perspective. This is a draft of history that seeks not to whitewash its most important participants.

In 2014, I was a life member of old-guard civil rights and social organizations like the National Association for the Advancement of Colored People (NAACP) and Alpha Phi Alpha Fraternity, Inc. Locally, I was a supporter of Urban League St. Louis and Organization of Black Struggle (OBS) events. I helped register voters, mentored youth in the community, and shared knowledge as widely as possible throughout the nation. I wrote notes or opinion pieces to politicians or officials when I thought something was unfair or unjust. I made it my business, however, to avoid confrontation with police my entire life because I had seen firsthand what they could do. By avoiding confrontation, I mean to say in the nearly thirty times I have been pulled over or "contacted" by the police, I tried not to piss them off—even when I felt humiliated. I was fortunate to have only received a few citations and nothing like what I have seen happen to others. Even though I abide by most laws and pay my

AUTHOR'S NOTE   XXVII

share of taxes, if pressed to say it, I can admit that I was afraid of the police. That was until August 2014.

I have always taken leadership seriously. In 2013, I was appointed director of the Black Studies program at Saint Louis University. In my scholarship, I wrote about the arrival of Black Studies as a discipline and the righteous scholar-activists who facilitated its birth. Students and faculty members in the 1960s risked it all for education. They fought, sometimes physically, against ideologues like then California governor Ronald Reagan and brutal law enforcement just to learn and teach about Black people in a systemic way. They allied themselves with street organizers, who wanted the systems to work for the people in the working class and low-income Black communities. When I took the position, I believed in that model; I thought that Black Studies should be linked to the people who could never hope to enroll in a private, predominantly white university. The Uprising demanded that I convert that theory into praxis.

IF WE DON'T GET IT

IF WE DON'T GET IT

INTRODUCTION

"People don't respect love; people don't respect kindness. People say they do, but they really don't. People respect fear. Up until America was scared, it wasn't no problem."[1]

—*Darren Seals*

In August 2014, a major point of contention for protesters and concerned citizens alike was the identity of Michael Brown's killer. It is vitally important to note that at the time of his death Brown had done nothing more than allegedly steal from a store and not follow police instructions. Media had portrayed him as a viable threat, but there was only one person in the altercation that had a firearm and used it to kill. If one only followed the mainstream news, one would have been satisfied knowing the threat—meaning the young Black male—had been neutralized. People in the Canfield Green apartment complex and similar complexes throughout the nation viewed the threat quite differently. The chasm in perspectives was the basis of mistrust. Ferguson police officials, for the safety of the officer, had withheld his name. That was maddening to Brown's family and peers, who only wanted answers to basic questions. Few in the community could understand why an unarmed young man could be shot dead by an officer wearing a bulletproof vest and who had a car, as well as access to several nonlethal weapons. The least they could learn, argued most protesters, was the killer's name.

On August 15, 2014, the Ferguson police held a presser. Chief Tom Jackson, red faced and white haired, appeared on camera in front of several Ferguson city police officers, who happened to be white and Black (that was quite a feat, as only a few of the fifty-four officers on the force were Black). Nervously, he apologized for being late and explained that he had been working hard to meet the many "sunshine requests," which were inquiries into the public record that citizens can make of government officials.[2] Early in the announcement, it seemed Jackson was in over his head. In trying to explain that he was making information available, he said: "I have made contact with someone who is in contact with Officer Brown's family."

Jackson, presumably, misspoke, but the slip set the stage for the remainder of the announcement. As he discussed the "strong-arm robbery" that took place at the Ferguson Market, so many of us felt the anxiety rising. Jackson lost his place when reading and had to pause before explaining that "the officer" met up with Brown on Canfield Drive at 12:01 p.m. By 12:04 p.m., the young high school graduate was bleeding out in the street. The chief paused the recounting of the events to let everyone know that he had plenty of packets with this information to pass out to whoever may want it. Then, almost nonchalantly, he stated: "The officer that was involved in the shooting was Darren Wilson." My breath caught. Even though I had never met Brown or Wilson, those two figures had sieged my waking thoughts for a week. Jackson made sure to share that Wilson had never seen disciplinary action in the six years he had been on the force. Those in the crowd that had amassed could not ask questions, as the chief explained he was giving them time to digest the information and that he would be taking questions at an event later in the day.

At the next event, Jackson brought more "information." Before answering questions, he wanted to show video footage of an altercation at the Ferguson Market that took place before Wilson shot six bullets into Brown.[3] The soundless recording revealed Brown seemingly in a confrontation with someone behind the counter before Brown grabbed a box of cigarillos and made for the door. At the door, he was confronted by a man whom Brown pushed aside as he exited the store. The recording did not show Brown paying for the cigarillos. In the previous presser, Chief Jackson had indicated that Brown had allegedly committed a strong-arm robbery. This video, viewers were to believe, was the proof. Jackson's choice to reveal the video just then was infuriating to many, including myself.

The timing of the exhibit was curious and only thinly veiled. Hours before, Jackson had stated the killer's name and professed his officer's clean record. As Jackson spoke at the first event, officers had handed out packets containing a picture of Wilson looking sharp in his dress uniform. Later that day, the juxtaposition of Wilson, the faultless policeman, next to Brown, the alleged strong-arm robber, could not have been any clearer.

The legal concept of "innocent until proven guilty" has, historically, not applied to Black people and especially young Black men. It did not apply to the Scottsboro Boys of the 1930s, the Central Park Five of the 1990s, Trayvon Martin in 2012, or Mike Brown in 2014. By divulging Wilson's name and showing the video on the same day, the Ferguson police attempted to highlight the criminality of the young citizen. This was a dangerous play because it appeared that the Ferguson police were justifying killing an 18-year-old American for stealing. If that were the case, then the nation's democracy was unquestionably broken, as it is not the place of the police to punish any citizen accused of a crime, only to detain them so that a court of law can adjudicate the matter. With respect to Black youth and crime, fear is always a factor for wider America. The idea that if Black crime is left unchecked it will eventually invade white communities was powerful enough for many to justify Brown's death.

Reporters who viewed the video evidence asked reasonable questions. "Why release the video now. . . . what's the explanation for the timing?"[4] a reporter queried. The chief, who had behaved quite nervously in the previous presser, now threw his arms open as if he were frustrated and annoyed, replying: "Because you asked for it!" Jackson, who had presented himself as unassuming and in search of truth, knew what he was doing. Reporters homed in on the chief's rationale. One asked if Wilson was responding to or knew of a strong-arm robbery call. Jackson, who had debriefed Wilson, said, "No, he didn't." Then why did Wilson have any contact with Brown, the reporters followed up: "Because they [Brown and his friend Dorian Johnson] were walking down the middle of the street blocking traffic." And, so it was. Another young Black man's death was precipitated by a traffic issue. In America, that scenario was ubiquitous.

Anger gripped many Black viewers because they understood what was going to happen next. They knew all too well that some of the people with whom they worked or associated would assign Brown's death as comeuppance for his alleged theft. The fact that the policeman did not know about Brown's alleged actions would not matter to those who intended to "back the blue." Black people also knew that victimhood only worked for them if one's character and behavior were spotless, like those of Rosa Parks. Of course, many Black people also understood that, in 1955, a fifteen-year-old Black girl in Montgomery, Claudette Colvin, refused to budge from her seat in the same way Parks had, but Colvin's case did not go forward because she became pregnant, dashing the claim of unassailable character and behavior.

Black people knew defending a young man who potentially committed a crime created an opportunity for non-Black people to claim that Black people condoned wrongdoing and a lawless society. The victim, in this case, was not "respectable." Perhaps most of all, anger arose within many Black viewers because this case would once again confirm that, in America, there was nothing a white police officer (or in the case of George Zimmerman, wannabe police officer) could do that was wrong when it came to the way they handled young Black people.

"The selective release of sensitive information that we have seen in this case so far is troubling to me," said the nation's first Black attorney general, Eric Holder, on August 18, 2014.[5] The previous week, community representatives, including myself, had been on a call with Senior Advisor to the President Valerie Jarrett, who, along with Holder, emphasized just how much the president wanted the Uprising quelled. They referred to an oncoming investigation. After all, a full-blown racial uprising was occurring on the watch of the first Black U.S. president. President Barack Obama, speaking about Ferguson, discussed racism and militarized policing broadly. Attorney General Holder was more specific in his opinions about law enforcement in Ferguson. "No matter how others pursue their own separate inquiries, the Justice Department is resolved to preserve the integrity of its investigation," he said.

Brown's last stand sparked a democracy movement throughout the country—in places like Memphis, Baltimore, New York, Dallas, and Minneapolis, and many others. More than the Justice Department or police precinct, young Black people in St. Louis and Ferguson rescued American democracy, and it scared the nation. Their agitation on behalf of eighteen-year-old Mike Brown, who fatally resisted an overbearing white police officer, brought the attention of millions of people to a sleepy suburb. The bold action of primarily Black demonstrators provoked Americans to seek answers to three fundamental questions: what is the precise purpose of policing; who will protect Black youth; and who is eligible for citizenship? In challenging the U.S. police state, young democrats called on people of good conscience to see the overreach of a militarized police force. As they pursued progress, the activists indirectly provoked a counter-protest movement, grounded in astroturf, known as Blue Lives Matter.[6]

When young Black people in Ferguson found that law enforcement seemed more interested in protecting property and capital than them, they and their peers elsewhere moved to protect themselves. They knew their intrinsic value as humans, even when they were not receiving those messages from larger society. Although they felt justified in destroying the systems that had neglected and abused them, Black youth, as citizens, influenced politics at every level. In that way, they fortified American democracy by making law enforcement recognize their constitutional rights.

In addition to the mobilizing and organizing that occurred on the streets of urban America, the youth-led Ferguson Uprising catalyzed a cultural moment that featured films like *The Hate U Give, Selma,* and *Birth of a Nation,* and the television series *Black-ish,* all of which helped to trigger a broader awakening around race and rights in America. Then, unquestionably, Ferguson activists revolutionized social media with their employment of Twitter, Facebook, and Instagram. With those platforms, they attempted to control a narrative about Black youth that had always been commandeered by those who were neither Black nor young. This brought social media to new heights.

Black Lives Matter as a phrase and campaign existed before the Ferguson Uprising, but it did not have the media notoriety that it gained in Ferguson in 2014–2015. The young people in eastern Missouri, protesting the brutal death of Mike Brown, breathed life into what is now an internationally recognizable movement. There was a distinction between local Ferguson and Black Lives Matter ideologies, tactics, and strategies that this book explores, offering depth and nuance to conventional understandings of the complicated roots of what has since become the largest mass movement for racial justice in history.

If We Don't Get It asserts that it would be a great mistake to believe that protest and activism were the only outcomes of the Ferguson Uprising. Young leaders took to heart the civics lessons that the municipal, state, and federal governments imposed on them with legislation and police enforcement. To be heard, they initiated a journey from protest to politics and eventually to policy making.

Labor organizer and activist Rasheen Aldridge marches to remind the world of his humanity and that of Mike Brown Jr. *Photo: Wiley Price*/St. Louis American

They achieved victories in the form of federal Justice Department investigations and sanctions on the Ferguson and St. Louis Police departments, bail and fine reforms, amnesty days regarding warrants, and revision of police protocols concerning mass gatherings. In the long run, they won victories at the polls as well, as young leaders like Alisha Sonnier, Rasheen Aldridge Jr., Michael Butler, and John Muhammad Jr. were elected or appointed to office in the wake of the Uprising.

The 2014–2015 Ferguson Uprising revealed the resounding effects of American racial capitalism. Black people in Ferguson, in St. Louis, and nationally faced over-policing, housing insecurity, and underperforming schools. The most vulnerable among them were young people, whom police targeted with traffic violations and warrants in North County municipalities, who had to attend unaccredited schools, and who had to fight for recognition as citizens deserving of Constitutional rights. These same young people, including college students and those whom America had written off as "thugs," reacted rationally to their circumstances on August 9, 2014, when officer Darren Wilson killed unarmed Michael Brown: they took to the streets, exclaiming: "IF WE DON'T GET IT, SHUT IT DOWN!" They meant nothing less than to block the entire legal system and town operations until they received justice.

Their message still resonates today.

In August 2024, the nation observed the tenth anniversary of the tragic shooting death of Mike Brown and the ensuing Ferguson Uprising. The time is right for those young people who organized, strategized, and mobilized in Ferguson to take their place in history: by bringing the fight to the Ferguson police station and the St. Louis County justice center, the midwestern agitators resembled the youth who had died to deliver the vote to Black southerners in the mid-1960s, those who squared off against tanks during the rebellions of the long, hot summers of the late 1960s, and those who became foot soldiers of democracy domestically and abroad. It is essential that readers today appreciate their efforts in proper historical perspective.

These young leaders picked up the legacy of Percy Green, who in 1964 chained himself to the skeleton of the St. Louis Arch to expose the lack of Black labor. They were in the lineage of movement stalwart Ivory Perry, who shut down a highway using his "stall-in" technique to protest police brutality. And the young Democrats traveled the roads paved by leaders like Jamala Rogers, who founded the Coalition Against Police Crimes & Repression (CAPCR St. Louis). Because it has only been ten years since Brown was taken from his parents, *If We Don't Get It* is not a history *per se* but rather a reframing of the contemporary narrative to center Black youth, the heroes and sheroes of the American tale. The Black youth of St. Louis—city and county—used protest to remind the nation and world that they, too, were citizens and that they, too, deserved freedom rights. *If We Don't Get It: A People's History of Ferguson* celebrates their story.

1.

RED'S RIBZ AND RACIAL CAPITALISM IN FERGUSON

St. Louis's North County had great perks. The homes were often spacious, with plentiful yards and attached garages. In the minds of some city dwellers, it was a whole different St. Louis. Charli Cooksey, the founder and executive director of We Power and a movement leader, grew up near Fairground Park in the urban environs of St. Louis city but attended Lutheran North High School near Ferguson. She perceived North County "as the area that middle class Black families lived who didn't want to live in the hood."[1]

That included Ferguson. Ferguson was the destination for those who participated in St. Louis's version of Black flight, the phenomenon of upwardly mobile Black people leaving the city to go to spaces where they saw more opportunities for themselves. That often required enduring the pains of desegregation, but to the families that persevered, it was worth it. Cooksey, who cherished her city experience, said that, growing up, she went to the county for school and to shop and "that's it."

Joshua Jones grew up in what he called a nice part of Ferguson, not too far from the Norwood Hills Country Club, which is about five minutes by car from where Darren Wilson killed Michael Brown.[2] Jones remembers having a diverse set of friends growing up and enjoyed playing sports in the area. His family was part of the Black middle class and was well known for its work in the clergy. Jones experienced a level of privilege that Mike Brown unfortunately did not. Where Brown graduated unaccredited Normandy High School, Jones graduated Lutheran North, a parochial school. Cooksey, who was an alumna, said that, unlike some public schools in North County, one had to know how to find Lutheran North, which was not far from the country club. Life there was very different than it was in North St. Louis city, but it afforded her much-needed exposure to resources. Along those lines, there is a running joke in St. Louis that goes: "You can get a really good education in St. Louis—as long as you pay for it!" That meant private school got one much farther in the minds of many local residents.

Clifton Kinnie was another North County resident who attended Lutheran North High School in 2014. Kinnie's mother had worked indefatigably to ensure he had the best educational opportunity possible, and the private Christian school was it. Unfortunately, Kinnie's mother succumbed to cancer in July of 2014. Despite the grief he bore from his mother's passing, Kinnie enjoyed school, at least until Mike Brown's death revealed elements he had not before recognized. Kinnie was a year younger than Brown.

Although Kinnie, Cooksey, and Jones had different educational experiences than Brown, that did not mean that Brown did not enjoy his time at Normandy High School. One teacher, Mama Lisa Gage, fondly recalled working with Brown, whom she found to be a dedicated student. She said, "For a two-week period in June, I spent a short but sweet moment in time with Michael Brown."[3] The young man needed some assistance completing his math requirements, and Gage, like so many committed educators, was there to help. Upon first meeting Brown, the mathematician remembered, two things stuck out about him: his "physique" and his "smile"; both were impressive. Gage told a beautiful story of a student with booksack straps around his shoulders, ready to learn by using a computer application. Brown, she said, was proficient with the technology and took his work seriously, bringing it home at night and returning it dutifully in the morning.

Importantly, Gage noted that Brown responded well to constructive criticism. "Do you think you could fix this for me and bring it in tomorrow?" she asked him. According to the tutor, "He never resisted or questioned huffily why he had to do this."[4] This is a crucial observation, as Brown responded well to authority figures whom he knew had his best interest at heart and who showed care for him. He did not resist, because it was apparent that Mama Gage was invested in his well-being and that she respected him. Mama Gage had much to teach.

In addition to the homes and private educational institutions, there were other nice amenities in the North County. For instance, there were great places to eat. At one point, there was a Sweetie Pie's soul food restaurant in Ferguson that my family patronized. There was also Red's Ribz, which had the most delectable rib tips. U.S. representative Cori Bush, who grew up very near Ferguson, concurred and was shocked that Ferguson was the location of protests because it was a relatively quiet place. She mentioned that it was home to "many [of the] businesses I patronized," which included "the salon where I got my hair done, the shop where I got my nails done, the restaurant where I got my barbecue, and another where I got my soul food."[5] Unfortunately, neither Red's nor Sweetie Pie's currently exists, but they were staples in Ferguson and North County. Besides going to enjoy the food, I was in Ferguson only a few times more. I visited a youth program that a community member and radio personality, Derrick "D-Rob" Robinson, helped operate. My work there eventually came in handy during the Uprising.

Racial Capitalism in the County

Police, for many working-class and poor Black youth in Ferguson, did not represent protection but rather a threat to freedom. That included the freedom to operate motor vehicles without fear of stops or imprisonment, and it also meant losing family members to what some Black youth believed were invaders, snatching the bodies of loved ones whenever law enforcement appeared. As journalists like Wes Lowery, who was arrested at a McDonald's during the early days of the Uprising (despite displaying his press credentials), quickly learned during the Uprising, the relationship between law enforcement and Black Ferguson residents was intensely strained because of structural inequities and racism.

Driving to Ferguson from the city and elsewhere required a certain kind of patience because there were always highway patrol officers on Interstate 270, Interstate 170, and Interstate 70 clocking drivers and issuing speeding tickets. Once off the freeway or when approaching Ferguson from the surface streets, one had to go through so many other municipalities, where local police (the majority of the almost 90 municipalities each had their own police force) awaited speeding motorists. It was bad business for someone such as me (a transplant to St. Louis), who *mostly* abided by the speed laws. I discovered quickly, however, that if one could afford an attorney one could get the speeding violations that were sure to come reduced to nonmoving violations, as long as the municipal courts got paid. Ferguson was a part of that network. Everyone knew it was shady, but it was just the price of admission, it seemed.

Police, in some communities, are invaders. In Ferguson, there was no residential policy for those on the police force. Many municipalities throughout the nation require their law enforcement officers to live where they police, reasoning that officers have more investment and attachment to the neighborhoods and city in which they reside. This ostensibly would improve what has been called "community policing," which emphasizes relationship building with residents. With stronger relations, law enforcement and neighborhood dwellers hope for increased understanding and more respectful interactions. That was, unfortunately, not the case in Ferguson.

Officers like Darren Wilson could live in the starkly white South County town of Crestwood, which consisted of 12,000 residents, 96 percent of whom were white and less than 2 percent Black. Crestwood is 17 miles from Ferguson, and it typically takes 30 minutes to get there by car. Based on distance and demographics, Wilson and other similarly situated officers (white or Black) were not part of the Ferguson community.

What must it have felt like for a 6 foot, 2 inch blonde-haired white law enforcement official to leave the new millennial version of "Mayberry" to come to an enclave that was twice as big, 33 times as Black, and decidedly younger in terms of residents? Ferguson was foreign to Wilson; to the people who lived there, Wilson was an invader.

A young Black man from Ferguson was interviewed in 2014 and recalled an interaction with white officers that was eerily similar to that involving Mike Brown. He and his friend were playing basketball in a street when patrolmen in a car ordered them to get out of the road. The friend did not immediately obey the directive, and instead stared at the officers. That apparently provoked the authorities to turn the patrol car around and assert their command presence. Demanding to know what the boy was looking at, an officer grabbed the friend and pressed him forcefully against the car's hood. When the interviewee pointed out to the officers that they were being too rough on his friend, the interviewee was told to "shut the F up!" Not all interactions with police were as intense, but Black people (especially youth) understood that the relationship between them and police was stressed.[6]

The young man's story had striking similarities to that of H.J. Rodgers, a longtime Ferguson resident-turned-activist. When asked if he had negative experiences with Ferguson, police, Rodgers, who had attended McCluer High School, responded, "Oh, most definitely!"[7] As an adult, he had been pulled over multiple times for alleged traffic violations. More poignantly, however, he remembered being seventeen years old and walking with two friends on West Florissant Avenue one night close to curfew, which was 11 p.m. A cruiser pulled up to them, with police demanding the youth stop walking. When Rodgers voiced that he did not want to stop, so that he could get to his destination, the officers called him disrespectful and demanded that he freeze. According to Rodgers, the officers then made the boy empty his bag of potato chips before placing cuffs on his wrists.

As no real crime had been committed (disrespect is not unlawful), other than a potential curfew infraction, the officers brought Rodgers and his friends to his family's house. Perhaps the officer thought that the young man would be in trouble, but Rodgers's family knew where he was. On August 9, 2014, when Rodgers heard that the Ferguson police had killed a teenage boy on Canfield Drive, his own run-in with the city's law enforcement replayed in his mind. Rodgers, reflectively, said what so many other young people thought—"That could have been me!" [8]

Ferguson, then, was the consummate study in racial capitalism, as members of the mostly white (all but two officers on the force were non-Black) force came to the city to earn their wages and salaries by suppressing elements of the community, and then took their money (and potential tax contributions) from the Black neighborhoods to bring them back to places like Crestwood. Once fined or arrested, the mostly Black offenders paid into a system that supported the careers of judges, attorneys, bail bonds people, towers, police officers, and law enforcement staff. [9]

Statistically, there was no doubt that law enforcement targeted and mistreated Black residents. According to a Department of Justice investigation, in the years leading up to Brown's death, Black motorists made up 86 percent of those to whom police issued citations after being stopped. Black drivers made up just less than two-thirds of those old enough to drive. White drivers made for a meager 12.7 percent of stops in Ferguson. Once stopped, Black motorists were twice as likely as white drivers to have their vehicle searched and also twice as likely as white motorists to be arrested even though the searches typically turned up illegal content in the vehicles of white motorists more. Black people in the St. Louis metropolitan area knew this all too well, and that is why when they met with representatives from the DOJ, they demanded an investigation, which resulted in revelations of racially biased patterns and practices within the Ferguson Police Department. That is governmental parlance for what the people who had to live with these circumstances knew it to truly be: racism.

Driving while Black. According to the Department of Justice report, Ferguson police, along with law enforcement in other municipalities, were guilty of "stacking" up citations on motorists. Officers were encouraged to issue tickets for multiple minor infractions at once, requiring motorists to either pay the fines, attend court, or lose driving privileges altogether.[10] The goal for Ferguson and the other municipalities that exploited drivers in this way was revenue. Some municipalities' budgets were almost entirely dependent on these traffic stops. Without the money from the fines and citations, the municipalities faced financial ruin.

This method of revenue enhancement was categorically unethical and immoral. As Jamala Rogers stated, "If you're [municipal officials] not gonna be creative about how your city raises funds, and you think the only thing that you can do or the main thing that you could do is use black bodies, something is definitely wrong with that picture!"[11]

The stops, citations, and arrests had significant economic and psychological effects. The fees from the tickets were costly, particularly for those who did not have much disposable income. In that case, one might be tempted to not pay the citation. That, of course, resulted in a bench warrant. Similarly, if one could not get off work or find childcare, one could easily miss the court date assigned on the tickets. That, too, triggered a bench warrant. Many in Ferguson understood that the way they were policed was not about safety but rather revenue. This was all, as Rogers indicated, part of a larger system of exploitation and oppression that most Black people in the area likely felt the effects of but could not clearly identify. For those working-class and financially challenged Black Ferguson residents who had warrants or fines, there was little in the way of representation in the courts and in elected office. From the public defender to the prosecuting attorney to the city council and mayor, there was little to no Black representation. Only one of the six city council members was Black in 2014.[12]

Realizing that policing had little to do with safety, some Ferguson residents lowered the level of respect and deference they offered to the police. Psychologically, for their part, white police officers coming from white enclaves viewed the subjects they were policing from a position of suspicion. It was a toxic relationship that engendered distrust, and Rogers rightly pointed out that "it had to be exposed." Brown's death, unfortunately, afforded the opportunity for that exposure.

2

TODAY *WAS* A GOOD DAY: MICHAEL BROWN ENCOUNTERS DARREN WILSON

Perhaps the most frightening part of Brown's tragedy was how quickly it escalated to a fatality. On August 15, 2014, Fox News 5 in St. Louis showed a video of Michael Brown and his friend, Dorian Johnson, entering a local convenience store, the Ferguson Market. Inside, Brown grabbed a package of cigarillos from the counter. There was no sound in the video, but there seemed to be words exchanged between him and the clerk. Brown made to leave and then pushed aside a store employee who came to stand between Brown and the door. That was when Brown and Johnson took the fateful walk down Canfield Drive, encountering Wilson patrolling in his cruiser. According to Wilson's account, at one moment, he was ordering Brown out of the street and minutes later, Wilson had fired six shots into the young citizen. Certainly, no one that day would have predicted that outcome.

In an interview I gave with the St. Louis affiliate of NPR, I made the case that Brown's death was a tragedy because it signaled that Black youth have no opportunity to make mistakes, that they could not have the time to figure out where they went wrong and how to get back on track—and, crucially, that the nation's unwillingness to see Black youth as budding citizens is cruel.[1] I tried to underscore the point by asking the interviewer: did any of the state and national politicians who were so committed to the faux Blue Lives Matter postures ever make a mistake when they were eighteen that could have gotten them sent to prison or killed? I expressed my gratitude for the opportunity to become more than what I was as a teenager. I pointed out that had we only measured Malcolm X's life by his actions as a youth, then we would not be able to see how personal evolution works. Surely, some would say, Brown was no Malcolm X and that it was sacrilegious to infer such, but if Malcolm Little could go from burgling houses to contemplating Black liberation with world leaders, why could not Mike Brown do it?

August has always been a significant month in the history of Black rebellion. Revolutionary leaders like Universal Negro Improvement Association leader Marcus Garvey, who was deported from the United States, and Black Panther icon Fred Hampton, who was assassinated by the Chicago police and FBI, were both born in August. The Haitian Revolution started in August 1791, and it led to the creation of the first Black nation in the western hemisphere. Nat Turner led a revolt in August 1831 that put slaveholders and supporters of the "peculiar institution" on notice that enslaved people were not satisfied in bondage. That also led to harsher forms of punishment and legislation aimed at rebellious Black people. In 1919, Black Chicagoans took to the streets in protest of the drowning death of seventeen-year-old Eugene Williams, whom white segregationists had stoned in the water at a beach near 29th Street. In August 1943, a white police officer in Harlem shot a Black soldier who had attempted to protect a Black woman from the police, who were brutally handling her. In honor of the GI who was serving in the midst of World War II, Black Harlemites rebelled in such a way that the mayor called on the U.S. Army to quell the uprising, which listed six people dead and five hundred arrested.

Mamie Till, in August 1955, made the unlikely decision to allow the publication of pictures of her son, Emmett Till, whom white men, seeking vigilante justice, kidnapped and murdered to send a message that disrespecting white people (and especially white women) was unacceptable and that Black boys had better learn their place of subservience early. The message was that they had better comply with the written and unwritten laws of white people. To show what racism did to her "Beau," Mamie Till released to the universe the gruesome image of her boy's body that the white vigilantes tortured and tied to a cotton gin fan. It set the world ablaze. Onlookers from different continents wondered if America ate its children, since it allowed such tragedies to occur unchecked. That image of a boy with an unrecognizable face was shocking and unsettling to civilized people everywhere.

Till's death set the stage for what historians called the modern civil rights movement. On the same date white racism killed Till, the Rev. Martin Luther King Jr., in 1963, gave his famous "I Have a Dream" speech. The late Representative John Lewis also declared, "We are tired of being beaten by policemen. We are tired of seeing our people locked up in jail over and over again. . . . We want our freedom and we want it now. We do not want to go to jail. But we will go to jail if this is the price we must pay!"[2] Two years later, in August, Black people in the Watts neighborhood of Los Angeles pushed back against the police, whom they'd observed brutalizing twenty-one-year-old Marquette Frye and his mother after a traffic stop. The outrage and rebellion spread to wider Los Angeles to cause $40 million in damage. The city called out the National Guard to suppress the uprising and subsequently enhanced its law enforcement mechanisms to military grade. That uprising was part of the long, hot summers that featured Black people rising up throughout the nation.

America made Black citizens pay the price of imprisonment over the course of the next decade. On August 7, 1971, in a Marin County (California) courthouse, Jonathan Jackson led an effort to free members of the Black Guerilla Family, which his incarcerated activist brother George Jackson had founded. In the altercation, Jackson and the men on trial took the judge, attorney general, and three jurors hostage. As Jonathan Jackson attempted to flee with the hostages, police killed him on the scene. Later, investigators found that the firearms that Jonathan Jackson had brought to the courthouse were registered in the name of Black Panther activist and philosopher Angela Davis. Less than two weeks later, Jonathan Jackson's revolutionary activist brother, George, was in San Quentin penitentiary facing a murder charge for killing a prison guard. George, on his way back to his cell after meeting with his attorney, had produced a pistol, taken a guard hostage, and initiated a rebellion in which other inmates participated. During the rebellion, three white guards were killed, along with two white inmates; another three guards survived, sustaining gunshot and stab wounds. George Jackson was killed in the prison yard. Jackson, in his will, stipulated the royalties from the books he had written be donated to the Black Panther Party.

Supporters of Black Power saw this rebellion as a revolutionary act that struck out against the prison–industrial complex that ravaged the lives of Black men. Between Jonathan and George Jackson's shooting deaths and 2014, America arrested and incarcerated millions of Black men and women, creating what attorney and author Michelle Alexander termed the New Jim Crow, a system that focused on controlling the Black community through law enforcement and incarceration.

High school graduate Mike Brown may not have known the history of Black rebellion in the month of August or the particulars of the prison–industrial complex, but he and his peers had certainly heard what had happened to Trayvon Martin and Jordan Davis when they did not comply with white vigilantes. Brown, although still a boy, lived in a city and country where law enforcement focused heavily on submission and compliance when it came to Black people.

The shooting death of Brown was deeply tragic, but the way that the police allowed his body to lie in misery for four and a half hours in the hot August sun drew a visceral response from

Canfield Green apartment complex residents. Canfield Drive is the only way in and out of the complex from West Florissant Ave. The road is wide enough for two lanes, but the sidewalks are quite narrow and often blocked by protruding cars from residents' driveways. Walking around the cars and in the street was not at all unusual for those who lived in the enclave. That, as noted in the previous scenario concerning the young men playing basketball in the street, was a point of contention for officers, who policed by car and not on foot.

The image of Brown's body on the ground spurred so many young people to activism. The original post, and the many reposts of the image on various social media platforms, added fuel to a war over narrative and for the control of the streets. As Ashley Yates, the co-founder of Millennium Activists United (MAU), noted, "Twitter was largely responsible for getting the word out about actions and movements in the first week. That was the way in which almost every one of us got the news that Mike Brown had been murdered and its importance in the early days cannot be stressed enough."[3] The social media platform allowed the young people a modicum of control in the chaos. With that in mind, according to Yates, they were "determined to get in and continue to tell our narrative" without the filters, interpretations, and translations of mainstream media.

"Thankfully for this generation, instead of waiting for a letter in the mail from Malcolm X, we have social media to drive this movement and get the truth out to millions of people, live," said Ferguson resident Johnetta "Netta" Elzie, who began tweeting furiously immediately after Wilson shot Brown.[4] In seeing the image and the scores of reactions, youth of all backgrounds wondered what they should do. Local St. Louis rapper Tef Poe's first thought was to contact Jamala Rogers, founder of the Organization of Black Struggle (OBS), a group started in 1980 to carry on the legacy of liberation in St. Louis and elsewhere from the earlier Black Freedom Movement. Poe now found himself in a situation that warranted Rogers's expertise. He said in a September 6, 2014, tweet, "Before I left the house to go to Ferguson . . . I called her and asked for guidance." That was ingenious and showed great humility on the part of the young leader. Where many young protesters believed that they were alone in their campaign for justice, Poe knew he had the backing of Rogers, whom he called "my personal elder."

Rogers told Poe to lean into community, and he, along with other young leaders, did exactly that. On August 10, they took their fight back to the police department, where they staged a peaceful protest. On Twitter, Poe made a request for food and water to sustain the activists, and in true community fashion, the people provided.

A young professional, Charli Cooksey, who co-founded the Young Citizens Council, was enjoying the sun on a boat as part of a retreat with the staff of InspireSTL, a nonprofit she directed, when she first saw the image of Brown.[5] It changed her life. Without hesitating, she left for Ferguson, where she landed in front of the police department. There, she and one of the most "diverse groups of Black folks" she had seen made their protest. People from "the streets to the boardroom" were there. Cooksey left before night fell on the first day of protest, when the police popped open cans of tear gas. Not to be deterred, the nonprofit leader returned the next day with the leader of the area Teach For America, Brittany Packnett Cunningham. Like so many professionals who wanted to protest, they came directly after work. Cooksey, because she was still in heels, had to borrow sneakers from Packnett Cunningham. They arrived to what Cooksey recalled "a very peaceful" rally that was quickly met with police resistance. To suppress the crowd, the police, once again, used tear gas.

Josh Williams was a day-one activist. Eighteen at the time and living in Jennings, he had recently run away from home. Before that day, Williams had mowed lawns for money and had never been in any legal trouble. He had certainly never protested or participated in demonstrations before August 9. Williams, acquainted with Brown and having learned that Brown had been killed and left dying on the street, made his way to the Canfield Green apartment complex in Ferguson. In a soft voice, Williams, who is currently imprisoned in a Missouri state penitentiary, remembered out loud what he saw: "When I showed up, he [Brown] was still on the ground [with a] white T-shirt, khaki shorts, Cardinals cap, and Nike flip-flops. He had been dead, you know" for hours.[6]

The sight of Brown's body was traumatizing for Williams, but what moved his spirit most was Lezley McSpadden's (Brown's mother) reaction in the moment. He reported that "everyone was crying and yelling."[7] That he "stood next to Lezley McSpadden" stirred his soul. In the grieving mother's presence, he observed something that radicalized him, changing him from a runaway to an activist. "I could feel her pain" as she hollered: "That's my baby! Y'all killed my baby!" Williams remembered her saying. Although he was troubled and struggling himself, hearing a Black mother mourn in such a heart-wrenching way provided Williams with a new purpose for his life. "That's what motivated me even more to stay out there," recollected the young leader. Eventually joining with the Lost Voices, Williams stayed in Ferguson, searching for justice for Mike Brown and solace for Lezley McSpadden.

Reporter Trymaine Lee discussed an emotional moment with the young leader when Williams was featured on MSNBC in September 2014. In Ferguson, Williams had squared off with police who had deployed tear gas and shot rubber pellets into the crowd. Unafraid, and perhaps a bit reckless, Williams, shouting angrily, began approaching the police line. That was when Pastor Willis Johnson of Well Spring Church, which is down the street from the Ferguson Police Department, caught Williams and hugged him in an effort to prevent any further escalation. The young man did not pull away from the embrace and, feeling the weight of the moment, shed tears. When asked about it later, Williams told the reporter that "I was really upset. I saw children, little kids getting tear gassed and stuff. I just couldn't take it." [8]

High schooler Clifton Kinnie arrived at the Canfield Green on day one as well. Still reeling from the death of his mother, "seeing his [Mike Brown's] mother scream, seeing his body on the ground, it put me in a traumatized state again," he remembered.[9] "It reminded me of my own mother," he said. He felt the aggression of the police, saw them in riot gear, and heard the growling, snipping dogs. Still young, he could not understand how this could be happening in the United States, in 2014. Moved by the experience of August 9, Kinnie joined the protests each night afterward.

Because pictures of young men throwing canisters of tear gas or carrying upside-down American flags are so ubiquitous in reference to Ferguson, it is difficult to remember that the earliest protesters were not men at all but rather mothers, grandmothers, aunties, and younger children. They did not know chants and had no real action plan other than to make their displeasure known to the people who had killed an unarmed young man and left him to cook on the pavement where his family lived.

Those women eventually teamed up with the young men in the community. Darren Seals of Hands Up United and Williams were similar in that they could not bear to see children and elders threatened. As Seals recalled of the first collective confrontations with police in Ferguson, "It's women and teenagers and they screamin', cryin', cursin' " in anger and fear.[10] That triggered his instincts as a protector. A resident of Ferguson, he told his friends, "Look we're the men; we gotta make sure they [the police] don't hurt these women and children." This was the approach that groups like the Deacons for Defense and Justice took when they armed themselves in Louisiana and the South or the Panthers took when they created neighborhood patrols in Oakland and Chicago.

Some observers cringe at the idea of men seeking to protect women. Many Black women in Ferguson, however, appreciated the idea that Black men, some of whom had done legitimate harm to the neighborhoods with their behavior, took responsibility for the protection of someone other than themselves. Black women and men stood together on the streets of Ferguson. Seals, in August 2014, did not take the time to poll anyone's opinions about gender narratives. Instead, he led a group of men to form a line between the police and the mothers with their children.

Seals and Williams, who were strangers to each other before August 9, came together as protectors. The line they formed forced the police to back down, but that line was effective in other ways as well. "We were out there with the street dudes," Seals said.[11] Making sure to clarify the class dynamics of the situation, Seals pointed out that, in his estimation, "it wasn't the conscious college students" on the street at the time, "it was drug dealers, killas, robbers, [and] cutthroats." In this moment they were dangerous people not because of their abilities to circumvent the law or potentially take lives but because, as Seals eloquently put it, "we was all together."

The danger in this moment stemmed from the fact that individuals who had regularly placed their own survival above everyone else's chose to be part of a collective. Williams remembered the sight of a member of the Crip gang tie his blue flag (bandana) together with the red flag of Blood gang member to symbolize the need to put down old differences and prioritize the most pressing danger: militarized police.[12] "I seen enemies, I seen cats that I had beef with growin' up, and they seen me, like 'Bro, bro, come give me a hug.'" That was a bold step in movement making, and it did not go unnoticed by law enforcement. An August 20, 2014, *Time* magazine article reported that there were, according to "enforcement officials, . . . multiple gang members from Chicago and East St. Louis who have forged an uneasy truce to pursue a common enemy."[13] The enemy, in this case, was the occupying police force, and that show of solidarity for the movement was revolutionary.

Unity and solidarity amongst the Black *lumpen proletariat*

(those in the underclass), *proletariat* (those in the working class), and *petite bourgeoisie* (those in managing class) was a great threat to America and of much concern for the Ferguson police. In the past, as shown by the duplicitous and debilitating reaction of law enforcement at the federal, state, and municipal levels to groups like the Rainbow Coalition in Chicago, the Council of Federated Organizations in southern states, and the clandestine Revolutionary Action Movement that had units all throughout the nation, overstepped legality. Police captured members, imprisoned them, and assassinated them for daring to stand in solidarity, resisting abuse and exploitation.

"We're in a gang too, just because of the uniform we wear," admitted a policeman for the *Time* article.[14] Indeed, it is not uncommon to hear Black and brown people in working-class and low-income neighborhoods refer to the police as a gang. The efforts to impose will, target enemies, protect territory, and exact retribution are not traits exclusively reserved for Black and brown youth gangs. The way that law enforcement operated in Ferguson warranted that comparison. MAU co-founder Ashley Yates bolstered the officer's claim. "Several of them [officers] told me on August 10th that they are a fraternity. That reality really hit home when I realized some of those same officers that were so civil in the daylight were pointing rifles at my head in the night and would not hesitate to shoot me upon command."[15] Gang or fraternity with lethal weapons, the officers were potentially deadly.

Unfortunately, history dictated that because these citizens happened to be Black, no help was forthcoming. That is why young people in Ferguson had to act on their own behalf. In August 2014, rather than the police deciding how to deal with Black youth, those young men and women declared: "You're not touching these kids, and we gonna all protect each other," Seals said.[16] And, valiantly, they did.

Williams and Seals, like Fred Hampton, the assassinated chair of the Illinois chapter of the Black Panther Party for Self-Defense, had a heart for the defenseless. Hampton, on December 4, 1969, sacrificed his life because he dared to resist the legal system that economically, mentally, and physically oppressed Black people. Williams, more than fifty years later, was willing to sacrifice himself for the very same cause. That day the pastor caught him, Williams was willing to die to protect justice and the people with whom he stood. In an interview nearly ten years after that moment, Williams said, "I seen all my young people out there in this big fight everyday, and I asked myself, if they can do it why can't I?" [17]

Like Hampton, Williams was led to leadership. In the manner of young citizen-leaders who came before him, he explained that "the thing that mainly scared me was one of my people getting shot by a cop next to me." Considering that a policeman had shot an unarmed boy just weeks earlier, the potential for its happening again seemed relatively high. Williams, however, did not fear for his own safety, which was evident by the way that he led chants on the front lines of the protest and threw tear-gas canisters back at the officers who launched them at demonstrators. "Fuck me right now! I'm here for my people," Williams exclaimed. Looking back he said, "Me, I didn't care about nothing but my people out there, so I was more scared for them rather than my own safety"—words spoken in the spirit of freedom fighters throughout history.

"If you would have told me 'You'll be a leader,' I would've been like, 'Yeah, I don't know about that,' " Williams revealed. He said he had never really seen himself as a leader before then. In the way of the Greek tragedy, the moment seemed to choose the unsuspecting Williams, and he responded with vigor. As he came to terms with his role in the movement, he believed that he not only led his brothers and sisters in the streets of St. Louis and Ferguson but millions of people all over the nation and world who paid close attention to what was happening back at "Ground Zero." Williams took pride in the fact that people came from everywhere to be in solidarity with St. Louisans like him. Humbly, he said, "I thank God for it."

Williams joined up with a group of activists, Lost Voices, which chose to demonstrate by camping out across from the Ferguson Police Department. Williams and the members of Lost Voices committed everything they had to the movement. Shortly after VonDerrit Myers Jr., an eighteen-year-old Black youth, was shot running away from a St. Louis City police officer in October 2014, Williams and many others took their protests to the city. If the police were killing Black boys throughout the metropolitan area, then activists believed it their duty to disrupt the lives of decision makers. Williams attended another action, this time in Clayton, Missouri, which is where the St. Louis County justice center resides. Along with dozens of other activists, he demonstrated at the office of County Prosecutor Bob McCulloch to bring charges against Wilson and Jason Flanery, who shot Myers. A *USA Today* article captured Williams's sentiments from the time: "We need to keep putting pressure on him. He [McCulloch] might change his mind because he might get tired of seeing us. . . . He's the one who can make the order and change."[18] Incidentally, Flanery never faced charges but did resign amidst a scandal in which he caused a car accident while driving his police cruiser intoxicated.

Similar to Williams, Cooksey, and others, H.J. Rodgers came to the scene on Canfield Drive as soon as he heard on the radio about Brown's shooting death. "I pulled up like I was his cousin," said Rodgers, who had not actually "had the pleasure of meeting Mike Brown in person."[19] He did not need to be blood related to Brown to feel his spirit. The resemblance was strong, as both were tall, broad-shouldered, handsome young Black men who happened to live in Ferguson. The police had finally removed Brown's body by the time Rodgers arrived. For him, it was unusual to see people still outside protesting. In St. Louis, when someone is shot or killed, people tend to congregate, he said, but the "energy and whole mood of the people that day was just crazy." Like so many others on the street that day, Rodgers had never formally protested anything. This was completely different. The first night, Rodgers recalled, was exhilarating and exhausting because "it was a new feeling for me."

At work the next day, all he could think was "that could have easily been me." When he finished at his job, he went back, intent on raising his voice about what he viewed as injustice.[20] Much like St. Louisans Damon Latchinson and Kayla Reed, who left work for organizing, Rodgers knew that life moving forward could not be the same. He decided the second night he was on the street that he had to quit his job and give himself over to this cause. For Rodgers and the many others who did the same, walking away from a primary source of income to expend all of his energy and resources fighting for someone he had not actually met in person required an enormous amount of faith and sense of community. One can only wonder if Brown could have imagined the way he inspired people from all walks of life. "The spirit told me" to quit my job and join the others, Rodgers claimed, and that night he stood in front of the Ferguson Police Department, cementing his career as a protester. "It most definitely was the ancestors talking, God riling me up, pushing me into a different capacity. It was my transformation."

In front of the police department, Rodgers met up with like-minded activists who engaged him in "dope conversations," he said. Noticing that the activists he was speaking with donned the same color and style of vest, Rodgers eventually asked, "Y'all the Black Panthers or something?" The question was not unreasonable, as members of the New Black Panther Party had been on the scene. The young people Rodgers asked, however, laughed and responded that they were not the Panthers but rather part of a new organization, Tribe X. The group's mission was to educate, empower, and organize the people. Jonathan Pulphus and Alisha Sonnier were among the early members, who formalized their meetings and created a name. They invited him to learn more and join, but Rodgers was a bit leery at first because, as he put it, "I wasn't an organization [type of] person, you know, I move on my own time." It would not take long before he was in community with Tribe X, organizing for the benefit of the people.

A graduate of Soldan High School in St. Louis City and the University of Missouri–Kansas City, Derecka Purnell was in Kansas City attending an event on August 9.[21] The keynote lecturer for the event was Brittany Packnett Cunningham, who quickly became a primary leader and spokesperson of the movement. Purnell had known Packnett Cunningham from childhood when they both worshipped at Westside Missionary Baptist Church on Page Avenue. Purnell, who had just given birth to her first child, had finished her undergraduate degree and was enrolled in Harvard Law School. She was set to go on a date with her husband after the lecture, but when news of Brown's murder reached them the couple decided they had to get home to St. Louis as fast as possible.

After arriving on August 10, Purnell immediately got to work. The police had cordoned off roads leading into the Canfield Green apartments and other areas. Noticing what seemed to be a confrontation between a Black woman and an officer at one of the blockades, Purnell investigated to find out that the distressed woman was a Canfield Green resident having a panic attack and was in need of her medication. Purnell called for paramedics to help the woman, who desperately wanted to go home. (That is only one of several terrifying stories about residents not being allowed to leave from or go into the complex.) Purnell was perturbed, but more than that, she was affirmed in her desire to fight on behalf of the people of Ferguson, the city she knew so well. After helping the resident, she and her then husband made it to her in-laws' home, where she started calling people that could get her more information; they included Packnett Cunningham and St. Louis City treasurer Tishaura Jones.

I attended a community event in St. Louis City that featured St. Louis County police chief Jon Belmar, who responded to the question of why the police did not cover Brown's body and left it lying lifeless for so many hours. Community members made the very legitimate point that when dogs are hit by cars, their bodies are often removed quicker, and that it seemed unreasonable to leave a human dead on the ground for so long. Belmar responded that the officers made a mistake by not immediately covering the body, as there were family members, children, and onlookers there to see Brown's blood coagulate on the asphalt road. After hours, the police finally placed a sheet over the body before Brown's mother, Lezley McSpadden, arrived.

After conceding that the officers misstepped by not covering Brown's body, Belmar defended the police's taking four and a half hours to investigate. He explained that it was essential to ascertain all the facts and to thoroughly assess the scene in order to establish a logical narrative of how the shooting and death occurred. That could take forty minutes or four hours, Belmar said. That seemed like a plausible reason for the long span of time Brown's body spent on the ground, but the community—people who had been mistreated and taken advantage of by police—struggled to sympathize with the chief's response.

Lezley McSpadden, Brown's mother, rejected the explanation outright. The police would not allow her to cross the yellow tape to see her son's body. Every second that police refused to talk to her or blocked her path to her son was immeasurable torture for McSpadden. In her memoir, she remembered closing her eyes at the time and hearing Mike Brown say to her, "Mama, I need you, I'm scared." She felt disrespected by the lack of information she received on the scene and the way that the authorities stonewalled her. It would seem that there could have been more sympathy for a mother whose unarmed son had just lost his life.[22]

The Ferguson chief of police, Tom Jackson, eventually apologized publicly to McSpadden for the day that Brown's body lay so long in the street. "I'm truly sorry for the loss of your son. I'm also sorry that it took so long to remove Michael from the street," Jackson said. He, along with the department, knew they were wrong.

The chief also mentioned the repressive tactics of his police force with respect to protesters on the street. "The right of the people to peacefully assemble is what the police are here to protect. If anyone who was peacefully exercising that right is upset and angry, I feel responsible and I'm sorry." Unfortunately, sorry sentiments could not bring Brown back or displace the feelings of mistrust in those whose rights had been violated.[23]

3.

WHO LET THE DOGS OUT?: REPRESSIVE POLICE ACTION

"I never thought the small county of Ferguson, this little part of Greater St. Louis, would become Gaza."
—*Johnetta "Netta" Elzie*

Many of the contemporary takes on the Ferguson Uprising posit the actual death of Michael Brown as the spark that ignited the racial explosion. But it was not just Officer Darren Wilson's shooting Brown that led to regular citizens demonstrating their frustration in the streets: it was the response of the police to public grief. The decision to release dogs on a Black crowd catalyzed a reaction from all the demographics in the Canfield Green apartments and beyond. This history-laden act, reminiscent of similar methods in Birmingham or Selma during the civil rights era, led to the activation of so many people who would have never stood up to a police force in such a manner and who would have never participated in a social movement before that day. Arriving in riot gear and attempting to use military tactics to suppress the mourning of the community provoked a destructive response—which took the form of burning a QuikTrip convenience store on West Florissant.

Throughout the history of this nation, Black Americans have had an uneasy relationship with dogs. Those intrepid enslaved Black runaways did whatever they could on their journeys to freedom to avoid the dogs that enslavers employed. Nat Turner, who led a rebellion of enslaved people, was caught by a hunting dog. More than a century later, in the 1950s and 1960s, police and state troopers used trained dogs to intimidate and detain Black people in Alabama and elsewhere as they marched for their freedom. In recent history, dogs have regularly been used to detect drugs in the cars of motorists. Black drivers nationally make up a higher percentage of those dealing with canine searches. Although Black people love dogs as pets, many are keenly aware of the consequences when police sic them on citizens. The Ferguson police must have been aware of this.

"Tear gas and dogs going off Canfield smh please pray," rapper and Hands Up United co-founder Tef Poe tweeted just after 9:30 p.m. on August 10. The police rationalized the tactical use of dogs to contain an angry and grieving crowd. Many Black Ferguson residents, however, perceived it as a way to terrorize and punish them for having the audacity to stop smiling and shout out in pain. Young activists like Poe saw it as an act of war. "This was the first time I had ever seen police dogs ready for attack in real life. I felt as if time was rewinding back and showing me scenes from Selma, Alabama, in the 1960s instead of Ferguson, Missouri, in 2014," remembered Johnetta "Netta" Elzie.[1] For her, the police tactic seemed unfathomable. She said, "I tried to remain as calm as possible in such a volatile situation but seeing those police dogs snarling at young Black children filled me with anger and rage." She continued, "I never would've dreamed that on the same street I drive down to go to my nail appointment at Crystal's, or to the QuikTrip I get gas from, would be the scene of a police occupation." Poe, equally incredulous, wrote, "This isn't right man . . . What's going on in my city is not right." He begged for "somebody [to] fucking get here and fix this please." The somebody he needed, Poe sadly realized, was him and the others who could no longer allow themselves to be bullied and abused.

During the first two weeks of the Uprising, the world witnessed a test of wills in Ferguson between marginalized people and the enforcement arm of the nation's socioeconomic system. Police officials appeared to be resentful of the resistance they faced and manifested their resentment in the form of localized warfare. Few knew that Ferguson had armored personnel vehicles, tanks, helicopters, and enough tear gas and flashbangs to invade a small country; few knew that the more that the police arrested community protesters, the more that the law enforcement vehicles spewed nauseating gas, and the more that officers pointed their semi-automatic rifles at civilians, the more they radicalized onlookers and observers to participate in the movement.

"Bring it, all you fucking animals! Bring it!" Those were the words coming from the mouth of a balding, large-bellied white man in a Ferguson Police Department uniform in the first week of the Uprising. CNN caught the officer expressing himself on camera, but the news network's analysis was typical of the media's clumsy attempts at balance in these early days. After describing the tension of the moment, the reporter, on August 11, 2014, sympathetically stated that "even an officer . . . gave into his rage" when making the comment. Ferguson mayor James Knowles said of the police, "The officers did their best. They're only human."[2]

"A neighborhood in mourning was greeted by a clear violation of their human rights," North County resident Netta Elzie described.[3] "I am upset to know," she commented, "that my people seem to not even have the right to hurt, to feel, to care, to show love, to be one with one another, or to mourn the loss of another Black life." It was clear in those days that de-escalation was not a priority for the police. According to Ron Henry, a North County resident interviewed for an August 20, 2014, *Time* magazine article, police in the Canfield Green drew automatic rifles on his fiancée and three-year-old son when they tried to exit the complex at night.[4] At the time, police posted checkpoints on the edges of the neighborhood. As Poe noted on Twitter, "Shooting at ppl [with rubber pellets or lead bullets] will not make them go in the house." It instead turned them out into the streets to check the unabashed occupying force. Poe exclaimed on Twitter that "we're currently at war with the system."

Over the course of the next few days, Poe reported from the battlefield. He observed that "the power of the police force in the state of Missouri is being dumped in North STL County." To some who were not in Ferguson, Poe's claim may have seemed like hyperbole, but police mobilized the equipment of war onto the streets. "Tanks have officially arrived in downtown STL," Poe warned. The tanks were transported to Ferguson. Just as guerilla fighters had confronted empires in the past, overmatched and outgunned people in Ferguson attacked the system in every way they could. They did not have tanks, but they could burn the QuikTrip and raid the Walmart, disrupting the revenue that those who did not live in the neighborhood gained from the residents of the community.

That August, people around the nation took notice. An op-ed ran in the *New York Amsterdam News* with a title that read "From Ferguson to Gaza: We Charge Genocide."

An August 18, 2014, *Wall Street Journal* article reported on President Barack Obama's statements about the mobilization of military equipment in Ferguson in which the president explained how after the terrorist attacks in New York City on September 11, 2001, Congress moved quickly to arrange for communities throughout the nation to have military grade equipment to protect themselves in case of another attack.

Obama was partly correct in his explanation of why tanks appeared in an eastern Missouri suburb. More broadly, the militarization of policing stemmed from Congress's 1990 authorization of the Department of Defense's 1033 Program, which made armaments available to local police forces to fight the "war on drugs." That war hastily devolved into a war on Black people and a way to increase profits for weapons and military equipment manufacturers. There were no terrorists from the Middle East to test the training and weapons Ferguson received, so mourning Black people had to suffice. Police were empowered to act as soldiers. Intensifying matters, Missouri's governor activated the National Guard to turn on citizens exercising their First Amendment rights.

"There is a big difference between our military and our local law enforcement, and we don't want those lines blurred," Obama wrote. It was, unfortunately, too late. For those who evaded the tanks, looked up at the helicopters, felt the effects of chemical weapons, and clashed against the gear, the battle lines and combatants were drawn quite clearly. The president commented that local police forces acting in the fashion of the military was "contrary to our traditions." Surely, the MOVE Organization bombing in Philadelphia in 1985 and the battering-ram campaigns in south central Los Angeles during the 1980s slipped President Obama's mind at the moment. Even Fox News had to run opinion pieces questioning the need for the camouflage uniforms and military equipment. One article quoted Walter Olson from the libertarian Cato Institute, who sensibly asked, "Why would cops wear camouflage gear against a terrain patterned by convenience stores and beauty parlors?"[5]

On August 20, 2014, to find out more about the situation, the president sent Attorney General Eric Holder to Ferguson to make an assessment. Holder, originally from Queens, New York, attempted to disarm Ferguson residents with his charming personality when he arrived at Drake's Place, a Black-owned restaurant on South Florissant. It had been open for less than a year before Darren Wilson killed Brown. There, Holder chatted with a mayor from a North County municipality, who, dressed in a lovely pink sweater and white dress, did not want the area known for the Uprising but rather the "good" things that were occurring.[6] She discussed economic development and the Fortune 500 business headquarters that existed in North County but did not offer commentary on policing, which was the sole purpose of Holder's trip. Fortunately, young leaders like Brittany

Packnett Cunningham met Holder to confront the issue of law enforcement overreach.

The efforts of the Ferguson activists were resulting in action at the federal level. By August 24, 2014, the *Wall Street Journal* reported that "President Barack Obama has called for a review of the federal programs that supply local police departments with military equipment amid growing concerns about the heavily armed law enforcement officers who faced down protesters in Ferguson, Mo."[7] Apparently, the president was as shocked as everyone else to see the suburban battlefield. The article continued, "White House staff will lead the assessment of the funding and programs that allow state and local law enforcement to purchase military-grade weapons, vehicles and body armor," a senior administration official said. Incidentally, President Obama was at Martha's Vineyard when consulting with his staff on Ferguson. In a better world, he, like so many others, would have been enjoying an end-of-summer vacation with his family.

"I ain't been comfortable my whole life. I decided that day, August 9, that I was going to do something. I would rather die before I continue to live the way I'm living,"[8] T-Dubb-O, a local rap artist turned activist, said when explaining why he joined the effort, co-founding Hands Up United.

"It's B.S. and someone needs to stand up," said the mother of Joshua Williams in August 2014.[9] Williams responded to his mother's challenge by hitting the streets to confront the onslaught of militarized police charging into the neighborhoods of Ferguson and St. Louis. Williams was a courageous front-liner, squaring off with police regardless of the consequences, which included rubber bullets, pepper spray, and arrest. As did most young people who demonstrated in the streets, Williams learned lessons quickly in the chaos of the Uprising. He said: "I learned that the police don't give a care about us. And I learned that we have to stand up and that you can't get nowhere with violence but you can always move people without it." Proud of his actions and those of others, Williams expressed gratitude about the evolution of consciousness in the region. He remarked that before the dawn of uprisings surrounding Brown's death, "nobody really did anything about anything," but after, "everyone cares for one another."

Most media accounts of the Uprising have done well to capture differences in the ways that white and Black onlookers viewed the demonstrations and protesting. But there were also significant nuances within the Black community regarding the actions of youth on the street. Young Black activists, based on the op-eds in white and Black local periodicals, remarks captured from social media accounts, and the recollections of youth participants in the movement, faced questions about tactics and methods. Although most in the community shared concern about the reaction of law enforcement and people on the ground, there were differences of opinion regarding how to attack the problems. Positionality, in terms of socioeconomic class status, sometimes shaped responses to the actions of protesters. Even those who were not from the neighborhood or from the working class or from the younger generation conceived of ways to help the cause. As events unfolded, there was, however, no friendly way to demand rights and respect.

One of the most beautiful aspects of the Uprising was the way young people looked and smelled and sounded on the street at night. At the time, many young men from St. Louis City and County sported cornrows or locs. Some young women with braids or weaves wore bright colors in their hair. It was hot in Missouri, so white tank tops were ubiquitous. Young men and women were adorned with earrings, and some wore nose rings as well. The language they used was as colorful as the sneakers on their feet. But as beautiful as they were, they did not appear to mirror the carefully crafted image of activists from the civil rights movement that one might see in a history book.

Alex Templeton, whose personality bubbles with confidence

and a bit of mischievousness, recalled that when young, they "ran the streets with" their "daddy like a friend," and "that's where my masculinity comes in!"[10] Currently, Templeton is a male-presenting student at the Washington University School of Law. Unlike some others, they proudly proclaim themself to be a leader. When their partner questioned them during the interview, Templeton said, "Ask about me, they know. It is true. No one can deny that." Indeed, Templeton was a key leader of the Ferguson Uprising. They were a founder of MAU, and they have enough critique of the movement for every organization and everyone. They have definitely earned the right. As Alisha Sonnier pointed out, if Templeton would have been on an Oprah Winfrey show, or if they were a straight man, they would be one of the most recognizable stars in the world.[11]

Undoubtedly, Templeton was, by choice, as far away from traditional notions of respectable as possible. They were decidedly a "nigga," a word that offended the senses of many older and more conservative community members. Templeton said that they were pushed into activism because of the way that police were "fuckin' with niggas." For many who would have been considered respectable, referring to oneself or others as a "nigga" was unnecessary and distracting. For those who considered themselves to be a "nigga," they did not mind embarrassing those who worried about how they looked in the eyes of wider society. Not unlike Bayard Rustin, the pacifist civil rights strategist and Rev. Martin Luther King Jr. advisor, Templeton was a queer radical willing to challenge all who were determined to control the freedom chances of those society had deemed as "others."

"I feel like this: [If] you can't get the streets together, [if] you can't get the killas, the dope dealers, the hustlas, the strippers, [if] you can't get the people in the streets to come together, [then] you're not a leader" asserted Darren Seals, a day-one organizer.[12] He organized what the Black Panthers called the lumpen proletariat, society's most marginalized, those who operate outside of the strictures of norms, mores, and laws. In an effort to reframe the traditional perspective of civilized society, he said that "those are the people that count."

Damon Latchinson (who went by Diamond in 2014) remembered how dismayed some of his family and community members were with how young people and others reacted to Wilson's killing Brown. Some of Latchinson's family asked, "Why would they do that?" in reference to the way that angry people destroyed property and "looted" establishments. Those family members proclaimed: "That's totally wrong" and "That's not how you go about your situation." Furthermore, they asked, "If you want to riot and loot, why don't you go to the white people's area and do it?"[13] Latchinson logically confronted his family's position. With respect to why rebels destroyed property in the Black neighborhood, he responded with a question of his own: "Why would people drive all the way out to Frontenac" (an exclusive and wealthy city in another part of St. Louis County) and then come right on back?"

There were those older people and those in the professional classes who could not abide the tactics and methods of the street activists, but there were many others who encouraged the young rebels. Ashley Yates of MAU spoke of elders "snatching her aside" to say "we are so proud of you. Wherever you lead, we're willing to follow." Elders from St. Louis and Ferguson had lived through and experienced the trauma of abusive policing and racial capitalism for decades, and they resisted in their own way, often to no avail. For many of them, young people like Yates, Russell, and Poe were lifelines—the opportunity to get that much closer to freedom in a place that restricted Black people legally and illegally. If they could not achieve success in the struggle, then they believed they owed the younger generations their support. According to Yates, the supportive elders understood that it was the youth reaction that sparked the rebellion that created pathways for change.

One supporter of youth took on a motherly role. Cathy Daniels, the woman activists called "Mama Cat," went above and beyond the call of duty in providing assistance to the young defenders of democracy. "This is 2014, and we are still confronting the problems that our mothers and fathers confronted back in the civil rights era," Daniels, who was in her fifties, explained. "My generation came along, and we fed off what they did. We didn't fight and keep the fight going." [14] So, she believed, it was her obligation to, at the least, feed those who were willing to fight. Daniels was teaching the young people two valuable lessons. The first is best explained by the phrase that is often attributed to French general Napoleon Bonaparte, "An army marches on its stomach." Passion and adrenaline can carry a person only so far. Daniels saw that the demonstrators would go hours and days without caring for themselves; she made them eat. When not cooking she banged a pot on West Florissant or in front of the Ferguson police station. The sound lesson still rings in some people's heads. Although food was a necessity for battle, winning the war required something greater, Daniels instructed. Teaching the second lesson, she said, "The only way to combat problems sometimes is through love." [15] Mama Cat fed the young soldiers' stomachs and showed them love. They were ready for battle.

Amy Hunter, Tishaura Jones, and LaTanya Buck were other "mothers" who were ready to protect children in Ferguson. Hunter, who was at the time director of racial justice at the YWCA Metro St. Louis, showed up to protest with young people in the city and county. She came because she was hurt by the news of Brown's death. "Mike Brown could have been our son; in some ways, fictively he is my son," she wrote for the YWCA website. She continued, "As a professional and as a mother, I never want to see a young person die from violence." [16] In calling on people to see Brown as a son, Hunter explained that the dynamic may have well shifted in the interaction between Wilson and Brown. "Maybe," she suggested, Wilson "would have taken him [Brown] to the police station and booked him, or talked sternly about the

IF WE DON'T GET IT

positive responsibilities of manhood," if Wilson had seen the eighteen-year-old as a son. Hunter wanted all youth to be safe; she did not want to see "tear gas, police dogs or swat teams used on U.S. citizens who are protesting," so she went to Ferguson in an attempt to help. What Ferguson needed, she concluded, was a "mother's movement."

Jones and Buck were in the "mother's movement," as they too had Black sons. Jones struggled with explaining what was happening in the street to her elementary school–aged son. As an elected official, she, of course, felt a duty to act, but as a self-described "unapologetically Black mother" she was inspired to share in any way she could.[17] As St. Louis City treasurer at the time, Jones "preferred to work in the background," where she believed she could be more effective in keeping young Black men alive. Buck, who directed a new multicultural center at Washington University, was jolted into action by fear. She realized that her five-year-old son was nearing the age when he would be seen as no longer cute but rather as dangerous to society. The problem was she was naturally fearful for his life, but she was also scared of denying him the opportunity to be fully human, as she protected him from racism.

In a poem titled, "Protect All of Our Sons," published in the *St. Louis American,* Buck wrote, "A jet-black gem, passed through my womb, for whom I am responsible for polishing. I fear that I will buff his callous and curious edges so much that it strips his unique and natural essence down to concrete camouflage for sake of survival."[18] In exasperation, she asked, "But how do I prepare a jewel of five years for a lifetime of society that is not prepared for him? How do I allow a boy to be just that—in his most authentic state—when I am forced to articulate and reason adult male content in a childlike manner?" Being a mother, more than anything else, pulled her and so many others into the movement.

U.S. representative Cori Bush, who was a nurse in 2014, admired the tenacity of the young people and their willingness to teach her something. Years later, she said about her experience in

Ferguson, "I didn't yet know what it was to be an activist, but I knew how to tend to people in crisis and I knew how to pray."[19] She brought those skills with her to the Canfield Green apartments, where she got to know the community well. During the days she met the clinical needs of residents. At night, she followed the lead of young people as they demonstrated on West Florissant and in front of the police station.

In a statement that captured the sentiments of more than a few mentors and observers, Bush said she was in her "late thirties" and "loved to see so many young Black people with their fists raised, voicing their frustration with a system that has never been designed for us, or worked for us."[20] She felt deep pride as she watched the youth "grab that moment for themselves." They were willing to do what no one else could or would do. Unlike some, she did not attempt to apply the pressure of respectability on the young people. "I didn't take issue with their modes of expression, as some older participants did."

There were other elders, executives, business owners, and professionals of all stripes, defending and advocating for the young people at the highest levels. Among those was Tony Thompson, owner and operator of one of St. Louis's most respected construction companies, Kwame Building Group. Thompson did not mince words when it came to what he believed: "Anything short of arresting that white cop for murder is an insult to black people," he wrote in August 2014.[21] Thompson was a St. Louisan who had grown his company through hard work and community support. His own brother, who had been a police chief of a historically Black North County municipality, had been murdered, so Thompson was familiar with police culture and behavior. In speaking so forcefully and clearly on the issue, he placed his socioeconomic standing in the business community at great risk.

Thompson made it plain that he did not think that the looting of businesses and protesting were the same things, and he did not condone punishing business owners for the actions of the police. He also believed, however, that civil disobedience was absolutely necessary for the moment because the police department had facilitated the "cold-blooded murder of another black kid."[22] Thompson wrote those words in an email to area community leaders and business people. His statement would have been jarring enough to keep regional officials talking for weeks, but Thompson went further.

On August 20, there was a community forum held at Harris-Stowe State University, which at the time was headed by Dwaun Warmack, the youngest president in the university's history. I was in attendance. Various traditional Black leaders waxed poetic about the history of St. Louis and the problems of policing. At the forum, Thompson repeated a line from the letter that snatched the breath from members of the audience. "Ferguson City Hall and Police Department need to burn to the ground!!!"[23] Thompson explained that he was speaking metaphorically, but the words had an effect. Some in the audience applauded, while the faces of others soured. This was the same Tony Thompson who had received nothing but pats on the back from business executives and community leaders at an event at the Chase Park Plaza in which Kwame Building Group was featured.

That August day, Thompson likely lost some admirers but earned the respect of many because he made members of the audience decide which side they were on. He was unabashedly on the side of those who were participating in and organizing the Uprising. Those in the movement counted Thompson as an advocate.

Etefia Umana, the close mentor of Jonathan Pulphus and Alisha Sonnier, was also a supporter, but the Uprising itself caught him off guard. "I think the fact that St. Louis is the catalyst for a nationwide conversation is highly ironic" because "it's not where St. Louis typically is," he explained in an August 19, 2014, interview with NPR.[24] Historically, St. Louis (and Ferguson) was not home to rebellion, and it was shocking to see things burn in his neighborhood. He, like the Joneses, as well as the residents of the

Canfield Green and Northwind Estates, had to physically, emotionally, and mentally navigate all of the public reaction in the otherwise quiet enclave. Umana started by creating a safe space for activists, which included his own son, Etefia, as well as Pulphus and Sonnier.

At the time, I encouraged national media to interview those youth to gain the perspective of college-enrolled students who came from the area. Based on his education and prior community work in the area with youth at the all-Black Cardinal Ritter College Preparatory High School and Better Family Life, perhaps Umana should not have been surprised by the movement burgeoning in his backyard. The seeds of knowledge that he and other mentors planted were bearing fruit. At that point in the demonstrations, however, no one quite knew what the total harvest would yield.

Thompson, Umana, and Rogers did not represent all of the elders. There were some who were not only confused but deeply unnerved. One mother who lived in the Canfield Green apartment complex said that all of the commotion and anger made her "scared," but at the same time, she was proud of the work that young people were doing to stand up for Brown.[25] The mother had a college-graduate daughter who had worked with former Black Panther and philosopher Angela Davis among the protesters. She worried for her daughter's safety in light of the rubber bullets and tear gas. Other elders were more frightened than anything. One man, whose octogenarian father lived near Canfield Drive, said plainly in an NPR interview, "Old people don't understand younger people, and younger people don't understand older people."[26] People tend to fear that which they do not understand. The man was generalizing, but he could account for his father, who did not want to leave his home, especially at night.

According to St. Louis politico and Missouri State Board of Education member Mike Jones (not related to the Jones family of Friendly Temple Missionary Baptist Church), young people

IF WE DON'T GET IT   49

would not have had to activate had it not been for the failure of the older Black political class. Jones, who admitted to being a part of the political class for three decades, issued a biting critique in the August 14, 2014, edition of the *St. Louis American:* "the circumstances that created the events that resulted in" what he intentionally referred to as the "murder" of Michael Brown "can be placed squarely at the feet of black leadership."[27] The elders, Jones opined, had "to fulfill the only moral imperative of leadership— protecting and advancing the interest of the people you lead," and they had not.

The situation in Ferguson, a city that was two-thirds Black, would not have devolved to the point of eruption had the Black political class seized power, Jones argued. Having police who actually lived where they policed was public policy. Laws governing the rules of engagement for police officers was public policy. And the ability to effectively indict and convict an officer who misused his power was a matter of public policy, Jones exclaimed. "A change in public policy requires control, or at least major influence on government," Jones wrote, and Black people had neither in the majority Black city.[28] If things were to change, Jones advised, it would require that Black people and their leaders understand that "every major issue facing the black community has a solution, and implementing that solution begins with a change in public policy."

Not every interaction with elders was generative for youth. As the Uprising continued, Netta Elzie explained on Twitter that "it's so apparent why this generational gap is present in our community." She was irked by a meeting she'd had with leaders from the local NAACP. She asserted that "as far as the community goes? I feel they've dropped the ball in the 21st century." In her experience, she claimed, the NAACP was mentioned in the past tense, and she was beginning to understand the reason during the Uprising. Elzie said, "We're not stuck in the past. So the message between generations shouldn't be either." After meeting with the elders, she commented, "I can't listen to . . . advice from the 20th century that doesn't remotely blend with today's movement."

Frustrated and feeling as though she was being lectured to, Elzie wrote, "The NAACP leader we just met w/was talking as if he's been out for the past 76 days. Not even saying he has to be frontline but WHO ARE YOU?" She continued that an "older lady today told me that the old school way was the right [way]. I politely reminded her if the old way worked so well we wouldn't be here." Based on her interaction, she said, "I'm just stating the facts on how I see the NAACP. No slander, no anger. I simply don't feel anything about them as it relates to Ferguson." In the end, however, Elzie explained that when in counsel with the elders, she would "try to do my best to listen to what's being said and pick out the good parts."

The tension was unfortunate but almost inevitable. The NAACP

On November 23, St. Louis, Missouri, United States, key organizers and communicators DeRay Mckesson (not wearing his distinct blue vest) and Johnetta Elzie stand at the corner of S. Grand Boulevard and Shaw Avenue at the end of a protest march for VonDerrit Myers Jr. in the Shaw neighborhood and south St. Louis. Mckesson and Elzie produced a newsletter about protests in Ferguson and St. Louis related to police shootings. *Photo: David Carson*/St. Louis Post-Dispatch/*Polaris*

IF WE DON'T GET IT 51

leaders were interested in progress and supporting young people, but establishing trust and communicating effectively in the middle of a crisis is difficult under any circumstances. It must have been difficult for some young people to believe, but the NAACP, when founded and operating in its early years, was considered by many older Black people to be a radical organization. White racists certainly saw it as a threat and mobilized resources to undermine its efforts. As is almost always the case, living long enough leads to a certain element of conservatism in most people and organizations. That has to do with the recognition of what could be lost. For young people, who had little materially to lose and who were just beginning life, there was every reason to risk it all. Current St. Louis City mayor Tishaura Jones, who was then city treasurer, put it well: "Sometimes members of the older generations can't recognize the passion in the young people that once blazed in them." [29] The generations were of the same liberation lineage—they just needed a bridge.

Just as the elder state education board member Mike Jones realized it was time to pass the torch in hopes that the youth could carry it further, young activists wanted to move beyond the ministerial, messianic movement model that had worked for the elders. The Rev. Jesse Jackson and Rev. Al Sharpton came to Ferguson to a mixed reception. Many young people were unfamiliar with their past victories and organizational efforts on behalf of Black people. Jackson and Sharpton had been highly criticized in conservative media, but they have a well-documented record of garnering resources for Black workers and citizens.

The narrative surrounding Jackson and Sharpton in the conservative and even mainstream media was that they were "race hustlers" who sought ways to benefit from the struggles of Black people. That narrative was especially powerful when those on the ground knew little about the history of Operation PUSH (People United to Save Humanity) or Jackson's work as a student activist at North Carolina A&T State University. Consequently, Jackson, who ran for U.S. president in 1984 and 1988, upon arriving to

St. Louis was met with the suspicion of the younger generation. One man suggested that young people look to the hip-hop generation for their leadership and "not just some old Christian pastor who was around when Martin Luther King was around."[30]

Day-one activist Darren Seals claimed, "I ran Jesse out of the Canfield."[31] Seals described how he walked past Jackson's security and told the elder activist, "You gotta leave. . . . You gotta go. We don't need you here. We don't want you here." Shortly after, the Rev. Jackson left.

In addition to believing the answer to current problems did not lie with older leaders, some younger activists contended the solutions could not come from the political system as it stood. Desperate for immediate help, MAU leader Ashley Yates said, "We're not vying for political capital.[32] We're not vying for a political position in the world to, say, let us vote, or let us have this. . . . What we're vying for is actually our lives." Making it plain, she explained that "our level of commitment is what you would do to fight for your life." Tory Russell, several years after Brown's death, stated emphatically, "If we're looking for Black liberation through a ballot box or through city hall, then we're kidding ourselves."[33]

4.

DEMOCRACY IS IN THE STREETS: MOTHERS, THUGS, AND THE DISPOSSESSED

Mothers, grandmothers, aunties, and sisters took over the streets of Ferguson with their children. Alongside them were the type of people who terrify respectable America. These were the Black youth with neck tattoos, piercings, and sagging pants; they were the kind who smoked weed and cursed in public. Respectable people typically crossed the street when encountering them. But that Sunday, those young "thugs," as conservative America called them, were the consummate democrats, protecting the republic.[1] Those patriots marched with the women who had reared and protected them and those who had lost loved ones to gun violence. They walked the streets with a different mission: rather than money, product, or territory, they were in search of justice for Mike Brown, the young man they knew from the neighborhood.

My father, Alphonso Bradley, who was a retired U.S. Army command sergeant major and combat veteran of the Korean and Vietnam conflicts, happened to be in St. Louis celebrating his birthday at the time that Wilson killed Brown and left the boy in the street for hours. A dedicated servant at his home church, the elder Bradley enjoyed attending services when he visited. As it so happened, I had been invited to speak at Washington Tabernacle Missionary Baptist Church on Sunday, August 10. The topic was on African American education, and the discussion was to occur during Sunday school at 9 a.m. I presented alongside then Washington University in St. Louis assistant professor Lerone Martin, who had been working on a book regarding the innovation of Black preachers who, during the early to mid-twentieth century, recorded albums of sermons that were then distributed nationally.

The previous day, I had heard from a student, who let me know that an unarmed Black teenager had been killed in the Canfield Green apartment complex. The death of any youth but particularly Black youth always saddened me, as I helped establish and worked with Black male initiatives at area institutions. Tragically, in the St. Louis metropolitan area, the loss of life for young Black men happened enough for it not to be completely shocking. The student told me that it was a police officer who had killed the youth and that the officer had let the body remain in the street without cover for hours. This was disturbing news on every level. Based on earlier volunteer experiences with youth in the complex, I knew there were many children in the area, and the road on which the policeman shot the young man was essentially the only one in and out of the complex.

I could only imagine what they saw and how it traumatized them, as a body with skin color like theirs laid lifeless, bleeding out on the hot asphalt in the 100 percent humidity of the summer day. This image sent a message to young people about what they could expect from confrontational interactions with the police. The shooting also sent a message to parents, indicating that police would kill their children to ensure that everyone complied with commands. That Brown's body lay uncovered for so long sent the message that he—and potentially all Black people who faced police violence—was not worthy of the respect and decency a sheet would have afforded to the deceased.

Before beginning my part of the church discussion, I asked for a moment of silence and prayer for Michael Brown, whom the Ferguson police had killed. The congregants obliged, and I embarked on a lecture covering the systemic racism at the root of American education and how Black youth challenged discrimination at every step—even when adults could not or would not rise up.

In particular, I discussed the teenager, Barbara Johns, who shamed the adults in her community of Farmville, Virginia, into action when she led a student strike that resulted in a lawsuit against the school district. That suit became an anchor for the nationally famous U.S. Supreme Court case *Brown v. Board of Education* (1954). It was not lost on me that young people were some of the first to respond to Brown's death and that if anything came of it, young people would be at the forefront.

On the afternoon of August 10, after church ended in the city, I drove my family through Ferguson. There was still daylight, and the expressions of determination, anger, and pain were especially clear on the faces of the people who lined the sidewalks and parking lots on West Florissant Avenue. In addition to the patriots, there was a heavy police presence. Overhead, the propellers of helicopters thumped, while law enforcement cordoned off streets. My father, who as a soldier fighting the Cold War in Asia took up such practices on behalf of his nation, shared his thoughts out loud, declaring: "This place is occupied!" His head swiveled back and forth watching the people protesting and the Ferguson police posted in certain sections. At the time, the citizen-activists shouted: "Hands Up, Don't Shoot!" and whenever a car honked its horn, marchers threw their hands in the air in the way they imagined Mike Brown doing when Darren Wilson drew his firearm. My family drove, honked, and put our fists outside the windows in solidarity. It was a remarkable scene for St. Louis, one that featured a sentiment that I had not witnessed in my lifetime.

When my family made it home, we watched the news incessantly, checking to make sure the police did not harm the protesters. I received an email from a local nonprofit leader, Charli Cooksey, calling for a meeting of young leaders at the office of the *St. Louis American,* the perennially award-winning Black weekly, that was to take place the next morning. That night,

I let my father know about the meeting. I could not sleep that night and stayed up watching coverage of the QuikTrip on West Florissant burning.

Sometime after 11 p.m., I received a frantic call from Christopher Walter, a good student of mine from Saint Louis University. Two years before the Uprising, I was his professor and mentor when he went through the Billikens Bridge to Success summer transitional program for first generation and underrepresented students. Walter was a graduate of Metro Academic and Classical High School in St. Louis and starting his sophomore year at the university. He was popular on campus, and his peers (as well as faculty and staff) greatly respected him as a leader and friend. He had grown close to another sophomore, Jonathan Pulphus, who had graduated from Crossroads College Preparatory Academy. Pulphus was quite familiar with the campus of SLU, as his mother was employed there. Like Walter, Pulphus was very dynamic and could, with ease, capture the attention of groups large and small with his smile and wit.

I had both young men in a class based on the Black Freedom Movement, and we frequently met to do service projects in the St. Louis Black community. Pulphus, at the time, was dating a recent graduate of Cardinal Ritter College Preparatory High School, Alisha Sonnier, whom I had met on a few occasions but did not know as well. Sonnier was an incoming first-year student at SLU. All three young people were in Ferguson protesting the immense police presence that night.

As neighborhood people rose up to resist the increased police presence and activity, the students joined with the people. Not surprisingly, they found themselves leading chants and in confrontation with the authorities. Pulphus, according to Walter (who was on the phone with me), had engaged in an altercation with police and refused to back down. Pulphus remembered asking the police "what the hell they thought they were doing" pointing weapons at children. "Get the fuck back," the police

IF WE DON'T GET IT

ordered Pulphus, and then they pointed their firearms at Pulphus and doused him with pepper spray. Walter also said that officers were shooting rubber bullets.

Stunned, I told them to get away as fast as they could, but Walter assured me that they had already reached safety. Sonnier had picked up and dragged Pulphus to the first house available, where the resident attempted to help by spraying the young man with water. That seemed to worsen the effect of the pepper spray. Sonnier, once again, carried Pulphus, this time to the home of Etefia Umana. I told Walter I was coming to get them. In a calm voice, Walter told me that "Mr. E is taking care of Jonathan" and that they were okay for now. I asked to speak with Umana (Mr. E), whom I had known from SLU Black Alumni events. Umana, in a hurried tone, said that he had the young rebels and that they were trying to figure out how to get all the pepper spray off the skin of the "baby."

Pulphus later said that the pepper spray felt like "if you have a scab on your wrist or your arm and you pour hot sauce and salt on it" except it felt like that all over his body.[2] Sonnier went on Twitter to find a remedy for neutralizing pepper spray; a Palestinian activist counseled her to use milk. The remedy worked, and the young rebel found some relief. In spite of a harrowing night, Pulphus had orientation for resident advisor training the next morning. Coincidentally, less than two weeks later, Pulphus paid his debt to Sonnier, Walter, and Umana forward when Cassandra Roberts courageously knelt in protest in front of oncoming armored personnel vehicles that ejected tear-gas canisters. After pulling her to safety, Pulphus used milk from the McDonald's on West Florissant to help Roberts. On August 18, at 12:35 a.m., a photojournalist from the *St. Louis Post-Dispatch*, Robert Cohen, shared a picture with the words "Cassandra Roberts gassed, helped by strangers in #Ferguson" on Twitter.

I showed up to the meeting at the *St. Louis American* with my father at my side. It was supposed to be a junta of young leaders, but I had always relied on my father's wisdom, and I was sure the attendees would not mind his presence. In fact, he was not the only elder there: Dr. Donald M. Suggs (owner/publisher of the *St. Louis American*) and Virvus Jones (longtime St. Louis politician and strategist) attended as well. The younger participants were Tishaura Jones (then St. Louis city treasurer); Brittany Packnett Cunningham (then an administrator for Teach for America); Charli Cooksey (who was executive director of InspireSTL, a nonprofit); Michael Butler (then Missouri state representative for District 79); Mark Butler (brother of Michael and a real estate broker in the city); Evan Krauss (then director of Faith Community Mobilization); Kira Van Niel (support and test systems chief of staff at Boeing); and Justin Hansford (assistant professor at the Saint Louis University School of Law). Many of the participants had received the *St. Louis American* "Young Leaders" award in previous years. As the meeting started, they quickly did introductions and decried what was occurring twenty minutes away in Ferguson. They all had ideas of what should happen and what they should be doing. Everyone in the room had accomplished much in their careers up to that point, and the way they thought revealed this. One of the suggestions Butler, Jones, myself, and several others made was for the city of Ferguson to have a citizens review board. Packnett Cunningham and Hansford concurred but added it needed subpoena powers that could oversee and sanction police misbehavior. Virvus Jones, who had at one point been the St. Louis city comptroller, remarked that the idea had great merit but that it would not go anywhere because of the grip that the police union had on politics in the county and city. Still, he said, it would be a step toward justice to have it.

One of the main themes of the meeting was the need not to calm the people down, but to encourage the people to express themselves and their anger. Their influence as leaders, they decided, would be misplaced if they attempted to rush the healing process by calling for peace before justice. They all, of

IF WE DON'T GET IT   59

course, hoped things would remain peaceful, but hope was all they had.

Another major theme of the discussion was that of narrative: who gets to speak for Black people and who would speak for young people around the age of Mike Brown? During that meeting, they committed to two action steps: the paper would cover in detail what was happening in Ferguson with a particular eye toward youth, and the young professionals would use whatever individual and collective resources at their disposal to uplift and amplify the voices of young Black people. They came up with a name on the fly. They would call themselves the Young Citizens Council. One of the council's first tasks was to construct an op-ed outlining its goals and purpose. They understood that because they were achieving in their careers, they could gain traction amongst those in the business community who were concerned about the reverberations of a violent uprising in the St. Louis metropolitan area.

Members of the council brainstormed whom else they needed to invite. Suggestions included Reena Hajat Carroll (director of the Diversity Awareness Partnership); Derecka Purnell (student at Harvard University School of Law); and L. Jared Boyd (graduate of University of Virginia Law and chief of staff to the city treasurer). As some of the members were beginning to receive media inquiries, they collectively decided on vital talking points and commitments. The primary commitment was to try, as often as possible, to encourage the news media to interview young people or to have young people with them when they were interviewed and to center young people in their conversations.

That Monday, the *Chris Hayes Show* on MSNBC contacted me for an interview. I accepted the invitation on the condition that I could have young people (in this case my students) with me. Several students met me in the parking lot where the QuikTrip burned. One, Josh Jones, son of Pastor Michael Jones Sr., who shepherded one of the largest predominantly Black churches in the St. Louis metropolitan area, met me. A DePauw University alumnus, Josh Jones was at SLU to attain a master's in social work. He had recently been hired to be the assistant for the African American Male Scholars Initiative (AAMS), a retention program that Jones's older brother, Mike Jones (who had graduated from SLU with bachelor's and doctorate degrees), helped establish a couple of years earlier. Along with LaTanya Buck, I co-chaired the mentoring group that sought to retain Black undergraduate males, which was the least retained demographic in higher education. The Jones brothers, Buck, and I worked hard to ensure that the general representation of Black men included formally educated young people as well.

During the interview, Hayes asked me about the political representation and relationship of residents to the police. I discussed the phenomenon of white flight from the City of St. Louis that occurred after the 1954 *Brown v. Board* decision and especially after the expansion of Interstate 64/U.S. Highway 40 to the northern suburbs. I mentioned the migration of Black people of means to North County but also those who were displaced when the large subsidized housing complexes in St. Louis, like the Pruitt Igoe, Darst-Webbe, and eventually Blue-Meyer, had their projects closed and destroyed after the federal and state governments gave up hope of maintaining the high-rise apartment units. The Blue-Meyer officially closed in March of 2014. Some residents, seeking affordable housing, moved to areas like Ferguson and the Canfield Green apartment complex for refuge.

I urged Hayes to speak to the students as well. They acquitted themselves and their peers wonderfully well, explaining that Ferguson was an unlikely place for rebellion. Those first interviews took place during the daylight hours on West Florissant Avenue, when the crowd was a beautiful mix of citizens and patriots. The crowd of demonstrators was categorically diverse. Racially, the crowd marching up and down West Florissant was mostly Black, but the age demographics varied greatly. I walked next to women who held their kindergarten-aged grandchildren's hands. One elder, as they marched, told me she could not understand why she had to do this again, that she thought she was done with all of this. As I turned to agree with her, she had tears in her eyes.

There, however, were not just grandma activists on the street. There were those marchers who passed blunts and fifths of cognac back and forth. Many school-aged demonstrators carried signs and shouted the loudest. Unlike the tears and sadness I saw in the elder woman's eyes, I saw determination and anger in the younger people. The anger I observed was not menacing but remarkably hopeful. Although it was universally understood that a tragic event brought everyone together, the young people exhibited a sense of positivity. Over and again, I heard the chant: "I Believe That We Will Win!" The chant, led by a Black woman, made me a believer. The people with whom I marched did not have guns or other traditional weapons, but they harnessed the essence of power: belief. They had full faith that what they were doing was right. That was enough for me; I knew then that I wanted to stand with them.

We ended the march at the spot on Canfield Drive where Brown died. There, people from the complex gathered along with the marchers. The Rev. Traci Blackmon, pastor of Christ the King United Church of Christ in nearby Florissant, as well as several other ministers offered prayers for Brown and his family and reminded everyone that we had to "pray with our feet."

It was inspirational, but that is not to say that it was a Kumbaya stroll. Regularly, I heard "FTP! Fuck the Police!" and "No Justice, No Peace, No Racist-Ass Police!" The elders, babies, high schoolers, thugs, professionals, pastors, and other concerned citizens were all there because they understood that what the police did was wrong. I was there not to debate whether Brown had tussled with Wilson but rather because Brown was unarmed and shot multiple times and because the authorities left him on the ground for hours and because the police treated community members (American citizens) as though they were not entitled to their freedom rights.

In the discussions I had with colleagues and friends, I made the point that if Americans were in a foreign country and the foreign officials treated those Americans the way that the Ferguson police treated people in their own yards and in their own residences, officials would have sent drones or troops to defend them or to exact revenge on the offending authorities. Therein was the problem; no one viewed these Black people at their homes and in their community as citizens.

The tenor of the street demonstrations shifted when day went into night. At a meeting of the Young Citizens Council, Tef Poe, the St. Louis–bred rap artist and activist, made a remark about the lack of "grown-man energy" in Ferguson during the night demonstrations. He was discussing the interaction between the police and the activists who stood off against each other on West Florissant and in front of the Ferguson police station. In the first days and even weeks of the protest, there were frequent physical clashes between front-line demonstrators and riot police who sought to clear the streets.

Although frequently in the crowd, I was never on the front lines. Many of the confrontations I observed occurred when a protester from the middle or back of the crowd threw a water bottle or other object that landed near or struck an officer. That often led to a violent overreaction by police, who grabbed the first protesters they could. In addition to being slammed and pummeled, the police zip-tied and arrested front-liners. Unlike some of the young people I spoke to on the street, I was determined not to go to jail. To that prospect, I thought: "Apparently these young people have never been to jail before; it's not a place one should want to go."

It was not that I was afraid of going inside (meaning go to jail); I had money for bail. I, however, could not see the sense in providing any more funds to the system that just killed an unarmed boy. So, I donated money to the bail funds that had been established and provided direct bail relief whenever possible. Because the Ferguson school district had delayed the opening of schools, there

IF WE DON'T GET IT

was a large contingent of teenagers who had nowhere to be in the mornings. As was always the case throughout time, young people determined to prove a point act fearlessly, courageously, and, at times, recklessly. That behavior definitely garnered national attention, but I remained fearful because the Ferguson police had already shown what they were capable of doing to a young person who resisted them. That was the reason that Tef Poe called for more "grown-man energy" on the street; there was a need for balance before the scales tipped in favor of fatal violence again.

As the Ferguson Uprising continued, going to jail became a badge of honor and a challenge to respectability. During the Montgomery Bus Boycott of 1955–1956, queer, socialist, and Black strategizer Bayard Rustin asked his friend, the Rev. King, why should he or anyone else be afraid to go to jail if the law or law enforcement was immoral. The shame, he explained, should be on the system, not the victims of the system. In that way, Rustin sought to neutralize the stalwarts of respectability who believed that if one were incarcerated, then one hurt the image of the family or the community. What if the perception of being arrested changed? That is the question that many young people asked.

As the Ferguson protests persisted, the police forces employed more weaponry. After spending several nights on the street, I was struck by the noisiness of it all. There was, of course, constant chanting in call and response but also the banging of pots and drums. Conversations between the chants and the constant thumping of helicopter propellers provided background. The bullhorns and sirens pierced my eardrums. More frightening, however, was the launching of military-grade flash bangs and smoke and tear-gas canisters; they traumatized my senses. Those sounds, along with the shrill voices of demonstrators cursing out the police to their faces, were the noises I heard in my dreams for multiple weeks.

Missouri senator Claire McCaskill, very concerned about the violence and disruption, wanted to check in with community members. The legislator called together several members of the Young Citizens Council, including Mike Butler, Tishaura Jones, Brittany Packnett Cunningham, Charli Cooksey, Justin Hansford, and me. A very well-respected elder hosted the meeting. It began cordially and affably. The senator discussed her education and background as a prosecuting attorney. The young professionals in the room were all top students who had done their homework regarding the senator. They already knew that she was a former prosecutor who was quite prolific in terms of convictions and that she prided herself on being a "moderate."

What they did not know was that she and her husband had a young Black man that they parented in their home in Kirkwood, Missouri. McCaskill said Brown's death affected her deeply because she could not help but think of the young man who lived with her. To prevent any misunderstandings from occurring (or worse) with the young man she was rearing, McCaskill had taken him to the Kirkwood police station to introduce him to the chief and other law enforcement officials so that they would know he was not a threat but rather her family member. This was all before Wilson killed Brown. The young citizens listened respectfully until she finished, and then Packnett Cunningham spoke the tongue of her peers. She first thanked the senator for being there and for sharing. Next, Packnett Cunningham explained that few Black people, and particularly those who reside in Ferguson, have the wherewithal or privilege of safely telling the police not to harass their sons. The status of McCaskill allowed her that access.

The politician took the point that Packnett Cunningham made, now aware that the citizens were younger but not naive. McCaskill shifted to discuss the death of Brown and what she was hearing. From her sources, she had heard that an indictment of the officer would be unlikely because there was an apparent struggle between Brown and Wilson that, in the mind of a prosecutor, would disincentivize charging the officer. The senator also said she knew County Prosecutor McCulloch relatively well, as they were

IF WE DON'T GET IT 65

both season ticket holders for the St. Louis Rams and because of their tenures in the profession. SLU School of Law assistant professor Justin Hansford spoke up to say that it is common knowledge that prosecutors could "indict a ham sandwich," if they had the desire. McCaskill said she knew that intimately but was dubious about McCulloch's intention, as she was also aware of his close relationship with the fraternal order of police.

Considering McCulloch's history, McCaskill concluded that things may get ugly if and when the decision was made to not indict Wilson. She requested that the young leaders in the room use their influence in the community to keep the peace. Cooksey, myself, and several other attendees pointed out that, first, even if they wanted to curb any ensuing violence, they could not. Second, and most important, the senator needed to share that message of peace with law enforcement, which seemed to choose violence. By that time, each of the young citizens had been on the ground to see what the police were capable of doing to peaceful protesters. McCaskill, hoping to end on a more positive note, discussed up-and-coming Black candidates for office. She asked the group to recommend young people whom the Democratic party could help to develop.

When McCaskill left, the remaining meeting attendees guffawed at the idea of controlling angry community members to prevent destruction. None in the room promoted violence; most agreed that Ferguson earned whatever it would receive, and that the municipality was fortunate more destruction had not happened already. For the Ground Zero demonstrators, it seemed like a strange request to ask people from a community that was quite literally being occupied to not resist by any means. Resisting oppressors was the basis of the American ethos, as the young people understood it. The elder in the room reminded the attendees to not be enamored of people in power positions but to always remain faithful to the people before all else.

Although I had read hundreds of books about elements of the

Black Freedom Movement over the course of my adult life, what I absorbed in the first weeks of the Uprising I could have never ascertained from those texts. I was humbled to be with those who were unafraid and willing to sacrifice for someone else's child and children. Having the opportunity to observe the different types of power at play was thrilling and instructive. Within the context of the Uprising, what I knew intellectually was reinforced in praxis: the most powerful rarely are formally elected, appointed, or have titles. Those with the most influence, I found, are those who could organize and mobilize the people to build. I saw that firsthand in the young people I observed.

These youthful citizens were the most serious young people I had encountered in my life. I had read many historical accounts about the amazing feats of people their age, but seeing activists, artists, organizers, and mobilizers answer the call of duty was plainly inspirational. When frightened by the police's shows of force, I could always look to the left and right and see demonstrators determined to outlast the opposition. They seemed to never tire, and that gave me the energy to show up with them. Their ability to be angry, laugh, strategize, philosophize, eat, text, and walk all at once was mesmerizing. Furthermore, it was the stuff of history.

5.

MOMENT OR A MOVEMENT?: YOUTH ORGANIZING FOR FREEDOM

"You were not put on this Earth with all of your genius to only help Black people on the weekends. If it is this change we want, we cannot only clock in part-time."

—*Umi Selah, Dream Defender organizer and mission director*

As powerful as the demonstrations were, they drew varying elements. There were, of course, committed activists and concerned citizens, but there were also thrill-seekers and what young people call "clout chasers." Determining leadership in a "modern" movement proved quite challenging when attempting to check patriarchy, traditionalism, and classism. The spotlight was very bright for people who had not gotten much attention prior to the Ferguson Uprising. What needed to be done, and who were the ones to do it? Why were they doing it?

Many people glamorize the sexiest parts of the freedom struggle, the loud clashes with police, the righteous indignation, the physical resistance, and the destruction. Many want to identify with the Panthers or the Combahee River Collective, with figures like Assata Shakur or Stokely Carmichael. It can be hard to see past the excitement to the methodologies of and rationale for particular protest actions or to the contingencies made in case the actions went awry. Where the news featured protesters marching in unison or chanting the same phrases, what did not make the

68   STEFAN M. BRADLEY

screen was the fear or anxiety that some organizers and leaders had. Perhaps they were fearless, but they were not dumb. To survive, they had to organize.

Hands Up United, one of the early groups on the ground at Ferguson, grew out of the Organization of Black Struggle (OBS) that Jamala Rogers had started thirty-five years prior. In much the same way that Ella Baker mentored the young people who started the Student Non-Violent Coordinating Committee at Shaw University in North Carolina in 1960, Rogers and Montague Simmons of OBS mentored the Black youth who created Hands Up United in Ferguson. Founding members included Tef Poe and Tory Russell. Poe, who was among the first contingent of people to show up in the Canfield Green apartment complex, did not know what to do when he arrived, so he called Rogers and asked: "Mama Jamala, what do we do?" Simmons, who had taken over the field operations for OBS, went to assess the scene. While there, Simmons met an angry and sad Russell, asking for direction. As Russell recalled: "I was blessed to meet Montague Simmons."[1] Simmons, the OBS leader, knew the area well as he had attended the same schools Brown did.

Another organization born of rebellion was Millennial Activists United (MAU). which was intentional about the role of Black women and queer people in organizing. Alex Templeton, Brittany Ferrell, and Ashley Yates were charter members. They noticed that the media focused almost exclusively on angry Black men to the exclusion of the women who had been in the street fighting and behind the scenes organizing. MAU followed in the footsteps of the women of the Combahee River Collective, who in 1977 expressed their political position thusly: "The most general statement of our politics at the present time would be that we are actively committed to struggling against racial, sexual, heterosexual, and class oppression, and see as our particular task the development of integrated analysis and practice based upon the fact that the major systems of oppression are interlocking."[2]

MAU sought to disrupt the traditional patterns of leadership selection and glorification that had been associated with the Black Freedom Movement of the mid-twentieth century. Cleverly and fortuitously, the name MAU provided a reminder of the Kenyan Mau Mau, a group of fierce Indigenous rebels and guerilla fighters who resisted British colonialism and paved the way for Kenyan independence. In that way, MAU, in Ferguson, may not have been able to overpower the police on the streets, but it could subvert and undermine law enforcement using social and traditional media. MAU members, unquestionably, were key strategists of the yearlong Uprising. Their insistence on recognizing women and queer leadership forced the movement to evolve in ways that threatened traditional values and the status quo. Their presence and protest at times frustrated other activists.

Tribe X member H.J. Rodgers, when asked if anything ever scared him, responded that he was regularly concerned about what could go wrong and who would be responsible. "The whole situation was dangerous," explained Rodgers, who a couple weeks into the movement went by "Huey" (à la Huey Newton of the Black Panther Party for Self Defense).[3] He said, "You gotta wonder about who's around you" when on the street. The police, clad in riot gear and shouldering firearms, were clearly the opposition, but most of these marches were gatherings of strangers who had not been part of the strategy sessions. Rodgers quoted rapper Nas's lyrics, when he said: "You gotta watch the company you keep and the crowds you bring." Rodgers candidly stated that as the crowds started to grow to the hundreds and thousands, he only knew personally thirty at most. Even amongst those he knew from organizing, there was no assurance that someone may not act out in such a way as to spark fatal violence, "so all of it was scary," he recollected.

When asked about the realities of organizing, people who have been in gangs, the military, fraternities, sororities, and justice movements highlight the inordinate number of meetings and sessions they had to attend. When there are no battles raging, movement making, if revealed for what it is, could be boring and tame. Of course, that did not mean that meetings could not get heated and combative. "Sometimes," Rodgers said, "you was agreeing to not agree and you was still going at the same time." Tribe X and other groups had a good working relationship, but the organizations sometimes parted ways philosophically regarding actions and strategies. These young soldiers of democracy discovered how to operate in spite of conflict. "We learned that, okay, we gon' bump heads, but when the police come, everybody [has to] tighten up!" he said. More than likely, Rodgers claimed, if it was a Tribe X action, the riot police were coming and there was no time for dissension in the midst of the chaos. Once the action was over and they confirmed that everyone lived, the members could "debrief" and discuss what they might have done differently.

These young democrats, providing a model for the nation, took special interest in not just the accountability of the systems they protested but also themselves. Rodgers explained that, according to its unofficial protocol, Tribe X charged those who had the largest critiques of or complaints about a completed action with leading the next action. This was a crucial concept on a number of accounts. First, it fostered a practice of constructive criticism because pointing out problems is necessary but rarely is that enough to achieve success.

Second, it forced the members to share leadership responsibilities and therefore share the risk of being criticized. This was important in terms of challenging gendered concepts of leadership, as men and women had to take their turns leading. Third, it required everyone in the organization to be a supportive follower. Anyone who has led anything understands that leadership is a difficult endeavor, but those who study movements know that following with a consciousness and devotion is an equally formidable task. Adding in challenges to traditional thinking and ways of operating only intensifies the difficulty of the task. Those who could not complete any of those requirements could not be counted on when it came time for the action.

For leaders like Hands Up United co-founder Tory Russell, a key factor of organizing was showing up and providing others the opportunity to do so as well. At 5:34 p.m. on August 9, Russell wrote on Twitter: "I got a plan to get some respect and answers" concerning the shooting of Brown and mistreatment of people from the neighborhood. A later tweet indicated that he was in contact with members of the St. Louis branch of the Nation of Islam (Muhammad Mosque #28, led by Minister Akbar Muhammad) and the Black Panther Party.

For Russell, it started the first night with his (and a small group's) entrance into the Ferguson Police Department to find out what exactly happened to Mike Brown. Just after 10 p.m., he tweeted: "Put your feeling to action," and implored everyone to meet him at the station. Once inside, officials told him that all the information would be shared the next day at a press conference. In a report to his virtual followers, Russell stated: "We came out together & united tonight. I got out and spoke to the ppl. We were angry with focus and that's what matters."

Russell learned an organizing lesson early: people can be unpredictable even if they show up in the name of the cause. That first night, he had to deal with the overwhelming anger of some protesters in order to prevent further lethal violence. The rage of the attendees was understandable, but "angry with a focus" became the primary theme of the Uprising.

The young organizer could have been satisfied with that initial demonstration; instead, he called for people to meet him at the police department at 9 a.m. on August 10 to prepare for the presser. More than one thousand people showed up individually and from other organizations in a display of strength that reminded the police that the young man Darren Wilson shot in the street was not alone. Russell's quick thinking and actions cemented his place as a leader early on in the movement.

As youth leaders emerged, they sought the help and opinions of mentors. For guidance, Russell looked to St. Louis area leaders like Jamala Rogers of OBS; Haki Baruti, who at the time was general president of the Universal African People's Organization; and Minister Anthony Shahid, longtime organizer and law enforcement critic. The elder leaders had been in the St. Louis struggle for decades and knew the streets well. Furthermore, they took pride in young people like Russell to whom they could pass their dearly bought wisdom. They could respect his goal, which was, according to an August 12 tweet, "to be the voice for the voiceless."

Russell and his Hands Up United co-founder Tef Poe constantly faced the question: "What's your plan?" Followers and opponents alike needed to know what the next steps were. That placed a pressure on the young leaders who, learning on the spot, had been too busy trying to survive each night to formulate a complete strategy. The plan the first week was to keep protesting. A mere thirteen days into the Uprising, an exasperated Poe said, "Two weeks ago I was just a rapper, now we're leading a resistance to get justice." Like so many others, he and his fellow democrats were developing and acquiring skills. Still, it was overwhelming at times.

On Twitter, Poe wanted people to keep protesting, but he candidly noted that "kids have misplaced energy[,] police are itching to shoot now at the slightest reasons." Although Poe, at one point, with a certain kind of bravado, claimed he was not afraid of anything, he was in fact fearful of someone who answered his calls to protest dying at the hands of the police. On August 18, he and some other leaders decided that "it's time to move the kids off of West flo [Florissant] so our kids can stop being mobile targets for the police."

As Poe had mentioned in his meeting with the Young Citizens Council, there were not enough officials and adults in the streets at night to contend with youthful rage. In terms of elected officials, he name checked representatives Antonio French and Maria

IF WE DON'T GET IT

Chappell-Nadal, but indicated there were not many others on the street. Poe made a powerful point about the generational and respectability gap. "Mugs [older and more respectable people] go flocking to the Sharpton speeches but these kids are listening to Boosie [the Louisiana rapper] and Boosie said Fuck the police so there's a disconnect." The differences were as stark as Ferguson in the day and Ferguson in the night. At around 4 a.m. on August 17, Poe further explained that "Their [the authorities'] only means of power is control by way of brute force and it's not working [because] people aren't scared anymore. . . . they [the authorities] are powerless." That put police in a very precarious situation. Fear and the sense that nothing could be done allowed the system to operate uninterrupted for decades in St. Louis; now the people were unafraid and locked in on justice. The police answered with rubber bullets.

In their willingness to do what the professional class would not or could not by taking the grievances to the street, high school and college-aged students learned civics the hard way, challenging the people and systems that most affected their young lives. Balancing their student and activist duties was extremely trying. By organizing on campus and in the streets, they exercised what I have termed Black Student Power, which was the act of using their privilege as college and high school matriculants to attain goals for Black freedom. In the past it involved sit-ins, boycotts, and takeovers; in Ferguson, Black Student Power featured die-ins, freeway shut-downs, and the disruption of public entertainment events. Their commitment sustained the year-long protest in the St. Louis area and beyond.

The Uprising unequivocally radicalized a generation of students in a way that would not have been possible in the area before August 9. A few weeks into the Uprising, I received a nearly four-page email message from a white student, Sarah Nash, who wrote from her study abroad. She apologized profusely for not being on the ground in Ferguson at a moment when people from her race could have been most effective. She wanted to know how to help from afar, and I told her that one thing she could do was spread the news. She promised to take my Black Male Identity course when she returned to the states. Student-workers in the African American Studies office, like Marissa Price, who was fiercely intelligent but painfully quiet by nature, worked overtime trying to learn about the various organizations in the street but also the types of bail relief resources available for those who were arrested.

Student Storm Ervin grew up in St. Louis but went to high school in St. Louis County. She currently works for a progressive think tank in Washington, D.C., but was a junior at the University of Missouri–Columbia (Mizzou) in August 2014. Ervin, who had spent her sophomore year of high school on the East Coast, was not new to activism or protest. The death of Trayvon Martin and the scandalous trial of George Zimmerman were fresh in her mind when she encountered the tragedy of Mike Brown. Although she was in mid-Missouri, preparing to begin her school year, Ervin remembered thinking, "I can't miss this moment; it's only two hours away."[4] She had to go home, she said. Ervin gathered a network of friends and caught a ride back to St. Louis on August 10. As soon as she touched down in her Delta Sigma Theta Sorority, Inc. jacket, she went to the Canfield Green apartment complex and to West Florissant. Although she had participated in demonstrations in Boston, the activities in Ferguson were more intense than anything Ervin had ever seen. To her shock, she observed and felt the heat of the QuikTrip on West Florissant burning. The experience that night was jarring, but it convinced Ervin that something needed to be done in Ferguson and back at Mizzou. Although she was without a car, she did her best to keep abreast of the movement. "I took trips to Ferguson with different organizers and activists throughout the entire fall semester." Ervin was not alone, as other students joined the resistance.

Saint Louis University students Alisha Sonnier, Jonathan Pulphus, Chris Walter, Trevor Woolfolk, and others had a challenge to meet. Although I fully supported their work as activists and organizers financially and with my minimal influence, I insisted on their submitting complete assignments on time. If not, then they received a late penalty fee of a lower grade each day. They attempted to resist the rigidness at the time because some other professors in the African American Studies program and throughout the university, understanding the great strain the student-activists were under, excused some of their late or incomplete work. I made it my business not to do so because I was clear-eyed about the history of Black student activism in higher education.

In the past, universities and colleges attempted to immobilize leaders of social justice movements. A favorite excuse was to suspend or expel Black dissidents and leaders for non-performance in the classroom. My students were indeed dissidents and leaders, who caused disruption in Ferguson but also on the beautiful campus. As I observed matters, they were targets of both conservative and liberal forces. Under my care, however, they would never be characterized as nonperformers. When they complained, I reminded them that I too faced similar scrutiny and that I would not give my employer or anyone else the opportunity to claim that I and the students did not perform excellently. The burden of the student-activist is fulfilling two roles that require nearly all of one's attention.

One of the most enduring memories of the Ferguson Uprising for me was the night I met with students Chris Walter and Trevor Woolfolk (an engineering major from Chicago), both of whom had been going to the street since the Uprising began. At that time, the police were trying to prevent people from accessing West Florissant. One thing I learned about young people is that they will find a way to have their voice heard. For Gen-Xers like me, deterrents and delays often work to dissuade. I, however, was determined to see about my students. After parking on a residential street, to avoid getting trapped on West Florissant or having my car harmed by an errant projectile, I walked to link up with them in a lot across from the McDonald's.

76 STEFAN M. BRADLEY

When they finally got together, they told me that Jonathan Pulphus was coming too but that he was late. In the face of a curfew (it was close to 11 p.m.) that Missouri governor Jay Nixon had levied, we joined the crowd marching up and down West Florissant. Around midnight, in an attempt to take back the street, the police, atop armored personnel vehicles, launched canisters of tear gas. Once the demonstrators got a whiff, most ran back toward the McDonald's. As an aside, by that point in their protesting careers, the students and protesters had learned the difference between the looks of regular smoke bombs and what my combat veteran father called "CN gas."

As the trio moved to an area that seemed relatively safe from the pungent fumes, Walter took a call from Pulphus, who said that he had wound his way through the neighborhoods and had arrived at nearly the same place that we just left. As I began to tell Walter to let Pulphus know he should reroute, Woolfolk spotted Pulphus through the fog of gas. They tried to holler at him, but their voices could not be heard over the warfare that the Ferguson police waged. Walter, rightly, declared that they had to go get Pulphus. I tried to stop Walter, who was already moving, and told Woolfolk to stay where he was. To my fright, fearlessly, selflessly, and courageously Walter ran into the billowing cloud of tear gas to find his friend. I saw officers closing in as well.

I followed Walter, holding my breath. About twenty paces into the cloud, I saw Pulphus running toward Walter. They made their way back toward me. Relieved, I foolishly sighed and took a deep breath, inhaling gas. By then my eyes were burning and watering. I bent over to breathe and felt a hand forcefully clasp my arm, pulling me backward. I thought it was an officer, but instead it was Woolfolk, who had disobeyed my direct order to come and save his foolish mentor and check on his friends.

The four of us got back up the street as fast as our feet would carry us. When we stopped, we could finally breathe, but our eyes were on fire. Someone we did not know saw us and produced bottles of water that they used to flush their eyes. At the time, I remembered being grateful for but also angry with Woolfolk and Walter, who gathered Pulphus and saved their professor. I was upset because I thought they could get hurt.

Looking back, I, again, underestimated these young people's commitment to the cause. Each day and night of the Uprising, youth manifested courage and selflessness. They were going to protest, and they were going to take care of each other. They fully embodied Assata Shakur's words that the street activists frequently recited: "It is our duty to fight for our freedom. It is our duty to win. We must love each other and support each other. We have nothing to lose but our chains."

One student, who quickly gained admission to the leadership class of the movement by co-creating the Millennial Activists United (MAU), dropped out of her university program.

As part of their Moral Mondays campaign, on August 11, 2015, Millennial Activist United founders Brittany Ferrell (atop barricade with arm raised) and Alex Templeton led a group of eighty demonstrators in shutting down Interstate Highway 70 in St. Louis County during rush hour. Among the sixty-four demonstrators whom county police arrested, Ferrell was eventually charged with felony property damage in the first degree, trespassing, and peace disturbing; Templeton faced misdemeanor charges of assault, trespassing, and peace disturbing. *Photo:* St. Louis American

Brittany Ferrell was a senior, majoring in nursing at the University of Missouri–St. Louis (UMSL), when Brown met his killer. A mother of a six-year-old, Ferrell was among the most courageous warriors on the street. She was featured in Damon Davis's exquisite film, *Whose Streets*, because of her intelligence and bravery.

Throwing herself headlong into the movement, Ferrell found that maintaining student status, meeting family obligations, and struggling for Black liberation was overwhelming on the best days and impossible on the worst. As an aspiring nurse Ferrell knew she had to triage and treat the issue before it got worse, but it took a particular moment of clarity before she did.

As did many of the students protesting, Ferrell remembered her hectic schedule: "I would go straight from class to the protest until 3 a.m. in the morning then wake up for clinicals after an hour of sleep." [5] That, in itself, was unhealthy, but she was willing to sacrifice rest to get justice for Mike Brown and the community. That was until the lack of sleep physically affected her ability to cover the duties of nursing. "I remember one day my hands were shaking and I realized I had to stop." Had she continued in that manner, she could have made a mistake and hurt someone. In addition to her fatigue, she was also frustrated that the UMSL was not acknowledging what was happening in its North County neighborhood. Taking account of what mattered most in the moment, she suspended her enrollment and became a full-time activist.

Even when she removed her student responsibilities, she was still a full-time mother, and her daughter needed rearing. In most cases she could, but Ferrell could not always count on the help she received before joining the Uprising. "There have been times when I've had my child out during the day to protest because my sitters didn't support my involvement in the movement." [6]

It cannot be overemphasized, the young people who led the Uprising went against all odds. That is why MAU co-founder Ashley Yates commended "the absolute dedication each and every

IF WE DON'T GET IT

one of us have to making sure this horrific tragedy is transformed into a revolutionary transformation of the system as it stands. For some of us that meant delaying school, others it meant quitting jobs in order to commit fully to fighting for justice."[7] It meant a movement was burgeoning.

Lutheran North High School senior Clifton Kinnie was one of the young people protesting at night. Kinnie was confronting two different realities in his young life. At night, he was a warrior for justice, fighting for Black liberation with his band of brothers and sisters. During the day, he was a student, preparing to take his next scholastic steps. Whereas everyone he agitated with on the street seemed to understand the assignment, some teachers and school officials seemed oppositional to his efforts. "I wish those people would stop looting and burning stuff," he heard his teacher say.[8] Weary and fatigued from nightly battles, his instructor's words jarred his ears.

The boy could have sulked and pouted, but instead, he organized. It started with him calling fellow students to his house to discuss what was happening on and off campus. There, under Kinnie's leadership, the students created an organization, Our Destiny STL.[9] The new group was active in the streets of Ferguson but also on campuses.

In addition to protesting at night, these young citizens, seeking to rescue the ideals of American democracy, registered eighteen-year-olds to vote at Lutheran North and other schools so that they did not have to feel powerless to the system that was complicit in killing their peer, Mike Brown. If anything, they had learned that "a high school degree wouldn't protect us from state violence," Kinnie told journalist Wes Lowery in an interview.[10] Kinnie, explaining why they were organizing, said to Lowery, "We [the students and young people] had to take a stance. Here we are, in these schools right around Ferguson, and Mike Brown had just graduated from one." Because of the violence imparted by poorly funded public education, poverty, and police, Brown would not go to college, Kinnie lamented. Our Destiny STL led a walkout of more than eight hundred high school students in November 2014.

Lutheran North High School senior Clifton Kinnie addresses a crowd of community members during a Ferguson Commission listening session. *Photo: Wiley Price/ St. Louis American*

College students had similar experiences and concerns as Kinnie. At places like SLU and Washington University, there had been issues of race and racism that preceded Brown's death. For instance at SLU, in 2010, a drunken white male student threatened to lynch a Black female student, provoking Black students to organize to protect their friend. In May 2014, members of the Black Student Alliance (BSA) at SLU issued demands to the university after several racist incidents occurred on campus.

Professors and staff members became mentors, as young people tried to navigate their new roles as activists. On the campus of Saint Louis University, the members of the African American Studies program stepped into new roles as well. At the time of the Uprising that included professors Katrina Thompson-Moore, Olubukola Gbadagesin, Chryl Laird, Jonathan Smith, and myself; staff member Aleidra Allen worked in student affairs. Other professors and staff at SLU provided guidance and showed up on the street as well. Assistant professors Amber Johnson in the Department of Communication and Kira Hudson Banks in the Department of Psychology supported students in multiple capacities.

The same was true of Washington University in St. Louis, where assistant professor of African and African American Studies Jonathan Fenderson showed extreme courage and compassion in participating in ground actions with young people. There were also assistant professors, Rebecca Wanzo and Jeffrey McCune, who counseled young people on and off campus. Administrators and staff such as LaTanya Buck, the inaugural director of the university's Center for Diversity and Inclusion, and Ashley Gray, a diversity coordinator, provided young people with a listening ear and support in their student lives.

Both students and faculty, as demonstrators, had to learn to operate in a different manner. There was a level of intimacy in movement culture that was not normal in regular society. In shutting down thoroughfares, running to or from confrontations with police and their equipment, and chanting, protesters learned much about each other, even if they were strangers before. For instance, because it was still summer in Missouri and people, essentially, spent hours exercising, most everyone on the street was at least mildly odorous and potentially musty. Then, of course, the constant chanting dried many a mouth, inviting some collective hot breath. Those smells were light in contrast to the smoke and tear gas that frequently wafted through the air.

Activists shared drinks, food, smokes, and laughs. Suffering in the heat for a superior cause tightened a bond that allowed people to draw closer in short amounts of time. As Darren Seals stated in 2014, "It was like 98 percent family reunion, 2 percent riot."[11]

Seals did not clarify what he meant by "riot," but the

physical conflicts with the police, even if they occupied 2 percent of the time, were powerfully traumatic.[12] Most protesters were not trained to hear loud booms or see bright flashing lights or feel rubber bullets bounce off their flesh. Those memories seize the minds of activists ten years later. "I still think about it every day," Lost Voices member Josh Williams said of the days and nights he spent as a protester in Ferguson.

Young Citizens Council member and professor Justin Hansford, even after the Uprising, experienced night terrors and disturbed sleep because of the intensity of street action.[13] In the midst of the rebellion, the battles could be all-consuming mentally. Less than two weeks into the Uprising, Russell described his experience plainly: "Getting tear gassed multiple days in a week makes you feel like America wants you to be dead. #Ferguson." Certainly, Darren Wilson did not shoot Mike Brown, and Jay Nixon did not mobilize the state police and National Guard, for Black people in Ferguson to thrive. So, what was the message the state was sending?

Seals wanted to keep the public narrative focused on community action and not frantic encounters with law enforcement. He said "on TV, it looked like a warzone, it wasn't shit like that." He was correct, to an extent. When watching Fox, CNN, or MSNBC, loops of burning and physical clashes ran constantly whenever they referenced Ferguson. That gave the impression to the world that an entire city was destroyed, when in point of fact, destruction took place largely on two streets in Ferguson and several in St. Louis City. Seals's point was not to minimize the harm to people's businesses and livelihoods that had occurred, but rather to emphasize the reality on the ground, which did not resemble what was represented on screen.

"Some people come to the protest and some ppl set up the protest," wrote Russell on Twitter several weeks after the Uprising began, explaining the difference between protesting and organizing. He was a leader and believed that "an organization without structure is just a association"; structure allowed for clear lines of communication and accountability. In this new turn of the Black Freedom Movement, activists did not respond to singular leadership as they did in generations past. Millennial and Generation Z participants wanted full access to decision-making. That could be frustrating for everyone as the pressures of doing something or anything to win freedom mounted. Russell made the point that "everybody wanna be Kobe but nobody wants to play on the team. . . . Unity will win this. Individualism will insure the enemy wins."

Freedom fighting came at an extreme cost, Russell discovered. On August 28, 2014, fifty-nine years after the brutal murder of Emmett Till and fifty-one years after the famous March on Washington for Jobs and Justice, the young Ferguson organizer, in a moment of vulnerability, tweeted, "My family life is terrible right now and fighting for justice ain't making it no better." How could it? If the struggle for justice was not a part-time affair, as Russell, Seals, Williams, Templeton, Latchinson, Rodgers, and so many others explained, if one had to devote oneself entirely to the cause, one was bound to fall short in other aspects of one's life.

Russell was not alone. I kept my job and did not sacrifice nearly as much as many of the young leaders, but I still met with difficulties as I neglected some family duties in my desire to be useful to the effort. Although my family was very understanding and supportive of the justice campaign, being out on the street in the evenings past midnight only to return home to leave for work before 9 a.m. necessarily led to friction, especially with a new baby in the house. I attempted to justify my absence by claiming that I did not choose the timing of the Uprising. For as true as that was for me and everyone else the movement consumed, I could not deny that by doing "good," I was not doing well in other areas of his life. My spouse lovingly reminded me of this with several four-letter words.

The families of civil rights and Black Power icons speak directly to this issue in John Blake's *Children of the Movement* (2007). Their recollections make clear that it was not just the organizers and activists who sacrificed. If one is not careful, working for the greater good can have unintended effects on loved ones. Even after considering his troublesome personal life, a week after his tweet about family, Russell remained committed: "This justice stuff is hard work but I know most ain't built for this #Ferguson," he wrote on September 3, 2014.

To help those who were not necessarily "built for this," organizers had to mobilize resources. Those included food, rides, housing, protective gear, and even party favors. An extremely useful service was bail relief. The longer one stayed on the street, the higher the chances of being arrested. In the early days of the Uprising, arrests were cause for crisis, as it required individual effort to get the activists released. When Russell got arrested the first time, Tef Poe went to social media to keep followers abreast of Russell's booking and eventual release. Social media created a space for crowdsourcing ideas and resources.

As protesters gained more experience with the police, their approach to arrests and activism in general evolved. The Arch-City Defenders, an organization founded by St. Louis attorney Thomas Harvey to provide "holistic legal representation," stepped forward to help the organizers by utilizing their litigation skills to protect protesters. Kris Hendrix, whom I had met while we were students at the University of Missouri–Columbia and saw on the streets in Ferguson, spoke to the importance of the courtroom as a place of resistance.

Like Brittany Ferrell, Hendrix was a mother but still active on the streets of Ferguson. So much so, she was tased and arrested. She, like so many other activists, made use of the *pro bono* services the ArchCity Defenders provided. "I think a lot of times, people only understand the 'sexy' part of protest, which is being on the front lines, yelling at cops, you know, being in the action and the thick of things. But really, a lot of civil rights cases, a

IF WE DON'T GET IT 85

lot of legal battles are done in the courtroom," Hendrix said.[14] Activists could go to the ArchCity Defenders for help with their individual cases, but the organization also attempted to achieve justice by bringing a class-action lawsuit against the City of Ferguson for the fines that it imposed on activists seeking to exercise their First Amendment rights.

By the second week of the Uprising, organizers instructed protesters to write the number of bail relief services on their arms or somewhere on their bodies in permanent ink. Brittany Ferrell tweeted in all caps: "ALL PROTESTORS! PLZ WRITE THESE NUMBERS ON YOUR ARMS & CALL IF YOU ARE ARRESTED TONIGHT." Leadership meant caring for those who followed.

On the one hand, allowing protesters to languish in jail was bad for morale in the protest community. On the other, police, by holding key activists in jail, created the prospects of martyrdom for figures who likely did nothing more than impede traffic or disturb the peace. The last thing law enforcement needed was modern figures getting the attention that historic freedom fighters like Huey Newton or Angela Davis received in the local jails. In an earlier period, civil rights leaders like the Rev. Martin Luther King Jr. and Bayard Rustin used law enforcement's desire to jail Black people as a weapon to overwhelm and disable the system.

In places like Montgomery and Birmingham, during the civil rights movement, that tactic had worked well, but in Albany, Georgia, in 1961 and 1962, the white sheriff, Laurie Pritchett, realized that as long as there was space for those detained, the system could still function in spite of increased activity. In Ferguson, in 2014, police who arrested activists brought them to the Ferguson facility, and also to the justice center in Clayton, the governmental seat of St. Louis County, which was nearly thirteen miles away, to ensure there was room for all.

SLU School of Law Professors Justin Hansford and Brendan Roediger were activists and attorneys devoting their time and energy to the cause. Hansford said that being a professor afforded him some privilege because class had not started when he first hit the street. Coming from the Washington, D.C., area, he did not know many people in St. Louis. Still, he was determined to make himself useful. "Being a young Black law professor, who worked on civil rights and critical race theory, . . . it was really easy for people to know who I was" because "it was really a small community there." Roediger, who was white, had been working with the SLU Law School Civil Advocacy Clinic. The two worked to keep protesters free. Hansford became a Lawyers Guild legal observer who was on the scene to ensure citizens were not harmed for protesting.[15] Eventually, Hansford himself was arrested, which made for a wonderful discussion among his students the next day in class.

"I wanted to be more of an organizer than an activist or demonstrator," Russell said about his work in Ferguson.[16] As the Uprising progressed from reaction to planned action, the young leaders refined their methodologies and philosophies. That occurred, in part, because of their focused efforts to learn from one another. Russell discussed being "in the room" with freedom fighters and organizers of every stripe. He felt like he was one of the Avengers from the Marvel movies as he engaged in "the right conversations." He said he saw "Mama Jamala [Rogers], I see a Montague [Simmons] with the Black Power fist, I see this radical Jew over here, I see these young people with crazy hair," and he saw queer labor organizers. Russell and the other young leaders of the Uprising, because of their willingness to move beyond protesting to organizing, began to comprehend the vastness of the struggle for justice through such intensive and wide-ranging conversations.

Over the course of the Uprising, young activists took their place as leaders, organizers, and protesters. Not everyone had the same duties or the capacity to exchange jobs even if they had a desire. Some tasks came with more acclaim while others required behind the scenes dealings. Not surprisingly, there was rumbling

IF WE DON'T GET IT

among the street activists. One issue they had was that they were necessary for actions to be effective, but they were not always involved in the planning sessions. Student-activist and labor organizer Danielle Blocker had an interesting take on the tension. She pointed out that the leaders and planners were perfectly righteous and were quite focused on doing what they believed was right for the community. Blocker also suggested that there was a class division between some activists and organizers. For instance, those who had vehicles and reliable transportation had a certain kind of "privilege" to get places. Incidentally, Blocker claimed that she became an activist because she needed a ride and the driver stopped at a social justice meeting along the way. That along with the encouragement she was receiving from mentors like Washington University professor Jonathan Fenderson was enough to ignite the fire of liberation. She had the passion but not the car.

The timing of meetings also privileged certain activists in terms of access to information. In the movement, the clock worked differently for those with different duties. Organizers handling logistics, provided they had available time, operated during daylight hours. Shock troops, field generals, and on-camera communicators typically functioned through the night. Eventually, they moderated to offer commentary during the day as well. It was clear, however, that "the people who are outside [in the streets] can't get up at nine o'clock in the morning and have a meeting because they were outside until four or five o'clock in the morning," Russell recalled.

As necessary as the bifurcation of day and night duties was, when people are not included in conversations, there can arise feelings of resentment. As people were sacrificing their lives and livelihoods for the cause, getting arrested and inhaling tear gas nightly, they sometimes felt dictated to when action plans were revealed. They did not want the police, politicians, or anyone else dictating to them, and they certainly did not want their peers doing so—even if that was not the intention of the organizing peers. Despite great efforts to erase hierarchy and be fair in organizing, the phenomenon of detachment that ground soldiers feel is almost inevitable.

Leaders like Russell, Kayla Reed, and Montague Simmons wanted this to be a working-class movement, and organizers such as Templeton and Seals believed it should be a campaign for the "niggas." If that were the case, then it needed to address critique and concerns of the proletariat and lumpen proletariat. Those from the underclass, who could not afford cars or miss work to attend meetings away from the site, sensed that they were being marginalized for what they did not have, which was resources and time. The movement did not afford anyone perfect scenarios and options. Young organizers encountered the travails of leadership as they tried their best to show their commitment at night and to devote their resources and knowhow in the day. Ostensibly, the reward for their troubles would be justice, but before they arrived at liberation, they would have to travel through frustration. For as good as it felt when actions worked and objectives were accomplished, it hurt when their peers questioned the motivations of the young leaders.

6.

BRING TOILET PAPER: POLICE REPRESSION AND YOUNG PROFESSIONALS

In the early twentieth century, some Black professionals believed in "uplifting" those trapped in the working and underclass by offering themselves as a model and sharing their resources. Among some in the professional class, that involved paternalism and condescension when envisioning freedom. If the new millennium Black professionals were going to be more democratic, then they would have to meet the people where they were and listen to the voices of those most affected by the crisis that overzealous policing had created in Ferguson.

Few people exemplified this attitude more than Cori Bush, who lived less than ten minutes from Ferguson and used her influence to persuade the mental health services agency to deploy a mobile response unit to address the needs of residents.[1] She worked in conjunction with a very popular local community development nonprofit, Better Family Life (BFL). Bush collaborated with Jihad Khiyyam, who was on staff at BFL, to create a more sustainable model of assistance in the complex. (I knew Khiyyam from events and programs at BFL in which I participated. BFL was very popular with St. Louis City residents who took advantage of the year-round educational, health, financial, and recreational services it provided. Over the course of the Uprising, Khiyyam and I saw each other multiple times on West

Florissant.) "The collective hurt was palpable," Bush remembered of her time with the residents of the Canfield Green. Her mental and physical health check-ins with residents were crucial. As she put it, "the people were traumatized."

Along with BFL, the Urban League of St. Louis, operated by Michael McMillan, worked exceptionally hard to meet the needs of those affected by the death of Brown and the ensuing Uprising. That included providing materials and resources directly to residents in the Canfield Green apartment complex as well as Ferguson in general. Sometimes, though, it meant being in solidarity with the movement in ways not usually associated with CEOs of the Urban League. McMillan, along with organizer Anthony Shahid and thirty other demonstrators, was arrested when attempting to shut down Interstate 70.[2] McMillan, who had been an organizer earlier in life, reactivated for this cause, using his influence to draw attention to injustice.

The local chapter of the Association of Black Psychologists (ABPsi) also leapt into action. Dr. Robert L. Williams, one of the earliest members of the Black nationalist mental health organization, took up the cadence of the late 1960s when he—along with the leaders of the St. Louis chapter, Drs. Marva Robinson, Jameca Falconer (now Jameca Woody-Cooper), Kira Hudson Banks, and Traice Webb-Bradley—offered community mental health sessions with the residents and their families. The day after Wilson killed Brown, Robinson, the president of the chapter and member of the Young Citizens Council, received a call from Pastor Willis Johnson of Wellspring Church (on the same street as the Ferguson Police Department), asking the assistance of ABPsi in welcoming protesters into the church if they wanted to talk through the stresses of the moment.

Webb-Bradley remembered going after work, in heels, to the Canfield Green to knock on doors and inquire about the mental health of tenants. She recalled speaking with a woman who was "very, very pregnant" about how the expecting mother felt about everything happening around her. The pregnant woman, according to Webb-Bradley, slept on the floor to avoid any projectiles coming through the windows and to breathe clearer air because the tear gas wafted through the ventilation.

"There was no relief; there was no escape; there was no separation of themselves from the epicenter of trauma. They were steeped in it; they could not leave," Webb-Bradley said of the situation. Robinson also remembered being profoundly sad after hearing a grandmother explain that her grandson, whom she was rearing, had started wetting the bed after the Uprising started. Robinson, shaken, informed the woman that bedwetting was a trauma response and to seek therapy for the boy—when the occupation ended. Even if they could escape the neighborhood, they could not escape their own psyches.

"When the tear gas goes off, all the noise, it sounds like bombs," a twelve-year-old child told Ashley Gammon of the United Way of St. Louis.[3] In order to get rest, the boy slept with his seventeen-year-old sister. Children in the complex were not sleeping, as chants reverberated, sirens screeched, helicopter blades thumped, flash bangs popped, speakers blared, and gunshots rang out. Fear tortured school-aged children. Cori Bush remembered one boy, who told her, "I don't want the police to get me like Mike Mike," and said, "I don't want to go to school . . . because the police got Mike Mike."[4]

What made matters worse was that school was not necessarily a safe space for the children who were affected by the Uprising. According to Dr. Jennifer Mays, who was a counselor in the Ferguson/Florissant school district in August 2014, teachers were instructed to not allow discussions about the Uprising in the classroom. Officials were not confident that the educators had enough training to be helpful in this moment of crisis. After all, it involved death, allegations of crimes, charges of racism, and so much more. Because of that, by the end of August 2014, the United Way of Greater St. Louis, along with Behavioral Health Response and the

St. Louis County Children's Service Fund, orchestrated the mobilization of counselors to the Ferguson/Florissant school district.

To provide further relief in the Canfield Green apartments, Dr. Robinson brought bubbles, pens, and notepads and instructed the therapists to move around the Canfield courtyard, offering the materials and their services. The bubbles were for the smaller children who needed some sense of joy and normalcy. The pens and notepads were for the adults to try journaling to get their frustrations out on paper. Additionally, ABPsi held a mental health weekend where they offered yoga therapy and various activities to alleviate stress. Dr. Robert L. Williams, who coined the phrase "Ebonics," donned his dashiki and encouraged the residents to seek help and to remember that they were not "crazy," as he put it. Instead, he told them in his commanding baritone voice, they were at the mercy of an inhumane system that fostered racism and psychosis from legislation to law enforcement.

In October, former national ABPsi national president Dr. Cheryl Grills came to Ferguson from Los Angeles to certify the St. Louis–based therapists, who were seeking to facilitate "emotional emancipation circles." Stepping into a nearly fifty-year-old legacy of Black collectivism, the therapists of ABPsi allowed hurt and traumatized people space to relieve themselves of pressures that mounted that summer.

Just as there was extreme pressure on those who quit their jobs to join the movement, there was also a price to pay for professionals who chose to participate. Protesting took time, money, and energy. When keeping a full-time job, money may not be the heaviest burden, but having the time to drive to actions and the energy to confront police, march, or run could be too much. Robinson was committed to the cause; however, her employer (a Fortune 500 health care insurer) was not as understanding of the activists' points of view. She remembered the company making exceptions to employees, who happened to be white, not coming to work because they were afraid to drive through or near Ferguson.

IF WE DON'T GET IT · 93

"We're . . . in predominantly white spaces. They [the employer and many employees] are operating with fear," Robinson said. Knowing how beautiful the people who lived in Ferguson were made the employer's accommodations that much more maddening because, she said, "I have to share cubicle space" with these people, who "have the privilege and luxury" of avoiding a very real crisis. "It was mind boggling" because her "heart was with the people." Like so many other professionals in the streets, she didn't "get that luxury"; she could not run away from the scary situation.

Even when one shared a sensibility for the people with professional peers, there could still be conflict. For instance, some of Robinson's fellow ABPsi members wanted to help, but the requests for their presence and free work in the Canfield was sometimes too much for them. Not everyone was willing to sacrifice the time, resources, and energy to the extent Robinson and other professionals were.

Certainly, there were levels of activism. For people like Alex Templeton, Kayla Reed, H.J. Rodgers, or Tory Russell who had quit their jobs, being arrested was a sign of commitment to the movement. For those professionals who kept their jobs, being on site where Brown was killed or where protests were taking place was a sign of commitment. Nothing could compare to the work of activists like those in Lost Voices, Hands Up United, Millennial Activists United, and Tribe X, but professionals could garner the respect of the people by showing up whenever possible.

Professionals could also make themselves even more relevant to the needs of the people by providing resources from their places of employment. Young Citizens Council members like Kira Van Niel, who worked for Boeing, tried to bridge the gap between her work for a major corporation and her community concerns. One way she did so was by leveraging the $10,000 donation match that Boeing offered. As long as the recipient of the donations was a registered entity, Van Niel could direct funds to a charity of her choice. She had been president of the Urban League Young

Professionals group, so that was a natural destination for some of her matched donations.

Additionally, Van Niel brought forth an idea that she called "Corporate Activism," which would address the tension that existed between being a young professional with morals or ethics that may conflict or be misaligned with the corporation's mission. Job security was a concern for many would-be protesters who were also early career professionals. Perhaps a company like Boeing would not naturally support the anti–police abuse efforts of protesters, but Van Niel, innovatively, found a way to use company policy to assist those suffering in Ferguson.

Reena Hajat Carroll used her expertise as executive director of the Diversity Awareness Partnership. Although she did not take her protests to the street, she attempted to create space for dialogue between the business community and those participating in the movement. For instance, DAP provided free diversity facilitation trainings for businesses and institutions to ensure more meaningful conversations about race in light of Brown's death. Additionally, she helped arrange programming around the city and county. I had the opportunity to participate in a panel discussion, sponsored by DAP and the United Way, that featured a representative from the St. Louis Metropolitan Police Department, a Ferguson business owner, and a youth organizer. The organizer and I were loudly skeptical of the officer, who was doing his best to pass a narrative that made the police victims in neighborhoods. He was seemingly a good person and well intentioned, but police in Ferguson, particularly at night, represented themselves in a different manner. Carroll did the best she could to keep the peace and make the discussion productive for the wider group. She specialized in moving frustrating conversation toward useful dialogue, and that was a necessary process in those days.

Another Young Citizens Council member, Dwaun Warmack, was quite new to the region and to his work as president of a higher education institution. In the summer of 2014, Warmack came to

St. Louis to head Harris-Stowe State University in St. Louis, succeeding the previous president, Henry Givens, who had been at the helm for more than three decades. Following in the footsteps of a beloved leader is always difficult, but stepping in at a time when so many young people were rising up was a near impossible mission. Warmack had no previous ties to the region, but he had been in the business of uplifting Black communities his entire life. That he was still in his thirties helped him to relate to the sensibilities of his college-aged students.

As HSSU was a partially state-funded institution, it would have been imprudent for Warmack to use his position to advance his personal opinions about a white officer shooting an unarmed Black young man to death. Like Van Niel, he attempted to help by making the institution's resources available to the activists and concerned citizens. One way was to host community forums that allowed protesters and others to confront issues. He also allowed for the Young Citizens Council to host an event featuring youth activists like organizer Netta Elzie and Ashley Yates of MAU. With the students, they discussed what the key issues were in the crowded gymnasium. Black Studies scholar and news anchor Marc Lamont Hill was there to cover the event. At that revered institution of education, students got more than degrees and job preparation; they got an entrée to democracy.

Historically, Christian Black ministers, mostly men, have acted as liaisons between the Black community and white American power structures. The preachers' duties, necessarily, extended beyond care for the soul because the church was more than a place of worship. It has always been a sacred space of spiritual development, to be sure, but it is also a community center, school, and, most of all, place of refuge. At a time when Black people had little else to claim as their own, they had religion, and they held their spiritual leaders in high esteem.

Black ministers had to earn the admiration of the community.

Courageous men like Vernon Johns, Fred Shuttlesworth, and Martin Luther King Jr. excelled in that capacity; in the Nation of Islam, ministers like Elijah Muhammad and eventually Malcolm X earned the respect of followers, who understood the need to organize along racial lines to protect themselves. Those spiritual leaders were heroes by any measure.

St. Louis City and County is home to many influential faith leaders, some of whom embraced the movement. Those included the Rev. Traci Blackmon of Christ the King, Rev. Tommie Pierson Sr. of Greater St. Mark's, Rev. Rodney Francis and Rev. Leah Gunning Francis of Washington Tabernacle Baptist, Rev. Michael Jones Sr. of Friendly Temple, and Rev. Starsky Wilson of St. John the Beloved Community (also co-chair of the Ferguson Commission), and multiple others who came to the streets or made their churches refuges in the movement. Women and men of the cloth were present in Ferguson.

As was the case throughout the Christian world, by 2014, younger people were not as engaged in church activities as were young people in previous generations. Mike Brown's peers often expressed that they were spiritual, believing in God, but not religious or churchgoing. They did not maintain the same reverence for the clergy that their grandparents had. That is why some Ferguson activists vocally opposed looking to ministers for leadership. This was especially true of nationally renowned ministers like Jesse Jackson, who faced the ire of some street activists. The *Guardian* reported that "Jackson fell afoul of the generational gulf when he asked a Ferguson audience to donate generously to a church, prompting scorn."[5] Washington University student Danielle Blocker was an usher at the event and remembered hearing the grumble of the young members of the crowd after Jackson's request, and then someone began yelling at the venerable activist.[6] Believing he was out of touch, University of Missouri–Columbia graduate student Jonathan Butler reacted, "We were, 'What? People here are poor. And angry.' It was the wrong way to do it."[7]

To be sure, Jackson had earned his *bona fides* first as a student-activist at North Carolina A&T (home of the sit-in movement) and then as a lieutenant of the Rev. King. Butler, of all people, should have had sympathy for Jackson, as Butler later became a nationally renowned student-protester who led a hunger strike in the #concernedstudent1950 campaign at Mizzou. While most remained respectful of Jackson, many young people doubted the ability of pastors from the era in which the Rev. King operated to understand, let alone lead a new millennium movement. Ultimately, the message was clear: this was going to be a youth-led movement.

The sentiment that met Jackson left the local ministry in a precarious situation. Members had to determine how to best serve the movement if they would not lead it. In the end, they decided that their service would come in the way of unflinching support, providing space and resources. In North St. Louis County, for example, the Rev. Traci Blackmon was pastor of Christ the King. In much the same way that HSSU president Dwaun Warmack made his campus available to the forums and gatherings during the Uprising, the Rev. Blackmon opened her sanctuary for community conversations. The governor, city and county police officials, and federal authorities all showed face in the sanctuary of her church. She was also quite present during demonstrations. Later, she became a prominent member of the Ferguson Commission and a stalwart representative of the movement.

Certain houses of worship have become famous in Black history. Even the most casual observers of the past can name Abyssinian Baptist Church and Mosque #7 in Harlem, Dexter Avenue Baptist Church in Montgomery, Sixteenth Street Baptist Church in Birmingham, and Ebeneezer Baptist Church in Atlanta. They became movement organizing spaces. Several churches in the St. Louis area should be remembered in the same way. Those include city sanctuaries like St. John's United Church of Christ (the Beloved Community), where the Rev. Starsky Wilson was pastor. As he became a clarion voice in the cry for justice, he eventually co-chaired the Ferguson Commission. There was also Washington Tabernacle Missionary Baptist Church, where Pastor Rodney Ferguson and his formidable wife, Dr. Leah Gunning Francis, led the flock; Washington Metropolitan African Methodist Episcopal Zion, home of the Rev. Anthony Witherspoon; and Friendly Temple Missionary Baptist Church, pastored by the Rev. Michael F. Jones Sr. In North County, several houses of worship became refuges for the movement. They included Christ the King United Church of Christ in Florissant, Wellspring Church in Ferguson, and Greater St. Mark's Family Church. Just as Black mosques and churches of the past protected young people, these St. Louis–area faith institutions offered loving support and protection to activist youth.

At Greater St. Mark's Family Church, the pastor, the Rev. Tommie Pierson Sr., who was also a state representative, threw his doors open to protesters who were in need of respite from protesting or in need of medical attention. Young rebels, many of whom did not attend church regularly, found safety inside—for a time. Late at night on August 19, law enforcement officers surrounded Greater St. Mark's Family Church; in the afternoon the following day they raided the building. Award-winning journalist Jelani Cobb, who arrived at the church after police left, tweeted, "Witnesses say police came to the building which was being used as [an] aid station for protestors."[8] The police claimed that protesters were sleeping inside the church, which would have violated occupancy ordinances. Pierson denied that activists were sleeping or residing at the church but made clear that the church was a safe place where they could find healing. Cobb, in speaking to movement leaders, found out that the police had been engaged in the harassment of Pierson and the church. "Organizers saying this is the 3rd time police have come here. Last night they had assault weapons," he reported.

Dream Defenders executive director Phil Agnew, who had

IF WE DON'T GET IT 99

come to offer training sessions to organizers, said, "In no uncertain terms, this was a place where this community deemed, a place where we could come and feel—what? Safe." Agnew explained, "What they did today was tell us what? There is no safety here."[9] In 1963, that was the message that the white supremacist bombers of the Sixteenth Street Baptist Church and Fred Shuttlesworth's Bethel Baptist Church in Birmingham sent to Black citizens interested in exercising their freedom rights as Americans. It still resonated in Ferguson.

Amnesty International showed up to the church to offer its services and support. The actions of the police only cemented Greater St. Mark's place in the minds of activists as a major strategizing center of the movement.

Just as allies and accomplices like white Unitarian Universalist minister James Reeb met harm because of their support of the Black Freedom movement in Alabama in 1965, white advocates of the Ferguson activists were hurt as well. Police fired rubber bullets into the midsection of the Rev. Renita Lamkin, who regularly attended night demonstrations. Thankfully, her story did not end like that of the Rev. Reeb, whom white vigilantes beat to death. Although the Rev. Lamkin survived, she too, received a message about her participation in the movement.

The Rev. Willis Johnson and Rev. Tommie Pierson's churches were much closer to the action. Both pastors kept their spaces open to protesters. I remembered conversing with the Rev. Osagyefo Sekou over sandwiches at Wellspring Church one late night after protesting at the police department. We appreciated that the resource was available for those needing a rest from the noise and intensity of protesting. These churches offered programming and activities that accommodated the needs of the activists. Perhaps most significant, these and the other pastors mentioned did not pass judgment on activists but also did not feel the need to justify their behavior. They were Christian and believed in forgiveness, but they also recognized righteous anger and the need for justice as a principle Jesus appreciated greatly. With the Uprising, these churches and pastors had the opportunity to live out the words they had preached for years.

That rang true when it came time for Mike Brown's funeral, when the family selected Friendly Temple as the host church. Where other megachurches had moved out of the poverty-stricken neighborhood, Friendly Temple stayed. "We happen to be a church in the community," Pastor Jones explained.[10] Inasmuch, he believed it was the church's duty to the people in the neighborhood to "revitalize their hope and spirit by raising them, training them, giving them opportunities to be lifted up above poverty." I had addressed the Friendly Temple congregation several times regarding the role of the Black church in history and to celebrate graduates in the congregation. Like many others in the community, I knew that this pastor and church were the right place for Brown's homegoing.

The evening before the service, the Missouri History Museum hosted a "Ferguson town hall" event that addressed the death of Brown and the Uprising. There, social critic Kevin Powell addressed an audience, and local activists facilitated a community conversation. The president of Alpha Phi Alpha Fraternity, Inc. Mark Tillman, was also present. Tillman stated that the fraternity was proudly covering the cost of Brown's funeral. The first collegiate Black fraternity, like the other Black Greek-letter organizations, had a responsibility to protect young black men like Brown and Trayvon Martin, Tillman asserted.[11] The racially and generationally mixed crowd was palpably angry, sad, and confused.

When I parked for the funeral on August 26, I was amazed at the volume of people present. I saw and greeted Dr. Donald M. Suggs, publisher of the award-winning weekly *St. Louis American* and member of Alpha Phi Alpha. As we walked toward the sanctuary, we observed people selling T-shirts on the sidewalk. I saw Pastor Jones's son and graduate assistant for SLU's African American Male Scholars Initiative, Josh Jones, ushering. The younger

Jones, who spent nights protesting and days working, already looked exasperated and the service had not begun. Suggs and I walked in with Michael McMillan, the executive director of the Urban League of St. Louis, perhaps the largest nonprofit serving the needs of Black residents. Inside we saw many of the youth who had been active on the street in Ferguson.

I took a seat behind Dorian Johnson, the friend whom Brown was with when he perished. Johnson was there with his attorney, Freeman Bosley Jr., son of St. Louis's first Black mayor. Johnson, looking clean with newly braided hair, briefly greeted me with sadness in his eyes. A few pews ahead of me there was some commotion amongst the ushers about seating. I noticed the Rev. Jesse Jackson, waiting to be seated, and after some more consultation among the ushers, he was. The family and other supporters like the Rev. Al Sharpton and attorney Benjamin Crump sat in the first rows. Crump had been on West Florissant with protesters early on; I met him and a local attorney, Anthony Gray, at one of the few restaurants that stayed open after dark, the Ferguson Burger Bar. Behind me sat Mississippi rapper and activist David Banner, who greeted everyone around him with sincerity. He and other famous rappers had lifted up Brown's name in their music. Although it was a sad occasion, I was pleasantly surprised to see historian and activist Donna Murch at the funeral as well.

The family of Brown sat stoically in the front of the sanctuary as the service started. In Black homegoing ceremonies, most everyone can fight back tears until the music plays and the singing begins. That was true of Brown's service. Pastor Jones did his best to facilitate the ceremony, but there were many nationally renowned figures who had words to share at the pulpit about Brown's life and death. Most notable, though, was the ability of family members to remain strong and even humorous while telling stories about "Mike Mike." Although this ceremony was ostensibly about a young Black high school graduate who was on his way to trade school, it became clear early that it was a production for the world to see. There were many calls for justice in the speeches that luminaries gave. It was remarkable how much a young person from a relatively obscure neighborhood moved not only the St. Louis area but also the nation.

In taking note of all the cameras from various news networks, I could not help but think about the August 1955 death of teenager Emmett Till in Mississippi. He, like Brown, met his downfall resisting respectability and the policing nature of white supremacy. His mother, like Lezley McSpadden, wept uncontrollably when she discovered how he was treated in life and death. Images of the bodies of Till and Brown went everywhere as a representative of American-style justice when it came to young Black people. In the end, Till's death in that small Mississippi town, like that of Brown in the small suburb of St. Louis, commandeered headlines around the globe and catalyzed the movement for Black liberation. When the ceremony ended, I felt strange. It occurred to me that the funeral marked the longest amount of time in weeks that any of us had spent seated while invoking Mike Brown's name.

7.

THUG LIFE: REPRESENTATION OF BLACK YOUTH IN LOCAL AND NATIONAL MEDIA

During the Ferguson protests, the representation of Black youth as terrorists, thugs, and deviants was relentless not only in right-wing news outlets, but also in the general media, which seemed to contort itself to make police repression seem reasonable.[1] That made the role of Black media outlets that much more critical. Like *Freedom's Journal,* established in 1827 as the first recognized Black periodical, the nationally award-winning weekly *St. Louis American* specialized in uplifting the image of Black people in general and children especially. Former editor and current public information officer for the St. Louis County prosecuting attorney's office Chris King explained that the mission of the paper was to show Black people as they are without the lens of pathology or racial bias.[2] In pursuing that mission, the weekly allowed for a realistic take on the lived experiences of Black people, showcasing their diversity of culture and socioeconomics.

King shared his observation of the paper's publisher, stating "Dr. Suggs [and the *St. Louis American*] are passionate about youth. . . . On a regular basis, we covered youth. They were a regular beat." Rather than criminalistic or dangerous, Dr. Suggs and the *St. Louis American* viewed youth as valuable to society. "Nothing, I mean nothing excited him more than a talented young black person," King remembered. "So then if you were to add to that a talented young black person willing to stand up for his or her people, then you are in the most prized category for the publisher." The *St. Louis American* was unique in that it was well acquainted with showcasing intelligent and courageous Black youth in the area. The Uprising provided the weekly with the opportunity to model its technique for other media outlets.

Even before the Uprising, some young leaders' faces and stories graced the *St. Louis American's* pages. A byline of the December 13, 2012, edition of the paper read, "Brittany Packnett Comes Home to Lead Teach for America St. Louis." The Teach for America program had been a point of controversy in the educational community since its inception, but there was absolutely no conflict about Packnett Cunningham's fervent commitment to developing young people. That was clear during the early days of the Uprising when she met with her mentee Destiny Crockett in Ferguson. Crockett was born and reared in St. Louis, and on August 7, 2013, a year and two days before Mike Brown's death, the *St. Louis American* ran a story titled, "Crockett Is First Clyde Miller Grad to Attend Ivy League School," that boasted on the young scholar's achievement.

Crockett, in August 2014, was enrolled as a student at Princeton University. She was home for summer break when a policeman killed her peer. Looking for guidance, she contacted her mentor, Packnett Cunningham. Crockett had to return to school shortly after the Uprising started, but she took the lessons that her mentor had taught her and implemented them on Princeton's campus, where she founded the Black Justice League to address issues affecting Black students. The *St. Louis American* had already highlighted these movement leaders before many other media outlets knew who they were. Further, the Black weekly was able to capture Black youth in their glory, not just in their moments of crisis.

Covering the Uprising so thoroughly was not easy. The staff of the *St. Louis American* consisted of just a few writers and columnists, who by all measures worked well beyond the capacity of the

IF WE DON'T GET IT

resources available to them. The ever observant columnist, Kenya Vaughn, and the award-winning photographer, Wiley Price III, had their fingers on the pulse of Black St. Louis culture. The incomparably curious Rebecca Rivas and meticulous editor Chris King covered policy and education. They, along with other members of the crack staff, did whatever was necessary to present the news to the community. During the Uprising, that was a daunting task. The staff was being pulled in every direction. This gave the newspaper crew an uneasy feeling. "If we didn't tell the story in the way we knew how, nobody was going to do so. They [other news outlets in the region or nationally] did not have the access we did," Rivas remembered nearly ten years after Brown's death.[3]

"The responsibility was overwhelming because people's lives were at stake; you have so many people needing you," Rivas said of the time.[4] The staff had to be as careful and accurate as possible. Activists and the rest of the world took notice of how the Uprising was being portrayed in the media. After months of demonstrating, Netta Elzie, an organizer and leader, said on Twitter, "I've been calling the media and journalists out since August 9th and I'll continue to do so. Don't lie. Report the truth. Be UNBIASED." According to Elzie, the problem was that "journalists and media are at home SPECTATING what's happening while we protest. That's irresponsible." Staff members knew intimately that the *St. Louis American* "was the only source of news for so many people"; Rivas admitted that it was difficult because "we always felt like we could not do it all." In a time when people needed to trust the media, the staff realized that there was no choice but to sacrifice sleep in service of the community. Unlike those whom Elzie critiqued, the *St. Louis American* showed up to cover all aspects of the Uprising.

Activists had a give-and-take relationship with various media sources that was, at times, strained. CNN regularly sent correspondents to Ferguson. Don Lemon infamously sported a military-grade hard hat for protection, and did not always receive positive feedback from people on the ground. Elzie and others believed that correspondents were physically manipulating demonstrators. "@CNN cameras were standing behind protesters trying to use them as shields. That's why they got walked off the protest site," she tweeted in October 2014. Viewership of CNN and other networks spiked because of the domestic warfare that raged in Ferguson, and organizers were glad the nation was able to learn about their travails, but frustration arose when the young people felt like the media was going too far.

Activists noticed how coverage angles did not show how police provoked crowds or acted abusively. Fox News regularly showed angry youth throwing water bottles, bricks, or tear-gas canisters, but rarely if ever did activists actually see Fox News correspondents in front of the police station or on West Florissant during the night. Its coverage gave the impression that Black youth were destroying an entire American city when damage and confrontation occurred in the range of three blocks. Media outlets like Fox and others, however, had the power to present images of mass destruction to people who would never be able to verify the accuracy for themselves. That is why social media, live streaming, and media sources like the *St. Louis American* were so valuable.

Scholars like Khalil Muhammad, in *Condemnation of Blackness: Race, Crime, and the Making of Modern Urban America* (2010) and Tommy Curry in *The Man-Not: Race, Class, Genre, and the Dilemmas of Black Manhood* (2017) have done well to discuss the way that misperceptions and stereotypes have historically been dangerous to the life chances of Black males. Taking the deaths of Trayvon Martin, Jordan Davis, Sean Bell, Eric Garner, and John Crawford into account, some Black leaders believed there was a "war on young Black men." Former mayor of New Orleans and current president of the National Urban League Marc Morial wrote in the *Chicago Defender* on August 27, 2014, "Clearly, racial suspicion and harassment of Black men, especially by law enforcement, has become an often-deadly epidemic in many parts of the

IF WE DON'T GET IT

country." He said, "local authorities . . . have been slow to respond and quick to blame the victim."

Chicago Defender columnist Earl Ofari Hutchinson bolstered Morial's assertions in his opinion piece entitled "The Second Slaying of Michael Brown." He wrote, "Police officials dusted off a well-worn cover themselves template. They would either hold a press conference, publicly release, or leak documents that depicted Brown as having gang ties, smoked dope, dealt dope, had an arrest record, was a school trouble maker, or engaged in some kind of deviant behavior."[5] In Ferguson, on the day that police reluctantly revealed the name of Mike Brown's killer, the chief shared a video of Brown allegedly committing a "strong-arm" robbery at a convenience store. Even though the chief of police stated the officer who killed Brown knew nothing about the incident at the store, the chief still authorized the footage to be released. "The unstated but lethal message was that there was a legitimate cause, if not outright justification, for the deadly train of events that occur[red]," Hutchinson contended. As he and many others saw it, "the image mugging often works because it rests firmly on the ancient, shop worn, but serviceable litany of stereotypes and negative typecasting of young Black males." Indeed, in Ferguson, it was formulaic.

The stereotypes and typecasting to which Hutchinson referred found a sturdy vessel in Fox News and elsewhere. As soon as the video of Brown was released on August 15, the conservative media outlet put it on a loop and attached stories with titles like "Ferguson Police Say Michael Brown Was Suspect in Robbery." The still image above the article shows a towering Brown extending his left arm in what appears to be a shove of a much shorter man. Those images clashed with a quotation from a St. Louis resident that Fox extracted from the *St. Louis Post Dispatch* in the article below, which read, "I am incensed. . . . I can't believe this is the tactic they are using, bringing up a robbery to make the victim look like he was the person who created this whole mess."

The article also quoted Benjamin Crump, Brown's family

attorney, who said, "It's bad enough they assassinated him, and now they're trying to assassinate his character." Highlighting the efforts of the police to maintain peace in light of "looters" who "smashed and burned businesses in the neighborhood," the piece focused on law enforcement operations. Fox News ran articles the next few days with a perspective sympathetic to police, " 'Outnumbered Overtime': Police Response in Ferguson" and "Missouri Cop Was Badly Beaten before Shooting Michael Brown, says source." The police surely had a friend in Fox.

I was concerned about the lazy media portrayals of those who were protesting in Ferguson. True, this was an Uprising spearheaded by some of the most disenfranchised people in the region, and it was also a rebellion that brought different classes of people together in resistance into a unique and authentic mix of voices, characters, and political views. With that in mind, I began steering media requests to my SLU students who were on the ground. Jonathan Pulphus, Alisha Sonnier, and Trevor Woolfolk appeared on an August 19, 2014, episode of *All in with Chris Hayes*. Woolfolk discussed his desire to find out what was happening after seeing posts on Facebook. He saw, with his own eyes, peaceful protests and was surprised to encounter major coverage of destruction and looting of businesses, so he returned to confirm his initial observations. He appeared alongside Sonnier, who eloquently articulated the mission of the protesters: "to have the same citizenship rights for everyone, no matter what their position is, how much money they have, gender, whatever, race, to be held accountable and to have the same rights and to not be privileged in any sort of a way because of a certain position."[6]

Sonnier wanted for there to be a way to address these issues without having to be adversarial; "We shouldn't be enemies," she said. The problem, she believed, was systemic. "So I mean . . . if you're a police officer and you deserve privacy and your name shouldn't be released, the same way that other citizens who maybe were accused of looting, maybe their information shouldn't be released either because we're all citizens at the end of the day," she suggested. "Or is it because you are a police officer, you are more privy to privacy than I am?"[7] Phil Agnew, executive director of the Dream Defenders, fortified Sonnier's position by illustrating a disparity in treatment from the beginning of the tragedy. When Wilson shot Brown, Agnew said, the officer "was being rushed off and [Brown's] body was laid out there for five hours."[8]

The misaligned coverage of Black youth spurred young people to better control the narrative and speak for themselves. They took a crash course on how to make use of reporters and media appearances. Perhaps the most proficient communicators of the movement were Brittany Packnett Cunningham, DeRay McKesson, and Netta Elzie. The millennials brought social media to new heights with the thousands of posts they made, week by week. Some posts waxed philosophic while others were more functional, but all were available for the world to see in real time. This was essential when local or national news could not or refused to cover particular aspects of the movement.

The demonstrations had reached a feverish pitch when Missouri governor Jay Nixon made the decision to place Captain Ron Johnson in charge of security operations in Ferguson. Media reported that Johnson was a resident of Florissant (a municipality adjacent to Ferguson) and he happened to be Black. Activists who had been gassed, pummeled, and chased saw the announcement as a potential reprieve from repressive policing; after all the officer was local and even a member of the Black Greek-letter organization, Kappa Alpha Psi Fraternity, Inc. In an interview, Johnson said he intended to improve community relations and that "I plan on tonight myself walking to QuikTrip that has been called ground zero and meeting with the folks there myself."[9] He was optimistic.

"It was so happy; we thought we had won," said SLU School of Law Professor Justin Hansford about the arrival of Johnson.[10] Hansford commented on the fact that the news presented protesters as "despicable or wrong" for demonstrating. He said that the day that Johnson took charge, he understood that "us being there was not disorderly or bad," which was how activists were portrayed. Hansford thought that the police and media, who "saw [the protesters] as this big threat," would change their mood when they "put a Black face on the police." Laughing, he said that "everyone was smiling and doing the electric slide," and riding atop cars, chanting. Some media outlets, Hansford remembered, concluded that "our gathering was thought to be evil and bad and unruly and worthy of tear-gassing and arresting people, but it was because the police made it that way." The hope was that all of that would change with Johnson on the scene. I spoke with Chris Hayes of MSNBC that night, and we agreed, noting the lighter vibe and the absence of a looming sense of doom.

The move to place Johnson in charge, as it turned out, was in line with the power plays of white institutions and entities in the past. Ron Johnson had not been brought in as part of a fundamental shift in policy; instead, white officials hoped that he could prevent any further destruction in Ferguson by containing the scope and energy of the movement.

Police representatives asked if it were possible for protesters to demonstrate in certain "free speech zones." Then, they wanted the protests to be finished by a certain time. Then, they suggested, protesters should keep moving rather than congregate or stop for more than five seconds. Resisting these infringements on rights made young people appear to be unreasonable.

If one were blindly patriotic, one would claim that these compromises to solve the problems of protest were not the American way, that it would be ironic to institute such rules in a nation that got its start from protesting and resisting the British authorities. For those who are acquainted with this nation and its relationship to racism, however, it would seem quite American to restrict the rights of Black citizens for the purpose of law and order. To some, these stipulations for exercising constitutional rights were remarkably similar to the slave and Black Codes of the nineteenth century that, intentionally and with approval of the authorities, curtailed the freedom of Black people.

Sensible people balked at not only the unconstitutionality of the stipulations but also the unconscionable nature of the suggestions. While there was a friendly Black face on the police, law enforcement boldly and flauntingly violated the freedom of citizens. So much so that the American Civil Liberties Union successfully sued and won multiple cases regarding the curfews, free speech zones, and the five-second rule, as well the prevention of citizens' recording officers, confiscation of recording equipment, and destruction of recording equipment.[11] Captain Johnson likely did his best, but the system was not dedicated to protecting the rights of Black citizens. That is why Hansford and others became legal observers; they sought to ensure that the police did not trample any more rights, and, if they did, witnesses would be there to log the legal transgressions.

The Ferguson Uprising revealed that it was not the young Black citizens who were threats, no matter how bad the news made them appear. Rather, the law enforcement and the officials who authorized the abridgment of constitutional rights threatened American democracy. Thankfully, media outlets such as the *St. Louis American,* the *Chicago Defender,* and others were able to explore the nuances of this Uprising and the varied identities of the activists.

8.

WHOSE MOVEMENT AND
WHOSE STREETS?

"If you not really with the fight, then go home, 'cause this fight is for real and it's dangerous."

—*Josh Williams*

In some circles, it is impolitic to discuss internal disputes in a public way, but clarity is crucial for this aspect of the Ferguson Uprising. What started as a local campaign with specific objectives turned into a cause célèbre that attracted activists, visitors, and money from around the nation. This invited heated conflict and controversy on the ground, as local activists saw outsiders attempt to add items to their protest agenda and raise funds in the name of Ferguson. Those who lived in Ferguson and St. Louis respected Black Lives Matter leaders from elsewhere, but some locals distrusted the intentions of outsiders and bitterly battled against a changing set of goals, which included demanding queer rights and national police reform in addition to justice for Mike Brown.

As various groups and activists evolved as organizers, conflict arose. Although everyone sacrificed to be part of the movement, there was an element of parochialism that existed among those who called St. Louis home. To be sure, in times of peace, many St. Louisans were guarded around those whom they deemed outsiders. When the Uprising occurred, those defense mechanisms were fortified. That fortification, combined with an adherence to traditional values, became the basis for internal warfare.

Who is a real activist? Battle-hardened street soldiers gatekept activist status. Activism was taking a toll on the people who had given their lives to the movement. Fatigue set in, and there was little energy left for those who were superficially supportive or lightly committed to the cause. As is the case with nearly every struggle, there arose inner and outer group dynamics that challenged morale. In the past, these dynamics sometimes formed wedges between soldiers and veterans who had and had not experienced combat.

Those who had seen and felt the dangers of war could trust each other, in spite of differences, because of the bond they forged. They had troubles, at times, respecting and abiding by the decision-making and opinions of those who were in the rear guard. In Vietnam, this led to a lethal practice called "fragging," where enlisted soldiers intentionally set off fragmentation grenades in such a way as to kill superior officers who seemed to disregard the well-being of ground troops. No one was throwing grenades in Ferguson in 2014–2015, but metaphorical fragging took place in the form of comments and conflicts over social media as well as verbal threats.

There is much to be said about those young democrats who sacrificed their livelihoods and safety to be part of the movement, but those who closely study the Black freedom struggle are critically aware that not everyone who shows up at the protest is for the cause or the collective. I witnessed a university student at a demonstration on West Florissant fixated on the need to take a selfie in front of the police, as though the student had been fighting the power. That was, unfortunately, not the case at all. It was a performance of sorts for the student, who then put the images on social media and received thumbs-up and fist emojis. That type of behavior was annoying to young activists and organizers. Dismayed, Josh Williams, who is still in prison from an act he committed while demonstrating, said: "A lot of people was out there to be in front of a bunch of cameras."[1] He thought it was disingenuous and disrespectful and that those types of people should not have been "in the movement" because they "were out there for fame and glory; I'm out here for business and justice."

That mix of glory-seekers, onlookers, and movement-makers has always been inevitable. Once, when I asked a seasoned Black Power organizer about why he showed up to an action back in the 1960s, the former activist stated with a straight face: "Because a girl I liked at the time was there." Once the former activist arrived, however, he understood the gravity of the moment and eventually became an organizer and leader in the movement.

For those who became homeless and jobless during or because of the Uprising, it was infuriating to encounter clout-chasers or people playing at revolution. That sentiment led to friction with and distrust of newcomers to the movement. Additionally, in some circles, the sentiment raised the stakes on who was considered a real activist; one requisite that some presented was whether a person had been arrested for protesting. It was clear in the mind of Alex Templeton that if one was not willing to be arrested, one could not be a real leader. "If you [a leader] aren't willing to make that extra step to get arrested," Templeton said of that period in the Uprising, then Templeton and others could not trust the leader because so many were willing to give anything, including their freedom, to the fight.[2] Templeton, who on August 19, 2014, had been arrested and jailed while chanting "This is what democracy looks like," was not asking leaders to do anything they had not been willing to do themself. The August 19 arrest was but one of several for Templeton.

One organizer, who was gaining considerable attention nationally as an expert communicator, was DeRay McKesson. Born and reared in Baltimore, his mother, unfortunately, was not present much of his life. Exceptionally bright and intellectually curious, he used education as a vehicle for progress. McKesson graduated Bowdoin College in Maine and then worked with Teach for America before taking administrative positions in numerous charter and public schools and nonprofits. Easily recognizable by a beautifully white smile and bright blue Patagonia vest, he had developed an association with St. Louis native daughter Brittany Packnett Cunningham, who was working as a Teach for America administrator in the region, and several other Teach for America participants.

That McKesson was an "outsider" and not from the area made some activists immediately skeptical. McKesson, according to Pulphus, got in some confrontations with local activists and residents because of "the pull he had with media."[3] McKesson was quite talented at communicating with mainstream audiences, breaking complex ideas down into statements just small enough to fill timed news segments and soundbites. His approach to mainstream networks and outlets irked some street activists. Some felt that he should have never been at the forefront of the media stories if "he was not necessarily in the front lines." Pulphus explained being a frontliner meant being in Ferguson since August 9, and it was a guarded status amongst activists. Despite not being a frontliner during every action, Pulphus said he respected McKesson because McKesson, Pulphus remembered, "used his platform to get the word [out] about what we were doing, which was helpful."

McKesson compellingly narrated the scene when Tribe X and other organizations executed an action shutting down the Galleria Mall and holding a die-in; he also helped plan and advertise the "occupy the police" action that brought activists to the county police station. Pulphus, aware that McKesson could not fully represent St. Louis, believed that the movement needed those who could "articulate what's going on with our people," and "he did that very effectively." There was room in the movement for everyone to use their resources. Thoughtfully, on camera, McKesson articulated key talking points.

Not everyone was as charitable with their take on McKesson. Darren Seals said in an interview on Facebook that McKesson "had nothing to do with Ferguson. We didn't even know who he was."[4] Seals also remembered the Galleria Mall event but did not view McKesson's role positively. When police came for the protesters, Seals said McKesson "was hiding in the car, tweeting. He was scared to get involved." Unfortunately, McKesson's presence and identity irked Seals. "He just came from Baltimore and cliqued up with the other gay people that was out there," Seals claimed. True, McKesson is gay, and he found community amongst those who welcomed him.

It was disconcerting to Seals that McKesson went from several hundred followers on social media to hundreds of thousands in a relatively short period of time when covering the events of Ferguson. He thought McKesson and others were setting up to be "the next Al Sharptons, the next Jesse Jacksons." There was also the possibility that McKesson knew how to make use of media in a timely and efficient way. Conveying a message in a moment or two of airtime was not easy or natural for some activists, but McKesson mastered it, in part because he anticipated the reporters' questions and practiced responses.[5]

Undeniably, the media was attracted to organizers like McKesson, Packnett Cunningham, Elzie, and others. Activist Damon Latchinson described the way that some of the more recognizable activists presented themselves on camera and in print media as "a picture of respectability," which worked well for mainstream outlets.[6] That was likely palatable to middle-class Black as well as white audiences. Latchinson contrasted their affect to that of the members of Lost Voices, who, while sleeping on the streets throughout the Uprising, did not receive nearly as much media attention. Seals and Latchinson could agree that Lost Voices activists were "street niggas," who were "St. Louis to the bone." Latchinson explained that "they were really going to say what was on their mind, unfiltered and unadulterated. . . . They were gonna cuss" and upset the sensibilities of many viewers.

When it came to those who appeared in the media frequently, Latchinson did not believe that it was necessarily because they wanted fame but because media outlets were trying to find some-one who looked to be a "leader" to offer comment. It quickly became about "who looked good, or who was able to articulate the full situation better." That, apparently, bothered Seals, as he thought that historically, movements failed because they were un-dermined by people with "a white man's education," a "European mind," and a "European agenda."[7] He thought McKesson was "catering to a white audience" and wanting "to impress the white folks." The Baltimore native's growing following created more ac-cess for himself and not the collective, Seals believed.

Furthermore, Seals was upset that a "gay agenda" had been inserted into the movement. He referred to the attention that two other leaders, Alex Templeton and Brittany Ferrell, received when they chose to marry during the Uprising. For Seals, the movement was supposed to be exclusively about Mike Brown—and not gay rights. He felt, though, that queer people with ulte-rior motives hijacked the movement. It was clear that Seals was an outspoken, brave activist and inspirational leader, but he was also flawed. Incidentally, Templeton and Ferrell were arrested numerous times for the movement; at one point Ferrell even re-ceived a felony charge. They were day-one officials whose cred-ibility could not be questioned.

Queer people, despite Seals's misgivings, were effectively lead-ing and contributing to the movement. He, however, did not want their identities emphasized for fear it would detract from the original message of justice for Mike Brown. Seals directed his ani-mus toward organizers like McKesson and especially Black Lives Matter, the organization founded by queer Black women. They introduced the push for queer liberation and gay rights in the Ferguson Uprising, Seals suggested. "They [activists like McKes-son] used Mike Brown's death to launch solo careers and a gay movement. . . . They used Twitter to exploit the death of a young Black man and to make millions of dollars," Seals asserted. Seals's animus for McKesson and others he deemed as outsiders led to

Seals's threatening to slap McKesson in a verbal confrontation in Ferguson. Seals did not actually strike McKesson, but the fact that the conflict over insider/outsider status reached that point was sad and not generative.

Looking back, it deeply upset Seals that people like McKesson and the founders of Black Lives Matter gained acclaim and access to resources while Lost Voices member Josh Williams languished in prison because he did not have money for a quality defense. The issues that Seals had were bigger than McKesson and the few queer activists he could identify.

Although parts of Seals's critique of the movement held value, the now deceased Ferguson resident's words were homophobic and harmful to people who, like him, sacrificed for the cause. McKesson, Reed, Latchinson, Templeton, Ferrell, and Aldridge were queer and left their jobs or quit school to fight and get arrested alongside activists like Seals. Though a fearless warrior, Seals and his points of view were frustrating. Thinking back, Alisha Sonnier was resentful of the heteronormative, patriarchal box in which some people from the time placed leadership. "I started to feel that people had pre-baked and predetermined ideas of what leadership looks like, and if you didn't match this predetermined image, they pretty much discredited or attacked or disrespected" the leadership of people like Templeton, Ferrell, Reed, and even McKesson because they were women, queer, or both.[8]

Templeton agreed with Sonnier, stating that leadership "looks powerful; it looks pissed; it looks ready; it looks frightened; it looks fem; it looks masculine; it looks dyke; it looks trans; it looks nigga; it looks man; it looks woman; it looks Jewish; shit, it looks Christian. Yeah, it looks armed!"[9] The young people who rose up were socialized in an America that never associated most of those characteristics with leadership. It is not surprising that some would struggle with the challenge to what had always been normal.

Seals did not reserve his critique solely for queer activists; he also criticized older civil rights leaders. When asked why he fell out of contact with Mike Brown's mother, Lezley McSpadden, he believed that her interactions with the Rev. Al Sharpton influenced her to shift her goal from justice for Mike Brown to money for his death. Seals opined that the minister helped to douse the flames of her passion: "As long as she was mad, the community was mad." With the objective shifting toward a cash settlement, Seals questioned whether McSpadden remained committed to justice, whether that be policy-driven or street-based. McSpadden's later run for office and continued evocation of her son's story cemented her commitment to the movement—not that she had anything to prove.

Regarding the movement, local activists and organizers made it clear: Black Lives Matter, but this is not that. The leaders of Black Lives Matter were doing important and viable work nationally, but they were, in essence, visitors. The narrative that Black Lives Matter funded and masterminded operations on the ground in Ferguson was prevalent during and after the Uprising. Nothing could be further from the truth, and many movement activists take offense at the implications of such a narrative. The local organizers, as the youth say, "got it out the mud."

"I feel that I am the reason that people chant 'Black lives matter!' in St. Louis, contended Templeton.[10] The claim may seem like braggadocio, but both Sonnier and Latchinson bolstered it. Each of the three leaders, along with others, made it painstakingly clear that when they said Black lives matter, they were not referring to the organization (BLM) but rather the sentiment. Organizers on the ground were proudly in the vanguard of the Uprising and planned the actions that demonstrators executed. They did not request permission and most often did not receive operational support from the Black Lives Matter organization.

Multiple Ferguson activists pointed out that there was no chapter of BLM in St. Louis, even though there had been an attempt to bring one into existence. Few would deny that St. Louis is a

IF WE DON'T GET IT
121

cliquish city and that it is very difficult for those who did not grow up in the area to penetrate existing networks. Furthermore, as Seals demonstrated, it is unlikely for newcomers to gain the trust of many St. Louisans even if they have joined the networks. It seems cliché, but Black people in the metro area pride themselves on being from the "Show Me" state, and they regularly apply that principle to new relationships.

Contrary to what mainstream media outlets presented in fall 2014, as the protests persisted, there formed a stark line of demarcation between Ferguson activists and BLM organizers. There were fundamental differences but also nuanced variations of particular stances. For instance, some local activists took umbrage at BLM's call to include transgender and queer rights as part of the demands for justice after Brown's killing. Although a better quality of life for transgender and queer people was a righteous cause, it was not at the forefront of mind for Brown's parents and peers from his neighborhood. This was all complicated by the fact that some (not the majority) of the first people on the ground to mourn Brown and rise up on his behalf were, in fact, queer and trans.

In spite of their mistreatment, queer and trans people pushed through to the forefront of protest lines and organizational efforts to hold Ferguson accountable for Brown's death. In that capacity, several of the most vocal and identifiable queer and trans leaders did not associate officially or endorse BLM as an organization. It was with that in mind that Templeton could confidently claim to have brought the phrase "Black lives matter" to the lexicon of Ferguson protesters without claiming affiliation with the organization. They used it in chants, but not as a pronouncement of their allegiance to the organization. Emphasizing the point, activists in St. Louis and Ferguson stated that they were part of the "Movement for Black Lives" but not Black Lives Matter. The distinction, for the locals, was necessary to illustrate their sentiments. It was not until the third week that Patrisse Cullors and others commenced a "Freedom Ride to Ferguson" with the goals of supporting "the community inside of Ferguson and St. Louis, and then go[ing] back home and [to] organize."[11] Along the way, they were able to establish new chapters in not just the United States but also three other nations. BLM had been known to a subculture of Americans and activists before the Uprising, but in the first weeks of the resistance movement in Ferguson, it was able to vastly expand its membership and fame.

The distrust toward Black Lives Matter built up as the Uprising unfurled. To some local leaders, such as Latchinson, Reed, Sonnier, and Templeton, it seemed as though BLM as an organization had not recognized the true significance of the Ferguson Uprising. Latchinson was confused about the arrival of BLM, "Like at first it was about Ferguson, and then it quickly became about BLM. I don't recall us having a meeting about this. When did we become Black Lives Matter?"[12] He remembered meeting Alicia Garza and Patrisse Cullors in Ferguson and having positive interactions. Cullors, during Ferguson October, was arrested alongside attorney Justin Hansford and artist Tef Poe at a Walmart in protest of the police shooting of John Crawford, a young Black man in Akron, Ohio.[13] The young leaders appreciated the visit; however, they never conceived that anyone would situate the Ferguson Uprising under the auspices of BLM. Templeton explained, "I think that's why St. Louis people get so pissed because it's like, well, you don't even know what went on and what was sacrificed for you to enjoy the ride along protest."[14]

Years later, he and Alisha Sonnier recalled a "Black Lives Matter National Convening" in Cleveland during the year-long Uprising. Activists from St. Louis, including young leader Kayla Reed, boarded a bus to attend. There, they participated in workshops and other breakout groups, but were surprised at the lack of acknowledgment for Ferguson. Latchinson remembered Reed, on stage, saying something to the effect, "We are not included in this and we were the ones" who inspired the moment.[15] "You wouldn't have a convening without us, and you wouldn't have this without Mike from St. Louis, so acknowledge the family, acknowledge him, and acknowledge us," Latchinson recalled Reed explaining. As they had to do in Ferguson, St. Louis organizers Reed, Latchinson, and Sonnier had to "claim the space" at a BLM national event, even to be recognized.

A movement mastermind, Kayla Reed (on the right with the bullhorn) was at the forefront of protest during and after the Ferguson Uprising. Using her organizational acumen, she co-founded Action St. Louis to ensure that politics and policies worked for the liberation of Black people in St. Louis and elsewhere. *Photo:* St. Louis American

In a dramatic display of power, the St. Louis contingent executed an impromptu action outside the convening. A teenage Black boy had been detained by the Cleveland police near the venue. The battle-tested Ferguson organizers circled the police, demanding to know what the young man had done and that he be released. Although they were not initially acknowledged inside the building, on that Cleveland street, the police recognized the potential for the situation to escalate and released the boy.

Latchinson said, "Like us mobbing for him . . . was probably better than the whole convention." The two laughed heartily, stating, "We're not even from Ohio, but damn that; this is our space now!"

In spite of that encouraging moment, the Ferguson organizers left with a much less favorable view of Black Lives Matter. Although leaders like Reed, Sonnier, and Latchinson could not endorse Seals's perceptions of queer activists, they could all agree with him that BLM was making a great deal of money in the wake of the Uprising that St. Louis and Ferguson did not see. The scrutiny of the organization by rightwing media was relentless, but it was also revelatory in the sense that people donated tens of millions of dollars because of the Ferguson Uprising and the subsequent rebellions throughout the country. Understandably, Sonnier asked, "Would Black Lives Matter have gotten this amount of following and gotten this much support, which has a relationship to the amount of financial capital that they're able to raise," without Ferguson? The answer is a resounding no. Putting a finer point on it, Sonnier said, "I feel strongly that what we were intentional about doing was making sure that people understood the separation between Black Lives Matter organization, and us walking in the streets and saying Black lives matter." [16]

"Our work as the Black Lives Matter Global Network would not exist without the tireless work of Ferguson organizers," Patrisse Cullors admitted in 2020.[17] Black Lives Matter founders had to recognize the role of the Ferguson Uprising; it was the centerpiece of the new movement. "Every generation of Black resistance is launched by an uprising; Ferguson was ours and we are forever indebted to every single Black person (and all the allies) who decided to fight for their dignity," wrote Cullors. This was the acknowledgment that Ferguson organizers and Brown's family deserved in 2014–2015 because, as SLU Law School Professor Justin Hansford put it, "anything that you can attest to the Black Lives Matter movement, you really have to attest that to Ferguson, and that includes shifts in the culture, shifts in music, and shifts in television."

In addition to the recognition, the Ferguson and St. Louis Black community could have benefitted greatly from the resources BLM acquired during and after the Uprising. Organizers and activists, of course, spent most of their time trying to achieve justice for Mike Brown, but the issue of resources was not insignificant. Although they did not see the millions that BLM was raising, there were funds coming into Ferguson. Receiving and distributing those resources was not easy, because the St. Louis metropolitan area, particularly Black organizations, had not imagined they would need the capacity necessary to accommodate the flood of goodwill.

9.

LEADERSHIP AND MONEY IN MOVEMENT MAKING

"In the most necessary way, it was a leaderful movement."
—*Charlie Cooksey, 2023*

In Ferguson, people initially came together without concern for identities. When it became necessary to sustain pressure on the city and police, there arose conflicts over what leaders should look like and whose participation was most valuable. Then, young people, determined to move beyond the strictures of previous freedom movements, attempted to normalize queer and female leadership. In an attempt to address multiple issues at once, women and queer activists brought to the fore issues of misogyny and homophobia in addition to police abuse of power.

There have long been conversations in Black movements about who is best fit for leadership, and the Ferguson movement was no different. The Uprising featured many different individuals who said they wanted Black liberation. Some women and queer people felt that the goal was to recreate a heteronormative hierarchy with straight Black males on top. Comments that some male activists made about a woman's place were demeaning. Moreover, some male activists disrespected the relationship status of queer activists who sought to lawfully consummate their love. For queer and women leaders, there was constant challenge from those who were more comfortable with "traditional" models of leadership.

A progressive movement has to be as much about revelation as it is about revolution. The entangled identities of people revealed themselves along with traditional beliefs and expectations of what was acceptable in the form of leadership. The identity of young leaders and participants, not surprisingly, became the subject of controversy. Latchinson, at the time, identified as a queer Black woman named Diamond. Caught up in the nightly action and daily organizing, he had not given much time to reflect on his personal identity. Then, in October 2014, he attended a Black trans march, where he was forced, perhaps for the first time in weeks, to wrestle with his varied identities. Activists spoke about the spate of senseless killings of Black people and emphasized that some of those who were targeted and murdered were transgender.

Latchinson had done well to analyze the racism that led to Brown's death but had not given as much attention to the quieter deaths of queer people. At that march, Latchinson confronted what Kimberle Crenshaw termed *intersectionality,* which was the convergence of his race and gender as points of marginalization. Latchinson thought, "If I were to fight for just my Blackness, I will also leave out the woman part . . . and the queer part." He wondered, "Where do these two sections come in? Do we just leave them off?" It became impossible to dissociate from any of those identities, and instead, he proudly chose to embrace them. As he came to terms with his intersectional identities, he said to himself, "I don't feel like I can fully fight and fully participate if I'm not being honest with myself." He decided, then, in the midst of a movement, to come out to himself as well as to his peers and family. He came to know that "all of who I am is important to this movement."

The issue of leadership identities was caught up in a more general question of the very idea of leadership itself in Ferguson. Charli Cooksey, most aptly, thought "in the most messy and necessary way, there was no structure to leadership."[1] There were, she said, "microcosms of it [leadership]; I believe a shared vision

IF WE DON'T GET IT   129

was never explicitly named." Unlike portrayals of Black freedom campaigns of the past, Cooksey pointed out that, regarding the Ferguson Uprising, there was no single leader, "in a good way," as she put it. In the book, *Groundwork: Local Black Freedom Movements in America* (2005), scholars Jeanne Theoharis and Komozi Woodard, among others, have shown that local leaders and facilitators made the larger civil rights movement work on the ground. There may have been people who spoke on behalf of the movement at the national level, but in reality, there were those on the ground who had to make decisions about living and dying in the local communities.

Cooksey spoke to this phenomenon when she noted that there were different kinds of leadership. "There was a narrative leadership; there's a narrative power," she said. "Some could easily conflate this [style of] leadership" with operational leadership, "but to me it was simply we had narrators of what was going on . . . and then we had actual [operational] leaders." Tribe X organizer Jonathan Pulphus supported Cooksey's observation. He said that some activists "who were on their phones a lot" did the important work of "documenting a lot of what was happening." Their ability to "tell the story" got their "voice lifted up in a certain kind of way," according to Pulphus.[2] It certainly attracted many virtual followers and attention from news networks; some eventually got book contracts. Pulphus contended that, typically, those were not the ones who were doing most of the organizing. By Pulphus's estimation, for example, DeRay McKesson was an excellent communicator, but some frontliners did not consider him an operational leader. Cooksey was quick to point out that multiple styles were necessary, but they were not all the same. Narrators helped to cogently communicate what was happening from the streets. She commented, "The list was long in terms of leaders, and that it was "a beautiful thing."[3]

McKesson, Brittany Packnett Cunningham, and Netta Elzie were extremely effective messengers of the movement, sending clarion calls out widely. McKesson and Elzie especially manipulated social media masterfully by leveraging their personalities and followings. Additionally, all three took advantage of their administrative acumen to contribute to the cause. McKesson, who was a standout young professional who had reached executive ranks in school districts in two major American cities, knew well how to communicate through chaos. He remembers having eight hundred followers on Twitter before arriving in Ferguson. In retrospect, he understands that it is important to "do your little thing every day because the little thing matters. The little thing is the big thing." [4] For him, the little thing was communicating what he saw to social media, and it became a big thing. Religiously, he "tweeted to the wind" in hopes of illustrating the atrocities he was witnessing to a wider audience. Because he had been an organizer as a teenager and bureaucrat in his young adult life, he knew intimately the intrinsic value of providing the evidence and inspiration needed for change.

McKesson saw his role clearly: "I was the messenger." Admitting that some people viewed his rising presence on social media and in the mainstream media as annoying, he emphasized that "they [organizers] trusted me" in that capacity. He made tens of thousands of tweets because organizers sought him out to spread word of or be present at their actions. That was extremely useful to them and it gave McKesson further exposure. So, he said, "I went to a lot of stuff because people were like, 'we need you here because you will document what happens.'" Additionally, reporters were attracted to him.

He realized, with self-awareness, that because of the strictures of time and being new to the area, he was not going to be a primary organizer like some others. "There were people who all they did was plan incredible things. That wasn't me. There were people who came up with the chants. I didn't do that," McKesson explained. What he did, he noted, was not more or less important than anything anyone else was doing: "There were all these incredible people who managed to do huge things, but people saw me because the thing that I did was the most visible." In addition to his work on Twitter and Instagram, McKesson made use of that visibility to communicate to the virtual world and those who were on the ground with a newsletter that featured long form pieces on what occurred and what was upcoming.

Damon Latchinson claimed not to be a leader in spite of the work he did organizing various actions. Instead, he referred to himself as just a "St. Louis nigga . . . who has seen other St. Louis people go through it with the police and the system."[5] He saw himself as "somebody who got tired, and I just wanted to see Black people not struggling anymore." About his willingness to jump in the movement, he said, "This was just like the moment to do something."

Cooksey identified people like Tef Poe, Kayla Reed, Darren Seals, Brittany Ferrell, and Alex Templeton as prominent operational leaders. Templeton, who went by Alexis in 2014 but now goes by Alex, had an interesting take on leadership as well. Templeton, in the manner of Ella Baker with the Southern Christian Leadership Conference (SCLC) more than a half century before, questioned the authenticity of some leaders. One leader in particular stood out to them because he branded himself as a Black militant and a killer if necessary. Templeton, however, dismissed the claim as fantasy and bluster. They pointed out that there "were people claiming identities that they could not stand on."[6] Some leaders, and this one in particular, were representing themselves as "steppers" (those ready to kill and die for the movement) but that was impossible, according to Templeton, because "Darren Wilson is still alive."

A leader claiming to be a killer or stepper without following through was not inspirational or edifying for the movement but rather dangerous, Templeton believed. By not being realistic about one's identity, a leader violated the trust of the people who followed. When followers or fellow leaders question another leader's authenticity, conflict and frustration were sure to ensue.

Some of the conflicts that arose between leaders and organizations became personal, while others remained philosophical, but all conflicts that were not addressed constructively were potential threats to the movement. Philosophically, several organizations like MAU, Tribe X, Hands Up United, and Lost Voices sought to undermine the messianic and hierarchical leadership style associated with organizations like the NAACP, Urban League, and SCLC. The younger activists sought to diffuse the singular decision-making power of a particular leader and employ participatory democracy that ensured all voices mattered equally.

With the more flattened approach to leadership, some groups feature representatives or facilitators rather than traditional chairpersons. Because the groups were newly formed, they typically had advisors but no boards, and so they only had themselves and their followers to satisfy. Followers did not always mean people who showed up for actions; often they simply followed the organization or members of the group on social media. Regarding decision-making, some organizations pushed against the idea that a simple majority vote should determine an outcome, and instead relied on consensus.

Philosophically, young Ferguson activists in their various organizations pushed against an overarching centralizing network. They attempted to actualize the decentralized approach to movement that SNCC advisor Ella Baker proposed. They demurred on following the model of long-standing civil rights organizations and traditional institutions like churches, because they believed those who needed resources the most rarely had the opportunity to influence decision-making.

It is vitally important to remember that no one had been trained for an uprising of that nature, so young people were doing the best they could as events unfolded. Nearly ten years later, Templeton commented on the dire need for political education that was necessary but not present during the most pivotal times

IF WE DON'T GET IT
133

of the Uprising. Not having it led to some of the pitfalls that plagued movements of the past.

As an unabashedly outspoken queer person, Templeton knew this all too well. "I think that [Templeton was] discredited a lot and challenged a lot because [of] homophobia," opined Alisha Sonnier.[7] With a maturity beyond her years, Sonnier said, "Even those of us that claim to be forward-thinking, we challenged the leadership of people who don't match that picture of cis heterosexual white image of leadership." It was unfortunate, Sonnier believed, because "Ferguson could have . . . have gotten further if we could have accepted the various ways of leadership."

Because these young people were socialized in America, they learned to accommodate white male leadership—and to challenge it only when something egregious occurs. Sonnier pointed to the fact that when leadership took the form of a queer Black person, everything was up for challenge and it was more difficult to offer the benefit of the doubt. Essentially, for some Black people, questioning non-white, non-male leadership was too easy and comfortable. That phenomenon played out with women and queer leadership in Ferguson. And yet, according to Sonnier, the Uprising would have never made it to "movement status, if it wasn't people from all various backgrounds, and various types of people who usually don't have solidarity, rubbing elbows."[8] Recognizing the different identities was not easy and sometimes sparked conflicts, but "we were all in one space and found this . . . common agenda," she said.

Sometimes conversations moved beyond critique of leadership styles to personal ad hominem attacks. Once, when debate got heated, a male activist, attempting to make the point that he did not care anything about Templeton's sexual orientation, crudely remarked: "I don't care if you fuck monkeys," Templeton remembered.[9] Sonnier, who was a leader in Tribe X, remembered a similar degrading and infuriating scenario in which she was told that she "belonged in the kitchen," when she had painstakingly put together a plan for an action. "This is all my idea," Sonnier thought. They sometimes laughed to keep from raging.

Gender and sexuality were issues that could not be avoided with respect to leadership, but there was also the issue of leadership style. Strong personalities were common in the Uprising. Conflict, sometimes harmful, was bound to arise. Leaders like Templeton surely faced challenges because of homophobia and biases regarding queer people, but in future lawyer fashion, Templeton did not display a relenting personality when they thought they were right. That, of course, is the case with many, but Templeton was willing to push the issue to confrontation without fear of consequence. They explained that they would "become masculine at some point" to match the energy of their male critics. In that way, they forced their male peers to respect them, but it was telling that they had to display "masculine" characteristics to attain a modicum of respect.

The comments of male activists, Templeton revealed, escalated from disrespect to threatening at times. For instance, they recall being across from a line of police with male activists by their side. As they battled to maintain the line and space on the street, Templeton claimed to have heard a Black demonstrator yell, "I'm going to rape your wife . . . [and] just think about me fucking your daughter" to a white police officer. To be sure, Templeton did not know what the officer said to the protester; also, Templeton, and presumably all the demonstrators on the line, wanted to hurt and weaken the opposition. Additionally, the activist may have not been serious about the threat but was probing ways to unsettle the officer. According to Templeton, however, what the male protester said was frightful and, furthermore, detrimental because if those who occupied female bodies believed that the male protester was capable of doing such a thing, they could never feel completely safe in that activist's presence. Templeton had to ask if the protester was "yelling at the white officer how [he was] gonna rape his wife[, then] what the fuck will you [the protester] do to the people behind you?!"

IF WE DON'T GET IT · 135

At the time of the confrontations, tensions ran high, but later on some male activists admitted to having a lack of awareness and even maturity. One example, according to Templeton, is Tory Russell, co-founder of Hands Up United. Russell, one of the most committed and long-standing activists in the movement, like Templeton, is a take-charge leader who is unafraid to voice his opinions. He is still quite close to Brown's father and family. Two strong personalities clashing in moments of high stress can lead to resentful feelings. At one point, Templeton felt as though "I hated that nigga; I had smoke for Tory; [I] wanted to fight Tory, and told that nigga to pull up on Twitter" because of the homophobia Templeton believed Russell exhibited.

The blessing and curse of the Ferguson Uprising was the fact that confrontation was inevitable and unavoidable. Templeton recollected the time when they and Russell had a difficult conversation that led to an understanding between them. They claim Russell was sympathetic and even contrite with regard to his interactions with Templeton, saying, "I got you; my bad, dog."[10] Embracing the learning process, he admitted to not fully comprehending the effects of his attitudes and behaviors with regard to queer people and women but wanted to make sure that they all could move forward in the fight for Mike Brown. Nearly ten years after their meeting of the minds, of Russell, Templeton says, "That's my nigga!"

Templeton, as time passed, tried to heal from some of the harmful interactions. When catching the Metrolink (train), Templeton encountered a former member of the Lost Voices who told them, "No bullshit . . . we owe you an apology because we didn't know what leadership was." Templeton appreciated the sentiment and thanked the evolving male activist, but they also admitted that it was difficult to get beyond the hurt they felt when the male activists and his peers undermined Templeton in the height of the Uprising. These young people were learning as they were going, and they, more often than not, did the best they could with what they had. Their interactions were a microcosm of those in the wider America.

In addition to self-actualization, money helps fuel a movement. Nothing, of course, means more than a righteous cause and commitment, but operationalizing actions and organizing is not free. The Ferguson Uprising, minimally, brought hundreds of thousands of dollars to the St. Louis community in the form of donations and grants. The direct action and protest of young people attracted these financial contributions, but young people and their grassroots organizations were not fiscally or organizationally established enough to operationalize the funds effectively. Organizations established long before the Uprising, like Organization for Black Struggle (OBS) and Missourians Organizing for Reform and Empowerment (MORE), which were established as 501c3s and 501c4s, became the conduits for donors and financial contributions worldwide. This, indirectly, created tension. The funds were generated by the actions of young people, but they had no direct access or say as to how the funds were distributed.

"People wanted their coins!"[11] Labor organizer and community leader Rasheen Aldridge Jr., with those words described the context of an unexpected action that took place during the Ferguson Uprising. Solidly in the fight for a $15 minimum wage, he understood well the need for money to survive. After nearly a year of protesting, some of the activists were destitute and desperate for money, but they maintained fealty to the movement. Aldridge himself lost his job to be an activist, and he was hardly alone. "We have put our lives on the line; we lost our livelihood, our jobs, everything. This [the movement] became my job," Aldridge said. He and so many others risked their lives and freedom nightly with no access to the security and resources a job would have provided. There was a bail relief fund for those who got arrested, and food was often available, but all the other aspects of life were uncovered. To be sure, the majority of people who participated in the movement at the street level were not wealthy; most appeared to be working class. They, like the majority of Americans, lived paycheck to paycheck. Once they stopped receiving paychecks, life became precarious.

The Association of Community Organizations for Reform Now (ACORN) was founded in 1970 to see to the economic and political well-being of local neighborhoods. For methodology it looked to the model of famed organizer Saul Alinsky, who was a leftist activist and political theorist from Chicago. Of Russian Jewish descent, during the 1960s Alinsky inspired young people to use their passion and protest to confront institutional power to gain compromises and victories for low-income communities. Student and youth activists in the New Left took heed of his suggestions for social justice found in the book *Rules for Radicals: A Political Primer* (1971). ACORN benefited from the tactics that Alinsky described.[12]

ACORN met with national controversy in 2009 when a conservative right operative, James O'Keefe, claimed to expose the deep corruption of ACORN in a heavily edited video that gained great popularity among conservatives on Breitbart News. Although investigations found that the organization was not guilty of any form of deep corruption, ACORN lost partnerships with the federal government and major private donors, and eventually dissolved as a result.

St. Louis had a chapter of ACORN operated by queer labor activist Jeff Ordower. In light of the ACORN "sting" and ensuing fallout that led to the progressive organization's demise, Ordower established Missourians Organizing for Reform and Empowerment (MORE), which sought racial, economic, and climate justice.[13] MORE, along with OBS, became a recipient of national funding and resources. Money flowed in from different sources, ranging from people sharing inheritance bequeathals to billionaire philanthropists like George Soros.[14] Much of it was used for bail relief.

A list circulated with the names of donors and amounts given, which totaled in the tens of thousands of dollars. The staff of MORE, along with some organizers and activists, questioned the fairness of having Ordower, a white man, determine how funding should be used. Pulphus remarked that many felt that a "white man leading all these Black people to freedom wasn't a good look." [15] To be sure, Ordower did not make such decisions himself, and his organization worked in collaboration with OBS. The decisions, however, were made at the MORE office, which was nearly twenty miles from Ferguson. Danielle Blocker commented on the tension that arose around the fact that planning sessions happened so far away from where much of the action occurred, which privileged those who could participate in the meetings. [16]

Money has a way of providing but also breeding mistrust. OBS, which had existed for thirty-five years by that point, needed funds to operate. Jamala Rogers remembered that "our folks all volunteered," and by and large, "our organization volunteered." [17] That was not at all sustainable. Admittedly "overwhelmed," Rogers and OBS launched a fundraising campaign for $40,000 to assist organizers in their efforts. It is remarkable that the figure was so low, but that tracks with Rogers's belief that organizers and organizations should take only what they need and leave the rest for others. The fundraising campaign worked better than Rogers predicted; the donations they received were double the request.

"I think this is when we started to see that this movement could attract sizable amounts of money," Rogers commented. "People understood that we can't [just] do this with volunteers." Rogers clarified that OBS "got nowhere near the money that we now know that Black Lives Matter got and squandered. We got nowhere near the money that Color of Change got that is getting squandered. But there was significant money, and it came from local people." For the first time, OBS received donations from the Deaconess Foundation, where the righteous Rev. Starsky Wilson was president and CEO. He understood well the needs of citizens on the ground, and

IF WE DON'T GET IT 139

he helped his foundation make a moral contribution to a righteous cause. In addition to OBS, two other organizations received sizable donations. According to Rogers, the money was relatively unrestricted in that activists could use the funds for materials, training, travel, and other efforts, but the three organizations had to have representatives sign off before a check could be given. As Pulphus and Aldridge pointed out, OBS and MORE provided the infrastructure to distribute funds.

"No, I'm doing the work, I get the money." That was the sentiment that Aldridge perceived from activists who were frustrated with the bureaucracy, as an intra-movement insurrection began to brew.[18] Street protesters from Lost Voices, Millennial Activists United, and other organizations met at the office on Skinker Boulevard in St. Louis. "There was a group of protesters that said we want the money," recalled Rogers.[19] They did not want to appeal to three agencies but rather to receive the money "directly." The activists said, according to Rogers, "we coming to get our money, and when we get there, cut the check!" Between MORE staff and street activists, the campaign had reached Twitter. The hashtag was #cutthecheck.

Millennium Activists United, in a May 14 online statement, said, "Many individuals and organizations of the protest movement that began in Ferguson, Missouri, organized a sit-in in the office of Missourians Organizing for Reform and Empowerment (MORE). The demand was simple: Cut the checks." Tired and frustrated with having to survive to live to struggle for freedom, the statement contended that MORE and OBS established a joint account "in which national donors from all over the world have donated over $150,000 to sustain the movement."[20]

The activists were not upset that the money was raised. According to the statement, it was the idea that "the poor black [people] of this movement who served as cash generators to bring money into St. Louis have seen little to none of that money" that rankled. Jeff Ordower became the target for the activists' ire. "Money is typically in the hands of white people who oversee the types of services that the non-profit provides" to Black people who are "literally broke and starving." The statement asserted that Black people needed to be the ones who determined how funds were used: "If black lives really matter, justice and self-determination for black people would mean the black community would control it's [sic] own political and economic resources."

Reluctantly relenting to the will of the desperate activists, Ordower of MORE and Bukky Gbadagesin of OBS signed off on checks of $2,750 to seventeen young protesters.[21] The activists saw it as a victory for accountability and for Black agency, but not everyone viewed the campaign the same way. Rogers and others asked, "What about the people who made more sacrifices than these folks?" What did they deserve? "There's a certain amount of sacrifice that we all are making in order to participate and to move this agenda forward."[22] She exclaimed that "this is not a movement that is going to be pimped off of!"

To make her point clear, Rogers penned a piece in the *St. Louis American*, titled "#Cutthecheck Is Not a Movement."[23] In the op-ed she referred to the sit-in as a "shake-down" that "pretty much cleaned out a bank account designed to support movement activities." Rogers regretted that the organizations acquiesced to protesters: "It was an error in judgment for the heads of OBS and MORE to write checks to a few individuals under these circumstances." In reflection, she said, "There is no rationale as to why this group [the seventeen protesters] was entitled to the monies over the thousands of people who have been a part of the Ferguson movement." It was not, she admitted, "a good stewardship of community resources." Rogers, a longtime organizer, explained that many Black Freedom Movement activists and organizers, from the Student Non-Violent Coordinating Committee's Fannie Lou Hamer to Jim Forman to countless others, died penniless or destitute without pensions, and so many lived without health care plans.

Rogers emphasized that "the way we resolve issues among each other" has to be "very different from how we deal with the white, racist power structure." Because there was supposed to be a baseline of trust and respect, the activists and organization representatives should have been able to work the issue out without an insurrectionist action. That, she wrote, seemed like a "no-brainer," but the young people, who were new to movement making, still needed education and training. Youth energy cannot always be bridled. In the article's comment section there were supporters and opponents of Rogers's position. One commenter went so far as to say that by not endorsing the #cutthecheck campaign, Rogers had turned capitalist and was part of the talented-tenth, contributing to the cliquishness in the Black community.

Conservative media loved the debacle, claiming it bolstered conspiracy theories about this not being a grass-roots movement but rather a movement financed by frightful rich leftists. They played up the divisions between white Ordower and Black activists and old- and new-guard organizers. Right-wing commentators did not believe that the protesters deserved anything. This incident in particular gave them an opportunity to criticize progressivism and Black liberation work in general. They capitalized on the images of activists using the $2,750 they received for clothing, self-care products, and other items one might expect teenagers or young people to purchase.

Aldridge called #cutthecheck an "unfortunate moment in the movement." He wished there had been something like a "workers' fund" that was available when the fast food workers went on strike before the Uprising. The activists fund would have allowed quicker access to financial relief for activists, but that infrastructure was not available. Aldridge was not fazed by the fact that activists received the money or that they spent it on material items, stating that he did not think they got rich from it and what they spent the money on was their choice. Instead, Aldridge commented on the fact that "there were so many moving pieces," and that they were "building a house." Without taking a "moment to debrief or train together" they were not able to see "what are the holes in the foundation." Clearly, he said, "It was a leaky house."

Almost ten years later, Templeton revealed "I didn't agree with the action. I'm saying that on the record, I was telling Brittany 'let's go.' "[24] If anything, Templeton said, "I think it was powerful, because it was the people saying we can take our money back. But I don't think that was the best way of doing it." In essence, Templeton admitted, "I think we did an impulsive thing. And we were doing impulsive things all the time," but there was a reason. "Niggas [young Black activists] feel like they got hit for $50,000" when they found out about the account. The people sitting at the table were desperate for funds. Pulphus, who did not take funds although his name was on the list, said that, overall, #cutthecheck was "a bad look."[25]

10.

FUN IN THE FRENZY: COMEDY IN THE CHAOS

A movement where people hit the streets for over 365 consecutive days does not survive without joy. There had to be some fun in the frenzy. Joy could be found in the banging pots that an elder activist, "Mama Cat," provided as the movement chef, arranging community potlucks and holiday gatherings. Youth activists also participated in "self-care" retreats held by community members like Angel Carter. They enjoyed meeting entertainers like rappers J. Cole and Talib Kweli, who unexpectedly showed up to the Canfield Green apartments. And although they were in the struggle, the young activists could not escape the often hilarious and emotionally driven drama associated with the ups and downs of romantic relationships.

"The thrill of outwitting the police always gave us great joy," Jonathan Pulphus remembered.[1] No one had ever tried most of the actions that these young demonstrators executed, and it took a special kind of daring. With that in mind, H.J. Rodgers cackled as he remembered his favorite demonstration. One night Tribe X members and others shut down Interstate 44. They were "in the middle of the highway, with a spotlight tryin' to stop traffic," recalled Rodgers. He was "like this is not finna work; I'm finna die!" Yet, it did, and traffic stopped. Looking back, it is funny to him, but he now realizes the danger in the action: "That would have been literally suicide."[2]

144   STEFAN M. BRADLEY

For instance, Tribe X, along with the newly formed St. Louis Students in Solidarity, held a mock trial for St. Louis County prosecuting attorney Robert McCulloch at a Saint Louis University School of Law event weeks after he refused to indict Darren Wilson. Hearing that activists intended to demonstrate, university police placed barricades in front of the doors. Because there was a preregistration, Tribe X and Students in Solidarity members, as well as other activists, signed up. To go unrecognized, they donned business casual clothes and made their way through the doors. Once in, they spread throughout the room and sat down. I advised SLU president Fred Pestello to delay the event because it was McCulloch's first public lecture after the disappointing decision. Naively I sat next to my students, Pulphus and Alisha Sonnier. Pulphus coyly asked me if I was ready; I had no inclination what he meant by the question.

Shortly after McCulloch began his lecture, an activist shouted, "Here Ye! Here Ye! All rise!" The demonstrators had folded their protest signs and sneaked them in via manilla folders. Activists from Students in Solidarity unfurled a banner. Relatively calmly, the university police came and walked them out of the room. Livid, McCulloch began again, claiming that he was promised the decorum would match that of the courtroom. He must not have realized that he was being put on trial and that he was not the judge.

McCulloch began again only to be disrupted once more. This time Washington University student and Students in Solidarity organizer Danielle Blocker interrupted him.[3] She had worn a judge's robe beneath a long winter coat so as not to be detected. Blocker and another activist acting as "prosecutor" then moved down the stairs to be in the middle of the room and declared that McCulloch was guilty of not recusing himself from the Darren Wilson indictment case and thereby miscarrying justice. The police apprehended them as well. McCulloch looked piercingly at Pestello and law school dean Michael Wolff in exasperation, stating again, "I thought this was supposed to be courtroom etiquette!" McCulloch restarted his lecture, and a wave of chants began. McCulloch's supporters in the front row had turned around and were histrionic, hollering their dismay wildly. Blocker and her fellow activist were escorted out too. Convinced the commotion was complete, McCulloch, red-faced, tried addressing the audience again. Not more than seconds into his words, Pulphus and Sonnier hopped up and began loudly chanting. I was still seated, and completely surprised, as was the president, who had formed a relationship with the two student-activists. I put my phone in the air as though I was recording; although, I was not savvy enough to access the video app in time. I feared the police might harm the students and thought the appearance of being filmed might dissuade an officer from employing violence. The two rebels left with the police without any notable physical altercations. McCulloch actually stayed as well and even tried to explain how he made the decision not to indict an officer who pulled a young man over for walking in the street and then killed the young man. Admittedly, the event was much less fun with the protesters absent. Pulphus, Sonnier, and Blocker all laughed heartily retelling the story because the multiphase action went precisely as planned. Moreover, they lived to tell the tale. As it was, none of the disruptive demonstrators was arrested or harmed by the campus police.

There were other instances of comedy in the chaos of freedom fighting. It tickled Pulphus when police officers, attempting to pepper spray or tear gas protesters, misaimed and accidentally doused their fellow officers. He also chuckled when remembering his attempt to be cool and rebellious like Edward Crawford, whose image went viral. A camera captured Crawford with his locs flying behind him, in an American flag T-shirt with the sleeves cut off, holding a snack-size bag of Red Hot Riplets in his left hand, and a lit tear-gas canister in his right. Crawford had picked it up and relaunched it back at the police, inspiring the crowd of protesters and providing the most iconic and St. Louis–esque image of the movement. It was symbolic of the resistance and won the *St. Louis Post-Dispatch* a Pulitzer Prize for photography.

Pulphus, like so many others, deeply appreciated Crawford's commitment and wanted to pay homage to him. It did not take long, because the police shot tear gas out nearly every night for weeks. Seeing his chance, Pulphus saw a group of protesters running away from a canister spewing tear gas. With thoughts of Crawford, the hood hero, on his mind, Pulphus ran to the canister, grabbed it and flung it. As it flew, Pulphus realized that accompanying the hot metal was the skin on the inside of his hand that the canister had scorched. "It was not one of my brightest ideas," he recalled. The young democrat laughed at the fact that his teenage brain had not fully formed yet. Pulphus became quiet as he recollected that Crawford, who was charged with assaulting a police officer, was found shot dead in the back of his car three years later. As with any war, there were casualties and fatalities in the movement.

"We had to figure out spaces to deepen our relationships," Pulphus said about the times he and his fellow freedom fighters were not protesting.[4] They had to do so to build trust. MoKaBe's, a coffeehouse, became just such a space. The owners were white queer folks and avowedly supportive of the movement. Activists felt comfortable there as they could strategize or decompress in a supportive environment that did not make them feel bad or wrong for calling out police repression. MoKaBe's experienced police violence directly when St. Louis Metropolitan Police forced activists into the coffee shop and set off a tear-gas canister near the entrance on the night that Bob McCulloch announced that he was not indicting the killer of Mike Brown. The owners and activists found out that there was no "safe space" when it came to police repression tactics.[5] Fortunately, the grand majority of the time spent in MoKaBe's was positive for Ground Zero organizers.

Pulphus, Alex Templeton, and DeRay McKesson revealed that

IF WE DON'T GET IT   147

sometimes petty differences, personality clashes, and serious ideo-
logical disagreements forced wedges between activists. As Mizzou
student-activist and St. Louis resident Storm Ervin sagely explained nearly a decade after the Uprising, "When you're fresh out
of whatever childhood experience you dealt with and you haven't
really looked back and healed those parts of you or dealt with
those parts of you or even understood the parts of you that aren't
serving you, but you're still operating in those parts of you because
that's all you know and all you're familiar with, you strain your
relationship with folks." [6] For Ervin and so many other organizers
and activists, that manifested itself as "anger, defensiveness," and
an attitude "like I'm not going down without a fight." That same
spirit caused them to rise up against an unjust system, but inter-
personally it became damaging.

A large contingent of those who organized and activated had
not healed their childhood traumas, so it was natural that the hurt
would resurface. Healing was necessary. Art activist Elizabeth
Vega attempted to provide space for healing and understanding
when Pulphus and Dhoruba Shakur, both impassioned Tribe X
leaders, had major disagreements that nearly led to fisticuffs. She
put together a ceremony that required the young warriors to join
hands in unity and confront the emotions that prevented them
from communicating constructively and working efficiently together. It did not solve all their problems, but it helped them to
understand that they could not defeat the larger enemy if they
spent their time and energy fighting each other.

Several members of Tribe X and other organizations got to know
each other and unwind over food. Activist Charles Wade helped
arrange a self-care event where a chef, Angela Davis the Kitch-
enista (no relation to the former Black Panther and philosopher),
prepared a multicourse meal for hungry young democrats. They
supped and imbibed to their hearts delight. Mama Cat regularly
provided meals to the activists as well. Discussions and laughter
over meals brought back a sense of normalcy to the young people.

In their downtime they could joke about how serious some of the Tribe X members who occupied SLU's campus were about getting the university to buy them MacBooks. In the midst of negotiating scholarships, community centers, and budget allocations, the portable computers became a sticking point because, they claimed, they needed them to organize the work ahead, which seemed reasonable. SLU's president acceded to the request for the devices. Tribe X members took receivership of the machines, and some were used for work, others were sold, and others were lost. There was a deep disagreement between Tribe X members and the "mothers" or advisors over organizational budget concerns, resulting in some members cutting ties. The mothers asked that the MacBooks be returned so that prospective members could make use of them. Suffice to say, those laptops were long gone. After a cooling period, they realized that the fact that plastic and metal items meant so much to them as they were fighting to change a system that had been in place for centuries was laughable.[7]

Some relationships blossomed during the Uprising. Brittany Ferrell, who postponed her nursing program to focus on mothering and movement making, grew her romantic partnership with Alex Templeton, who also delayed their education. After courting on the streets of Ferguson, at police stations, and in jail cells, they made their relationship official when Templeton proposed to Ferrell on the steps of St. Louis City Hall. In front of friends and family, they expressed what the *St. Louis American* called "revolutionary love."[8] Because all of the key organizers and various leaders of the movement showed up to support their betrothal, city officials got worried. When an officer spotted DeRay McKesson, the officer asked if they were planning to shut down the courthouse. Journalist Rebecca Rivas reported on one friend who answered the officer with a sign that read, "All we want to do is take the chains off! (and put a ring on it)."[9] Jamell Spann, whom the couple would designate as their best man, eloquently remarked that "it's like watching poetry write itself." It was poetry and history and love combining to create change.

As young revolutionaries challenged traditional systems they sometimes struggled with traditional monogamous relationships. Sonnier and Pulphus were role models for movement relationships. They strategized and courageously confronted injustice together. Pulphus garnered much attention because of his personality and because he was a young man. Sonnier was equally extroverted but perhaps less daring than her partner in some ways. As the Uprising progressed, to share what they knew about activism and leadership, Sonnier and Pulphus traveled around the country like an "AAU (Amateur Athletic Union) team," they remembered. Jokingly, Pulphus said people would pay them to talk like they were "Jesse Jackson or Coretta Scott King" or some other notable historical figures. They met sheroes like premier poet Nikki Giovanni and actors such as Omari Hardwick from the hit show *Power*. That, Pulphus admitted, inflated his ego a bit. They were only teenagers, but they carried on like an old couple. I remembered each one, at different points, coming to my office or contacting me by phone to complain about the other. It was mostly funny watching them go through the throes of young love.

All was well until popularity and carnal desires worked against them. Although Pulphus was emotionally committed to Sonnier, he gave into physical temptation when a beautiful and slightly older member of another organization showed interest in him. Fully human, he had an indiscretion with the other activist. In the process, he crushed the feelings of Sonnier, who had remained faithful to him. It was not at all funny but unfortunately predictable because they were so young. Sonnier, who had done nothing wrong, was embarrassed and hurt because of the betrayal and because they, as a couple, had in some ways been placed on a pedestal as an example of a healthy revolutionary relationship. Pulphus was deeply regretful and sorrowful for hurting his first love.

It was remarkable that no matter how progressive the times were, the very real feelings of lust and emotional violation always remained the same. Ferguson taught that faith and trust are key components in movement making, but humans will always be human. Once faith and trust are broken, it is quite difficult to rebuild. As important as trust is, so too is forgiveness and restoration. Pulphus worked hard to reconstruct trust with Sonnier, and it eventually led to reconciliation; however, the seed of doubt had been planted. Still, they carried forward, showing that a productive relationship could recover from infidelity. Looking back, Pulphus joked with Sonnier, trying to gaslight her into thinking that he was but a naive sheep who was attacked by a cougar and that he was actually innocent. Neither she nor anyone else believed him, although his infectious smile was convincing. Ten years later, Pulphus and Sonnier are no longer together, but they remain cordial, having learned so much from each other and their shared experiences.

Rappers on Deck

Hip hop belongs to the youth, and in the midst of the rebellion in Ferguson, artists oriented their work toward the actions of the young people. Local artists like Tef Poe and T-Dubb-O regularly entertained and educated, but the Uprising brought many famous talents to town. They showed great humility and generosity in using their influence to highlight the injustice that was occurring. Even though they came for very serious reasons, there was always a bit of humor that accompanied them.

For instance, early in the Uprising, I brought my father to the Canfield Green apartment complex to show him the good work of various organizations and activists. While speaking with Derrick "D-Rob" Robinson on the sidewalk, I felt the intense glare of someone. There was a young man around the age of twenty-five with dark brown skin, cornrowed hair, and muscles abounding from the medium white tank top that fit snugly on his at least 6-foot-tall, 250-pound frame. He looked intently at me as Robinson talked, and then he abruptly asked, "Ay, bro, you from here?" speaking directly to me. Wondering what this was about, I, who weighed one hundred pounds less than the inquisitor, replied that I was not from the complex, and the young man cut me off to say, "I seen you before." The tone of voice gave me the sense that a conflict was soon to occur, and the fact that D-Rob and the others in the area had gotten library quiet did not help. In a blunt way, the young man asked, "You was the one on TV the other night?" Confused as to where this was leading, I tepidly said that I had been interviewed. The young man shot back, "Yeah, but that's not why I know your face!"

At lightning speed, I processed the memories of all the women I had crossed and men I had upset to grasp what could be wrong with the young man, who still had not smiled or eased his tone. Now facing each other squarely, he said to me, in what seemed to be the hardest way possible, "You was the one that was with those kids doing push-ups for money a while back." Because I had been expecting an entirely different charge, it took me a moment, but I explained that I had bet the young men they could not do fifty push-ups for $50. I then said I told the boys that if they were willing to do all of that for $50, what would they be willing to do for a $50,000 scholarship? Without speaking, the young man, in a fast motion, put his hand up in the air, and I got in my defensive set, thinking I was about to die for the cause. The young man roughly grabbed my right hand and with startling velocity pulled me in for a half-hug, hollering loudly in a deep voice, "That's what it is, Bro Bro!" I exhaled, realizing that I had not been breathing.

At just that moment, I could see a Mercedes-Benz van pull to the side of the road on Canfield Drive. It seemed odd, but then nothing was normal in the Canfield apartments at that point. Out of the van popped a lanky young man who was dressed as though he could have been cast as Shaggy in a modern *Scooby-Doo* with his baggy T-shirt, baggy basketball shorts, athletic socks, and slides. He walked to where I had just been released from the young man's death grip of love. There was a growing number of people following him. Upon his coming closer, I recognized the lanky man as the rapper J. Cole. So too did the young man who had interrogated me. In a falsetto voice that resembled Maxwell, Michael Jackson, or the Weeknd, the muscle-bound young man screamed, "That's J. Cole, that's J. Cole!" I was again confused; how did the young man's voice get so high so quickly? The young man from the complex then asked the artist to "spit something, J. Cole!" but Cole declined, saying quietly, "I'm not here for that; I came to see y'all." By then, it was like a chorus with people saying "J. Cole's here." I shook Cole's hand, thanked him for coming, and then rushed off to try to make sense of it all. Around that time, Cole put out a thoughtful song called "Be Free" that he dedicated to "every young black man murdered in America." [10] In a statement on his Dreamvillain website, he said, "I'M TIRED OF being desensitized to the murder of black men . . . I don't give a fuck if it's by police or peers." No matter how many times he heard of Black youth dying, Cole exclaimed that "this shit is not normal."

Another rapper came to check on the people of Ferguson as well. Talib Kweli, one half of the group Black Star, marched with protestors during the August nights. I, who had interviewed Kweli before, encountered the rapper on the set of CNN where we were both in queue to speak with CNN anchor Don Lemon. While waiting, I saw the Obama administration special appointee, Van Jones. We introduced ourselves, and Jones continued in his conversation with Kweli. I tried, to no avail, to remind Kweli of the time that I interviewed him a few years earlier. Lemon, finished with his segment, walked by and said hello to all three of us. After a brief period, someone from CNN came to situate Kweli with a microphone. The person brought Kweli in front of the camera, where Lemon arrived shortly afterward.

Once the camera rolled, chaos and comedy ensued. It started with Lemon mispronouncing the famous rapper's name. The artist was visibly annoyed and mentioned the anchor's faux pas on camera. Lemon seemed to take offense at his guest's willingness to call him out and responded that he was sorry for mispronouncing his name. This continued for what seemed like forever, with Kweli claiming he was going to end the interview. Off camera, Van Jones was whisper-yelling for them to stop arguing. I was snickering in hopes that they would physically fight. Knowing that both of the men on camera would be gone in a few days, I found it comical, entertaining, and petty all at once.

Kweli claimed that if Lemon had cared, he would have gotten the name right, and that the mistake was indicative of CNN's skewed coverage. He said, for instance, in an article the network presented as fact that protesters were throwing bottles at police, which provoked law enforcement to respond with violence. Kweli, who was in the crowd, said that characterization was patently false; instead, police began violently arresting and pushing peaceful protesters, and the crowd reacted. Lemon challenged the notion and justified the coverage by stating that what Kweli said may have been true but that Kweli did not have the exclusive vantage point of the protest and that the article was but one of many CNN articles about the demonstrations. Kweli conceded the point but explained that the media was complicit in allowing police narratives to go unchecked. The two went back and forth for nearly ten minutes, with Jones just off camera pushing his hands down toward the ground as if to tell the two famous Black men to calm down. The interview ended peacefully, but it went viral on social media.

I went on directly after Kweli. Just before the camera rolled, Lemon looked me in the eye, smiled, and asked, "How do you say your name? I don't want that to happen again." Lemon, after introducing me, showed a clip of Spike Lee claiming that there was a war on Black men and asked me about my opinion. I responded that life for Black men was perilous because of the ways that America was killing them quickly with bullets and chokeholds and how the nation was killing them slowly with food deserts, inadequate health care, and underfunded education. Lemon cut in to say that he was short on time but wanted to know what could be done to make the necessary changes in Ferguson. My first thought was, "Of course you're short on time, because you engaged a war of pettiness for ten minutes, and now you want the abridged version of how to fix systemic racism." To answer, I shared some of the talking points that the Young Citizens Council had discussed in the days just after Wilson shot Brown. Lemon, concluding the interview, said that in the Black community we needed to have these hard conversations and sometimes they get heated but that was just how Black people got along. Taking that to heart, I challenged Lemon to a wrestling match. We laughed and shook hands in peace.

They came together in tragedy, but young citizens and their supporters were able to find joy in various capacities. For instance, in an effort to place pressure on McCulloch to indict Wilson and to bring awareness to a world body, activists boarded planes and flew to Geneva, Switzerland, to meet with the United Nations Committee against Torture. Brown's parents, as well as organizers like artist Tef Poe and attorney Justin Hansford, spoke out about the atrocities that afflicted Ferguson. Brown's parents had never before been out of the country. In Switzerland, they felt the sympathy and love that parents of a child shot by police deserved. CNN reported that Lezley McSpadden said, "We've been received very well. . . . They've given us a lot of love and support since we've been here. Everything seems to be positive. It's a great experience." [11]

While there, the representatives from Ferguson shared a statement constructed by the Organization for Black Struggle and Hands Up United. Hansford, who had some experience with international legal cases because of his work to rescind the

IF WE DON'T GET IT   155

conviction of Universal Negro Improvement Association leader Marcus Garvey, helped the group navigate procedurally. Having assisted with writing the statement, he said, "Traditionally, if you look at the history of the Convention Against Torture, this is the correct location for claims of police violence."[12] Even though they were in grief over the loss of Brown, those devoted citizens took pride in the fact that they were doing everything possible to get justice for the young American who experienced state violence on the street in Ferguson.

In a similar fashion, young leaders Brittany Packnett Cunningham, Netta Elzie, DeRay McKesson, Justin Hansford, and Rasheen Aldridge Jr. at different times brought the issues of Ferguson to the White House. Packnett Cunningham remembered being conflicted with regard to being tactfully or brutally honest with President Barack Obama about what she had seen on the street. Always thoughtful and courageous, she said, "I was afraid of sounding like an angry black woman at the White House, . . . but I needed the president to know what middle-schoolers faced in their neighborhood."[13]

By then, Packnett Cunningham had been appointed to Missouri governor Jay Nixon's Ferguson Commission, where she specialized in telling truth to power. The commission's report became the political platform for several St. Louis candidates. In December 2014, Packnett Cunningham, along with premier St. Louis labor leader Aldridge and dedicated activist McKesson, took turns sharing their experiences as young people in St. Louis and Ferguson. They made onlookers from those areas extremely proud because someone was finally amplifying the voices of the unheard. The administration could not claim ignorance and had to confront biased practices. Packnett Cunningham, perhaps the most incisive communicator in the movement, caught the attention of the president and was appointed to the White House twelve-member Taskforce on 21st Century Policing.[14] During one of her numerous trips to D.C. for the meetings, Packnett Cunningham gleefully reported that she was wearing Air Jordans on the White House Lawn.

Ferguson Commission member and premier communicator Brittany Packnett Cunningham (left) brought the Uprising with her to meet President Barack Obama (center) and Rep. John Lewis (D-GA), in the Roosevelt Room at the White House during a Black History Month celebration on February 18, 2016. *Photo: Mark Wilson/Getty Images*

Organizers and activists had the opportunity to visit places and party with people they never imagined meeting. It allowed them to have a bit of joy in the midst of pain. Then, the work continued. Packnett Cunningham, Elzie, and McKesson, riding the momentum from the White House visits and efforts with the Ferguson Commission, came together to birth Campaign Zero, an initiative to reform abusive police practices. Using their scholastic skills that they honed as administrators and organizers, the trio, along with Samuel Sinyangwe, focused on using data to drive policy discussions. As McKesson remembered proudly, they "created the first ever database of police union contracts, the first ever database of use of force policies, and we made maps of police violence and the first activist-led database of killings."[15] He noted that these were the data that they discussed when meeting with Beyonce and Jay Z. The young people's activism, research, and reporting helped pass more police reform laws than had been passed in two generations; they deserved to party, revel, and decompress.

11.

SOLDIERS AND SCHOLARS: FERGUSON COMES TO SLU

"This didn't just start with us; we just made it a lot bigger. And, we took actions that had never been taken before."
—*Mizzou student Storm Ervin*

Historical narratives often delineate the roles that people play in movement making. For instance, some are portrayed as soldiers (those who physically risk their lives for the cause) while others are presented as disinterested scholars who are able to contextualize the need for action. The reality is that most Black freedom campaigns have been bolstered by soldier-scholars. In the case of the Ferguson Uprising, those were individuals who attended educational institutions and were in the process of garnering credentials; they, too, risked their freedom status and standing as students by protesting in the streets at night. The justice for Mike Brown movement reverberated throughout the entire city, region, and nation, with soldier-scholars activating in campaigns such as #OccupySLU and #ConcernedStudent1950 in Missouri.

By the beginning of the school year in 2014, the Ferguson Uprising had radicalized thousands of students nationwide. More than three hundred Howard University students tweeted an image of them with their hands up to show support, while the Harvard University Black Law Student Association issued a statement to Attorney General Eric Holder, "This is a moment for policy makers to correct the wrongs that have occurred and continue to occur in police interactions with Black Americans. Our nation must recognize the overt and covert biases that interweave our social fabric. The American promise of liberty and justice can be fulfilled through both policy and social change, but it will not be fulfilled if we stand idly by."[1] Ferguson, officially or otherwise, was on the curriculum of America's higher education institutions. Students from coast to coast, including those at Washington University and Saint Louis University, walked out of classes the day after Mike Brown's funeral.

Life moved quickly in St. Louis during the Uprising. Ten days after Brown's death, the St. Louis Metropolitan Police shot and killed twenty-five-year old Black man Kajieme Powell, whom the police claimed shoplifted and rushed toward officers while wielding a knife. It felt as though police were piling on.

As people in the city were grappling with the Powell incident, another shooting occurred on October 9. Off-duty officer Jason Flanery, not in uniform, shot an eighteen-year-old Black man, VonDerrit Myers Jr. The teenager was out on bond for a gun possession charge, and the policeman was moonlighting as a security guard in the Shaw neighborhood. Flanery claimed that Myers and two others ran from Flanery's security vehicle and the officer pursued them. After stopping the vehicle and chasing Myers on foot, Flanery claimed the two engaged in a "physical altercation," and then Myers shot at him three times. The officer returned seventeen rounds, killing Myers.

The family of Myers hired a pathologist to provide the details of the young man's death. The pathologist, who had investigated the deaths of John F. Kennedy, Elvis Presley, and JonBenet Ramsey, issued a report that revealed Myers had been shot six times (like Brown) on the back and side of his body, indicating that he had been running away from the officer.[2] Additionally, the pathologist did not find that the weapon Flanery claimed Myers used to shoot at him contained any of Myers's DNA. Police officials, not surprisingly, believed Flanery's version of events.

Myers's father, VonDerrit Myers Sr., worked at Saint Louis University. I had seen him on campus but had no clue of his relationship to the fallen young man. Students from SLU, however, felt a particular connection to Myers's son because of the young man's age and because of the moment. One afternoon, I brought several students to the site where Flanery killed Myers to pay their respects. There happened to be several of Myers's friends at the makeshift memorial. The students and I listened to the slain young man's neighborhood friends tell stories about "Droop," which is what they called Myers. As they regaled us with stories about Droop, they held in their hands bottles of hot sauce. Finally, someone who said Myers was his cousin shouted "Droop block!" and drank from the bottle of hot sauce, explaining that Myers loved the condiment. It was a moving tribute to a fallen friend.

The timing of Myers's death could not have been worse for St. Louis–area law enforcement, as activists had put out a call for reinforcements. In much the same way that the Southern Christian Leadership Conference called for people of goodwill from around the nation to come to Selma after the police killed Jimmie Lee Jackson and brutalized young democrats on Bloody Sunday in March 1965, organizers in Ferguson did the same in fall 2014. Just as goodwill activists responded to the call, so too did the police, who put forth every effort to contain protest in the city.

The city's urban setting added a new dimension to the demonstrations for police. Activists took advantage of the more condensed area of operation and the ability to cover more ground with less fuel and at a cheaper cost. The center of the newest action was in the Shaw neighborhood on St. Louis City's south side. The south side of the city was seen by many in the local media as safer and less affected by crime. There was a relatively high percentage of working-class Black people in that section, but many middle- and upper-middle-class white people resided there as well. Few were expecting the protests of Ferguson to make it to the Shaw neighborhood.

"No justice, no sleep," activists chanted after midnight as they marched through the streets. Like the agitators in Ferguson, those in the city wanted to disrupt the peace of people who may have viewed Myers's death as a tragedy but largely felt unaffected by it. In addition to chanting, protesters burned a flag on the ground. "Our children are being killed in the street. This flag doesn't cover black or brown people," exclaimed artist Elizabeth Vega.[3] In earlier protests, demonstrators broke the windows of police vehicles. Attempting to take a different tack than the police forces in the county, the chief of St. Louis City Police Sam Dotson said, "We will do everything we can to support everybody's right to protest and allow their voices to be heard as long as it doesn't infringe on other people's rights." In principle, his approach was righteous, but confrontation between his officers and the demonstrators was inevitable.

Hundreds of activists from around the region and nation showed up in the St. Louis metropolitan area to participate in "Ferguson October." One of the planners of Ferguson October was Organization of Black Struggle (OBS) leader Montague Simmons, who had grown up in North County and had had the same educational experiences as Mike Brown when younger. When Simmons and other leaders found out that the county's grand jury was expected to make an announcement about the potential indictment of Wilson in mid-October, they collaborated to put together a weekend, October 10–13, of demonstrations, education, and entertainment.

"We saw this as an opportunity to lift this from just being one moment, one case, to really take a stand on this national epidemic of police violence that's occurring in Black and brown communities," Simmons said of Ferguson October.[4] Understanding that the movement was at the center of the national stage, he said, they "wanted to draw a line not just here in Ferguson and St. Louis but . . . nationally" because "we actually have to change the way that police interact with us in our communities." Simmons attempted to compare and contrast the contemporary movement with that which took place in the South, stating that during the civil rights movement, white college students went South to help with the movement. In the new movement, "we're starting with indigenous [local Black] youth actually recognizing the need and

Millennial Activists United co-founder Ashley Yates (left) and Hands Up United co-founder Tef Poe commandeer the microphone at an event during "Ferguson October" at Chaifetz Arena on the campus of Saint Louis University. *Photo: Wiley Price/ St. Louis American*

their own power to turn around and fight back, to resist, to bring change and transformation into their own communities." In doing so, they placed themselves in a position to tie their campaigns to those of young democrats throughout the nation.

Organizers like Derecka Purnell helped make arrangements for the visitors. The overarching plan was to conduct large-scale actions throughout the metro area, applying pressure to county prosecutor Bob McCulloch to indict Wilson and for law enforcement to stand down. Many young organizers displayed great leadership acumen and style while connecting this local crisis to the larger issues of the nation. Ground Zero demonstrators like Tef Poe, Ashley Yates, Alex Templeton, Brittany Ferrell, Netta Elzie, Jonathan Pulphus, Alisha Sonnier, and so many more took their rightful place at the vanguard of the new movement. Poe rapped on stage with artists like Talib Kweli, Common, Jasiri X, and others.

The sight of activists from all over the nation convening on the streets of St. Louis and Ferguson was breathtaking. Local organizers, activists, and hosts were able to showcase the best of themselves while exchanging ideas and tactics with others. One of the most innovative and powerful symbols of protest was a mirrored casket, designed by artist De Nichols. Nichols, a recent graduate of Washington University, where she was an Ervin Scholar like Danielle Blocker, went on to receive an MSW from the Brown School of Social Work. She had been in discussion with the Young Citizens Council early on in the Uprising, but no one could have predicted the profundity of her artistic contribution. In an interview about her work, Nichols said she was haunted by images of Brown on the ground and police clashing with activists because she had seven brothers of her own. She was harmed by those images.

Nichols had recurring nightmares of men carrying a casket and needed to get the sight out of her head.[5] So, she sketched the idea on a napkin and called on artists in her network like Elizabeth Vega to actualize her vision. The glass on the cover of the eight-foot-long casket was intentionally shattered and the glass on the sides remained intact so that when people looked at it while it was being carried, they clearly saw themselves as culpable for ending a Black life. When tilted forward to face police, the shattered glass presented countless distorted and disturbing images back to the officers.

Nichols said she wanted to "provoke this question of our own accountability and our own complicity in the murders of young Black people."[6] It begged the question: "What part have I played in not only perpetuating police brutality but this sense of violence in communities at large and the systemic issues that cultivate a space for people like Mike Brown to be murdered?" During Ferguson October, activists carried the casket from the spot where Wilson shot Brown dead to the Ferguson Police Department. Nichols's artwork is currently displayed in the Smithsonian National Museum of African American History and Culture.

The Shaw neighborhood is a relatively short distance from the campus of Saint Louis University (SLU). People who lived near or got off the bus near SLU know not to cross through the beautifully pristine urban campus. Founded in 1818, the private, Catholic Jesuit university rests in a space that was once the home to Mill Creek Valley, a working-class Black neighborhood, before the school overtook it in the mid-twentieth century. In 2014, poor and working-class Black people resided around the university in every direction. Many had never actually been on the campus, but they could see the magnificent St. Xavier College Church steeple that was part of the city's skyline. The university took pride in being the first major university in the state to admit Black students in 1944. Their presence challenged the status quo even then.

Black students in 2014–2015 continued to challenge the status quo at SLU and in the St. Louis metropolitan area. On Sunday, October 12, 2014, local activists and those who were in town for Ferguson October attended an event at SLU's relatively new Chaifetz Arena. There, they heard from nationally and locally renowned leaders, such as NAACP president Cornell Williams Brooks and the famous scholar (who became a presidential candidate) Cornel West. West said that he had not come to Ferguson for speechifying but rather to go to jail, and, in fact, he did get arrested with seventeen others earlier that day. I admired West but believed that making his arrest the stated mission was dangerous for others. West had bail money and tenure at his workplace; his life was stable and he knew he would have a home and food to eat. That was not the case with everyone who looked up to him as he boasted about wanting to be arrested. Those who did not live like West had a higher price to pay if they were arrested and convicted. West was nearing retirement age, and the young people had their lives ahead of them. Being arrested was not the worst thing that could happen to young people, but it would be much more of an inconvenience for them than it would be for the world-renowned philosopher and theologian.

Although the event was organized by area ministers like the very well-respected Rev. Starsky Wilson and Rev. Traci Blackmon, as well as academicians like SLU's Associate Professor Norm White, it could not quite meet the moment. Wanting to feature the visitors and "adults," which included ministers and civil rights leaders, the event did not center the voices of the local youth who were going to jail, losing jobs, contesting police repression, and uplifting Brown's name. The young people present turned the event out, commandeering the microphone. A reporter from the *Detroit Free Press* described how "a raucous Ferguson October crowd turned a mass protest service on its head Sunday night, heckling the president of the NAACP and successfully demanding that young demonstrators get a place on stage to address an audience of hundreds."[7]

"This ain't your daddy's Civil Rights Movement," Tef Poe infamously exclaimed, urging the clergy and elders to "get off your ass and join us."[8] The "us" to whom he referred was the working- and under-class Black youth who risked life and limb on the streets nightly. Poe's sentiment was not at all different from that of those young people who ushered in the Black Power Movement in the 1960s.

Younger activists in the late 1960s saw integrationist preachers and leaders like King of the Southern Christian Leadership Conference (SCLC), Roy Wilkins of the NAACP, and Whitney Young of the National Urban League as important figures but representative of different goals and tactics with respect to the movement. Whereas King's cadre believed that the American political and economic system could eventually yield justice, young activists in organizations like the Student Non-Violent Coordinating Committee (SNCC), the Congress of Racial Equality, and the Revolutionary Action Movement were dubious. They believed that it would take much more than the vote and the love associated with King's vision of a "Beloved Community." Black Power advocates, frustrated with King and his allies' admonition to let love conquer hate, said "too much love, too much love, nothing kills a nigger like too much love!"

Of course, the "daddies" that Poe referenced were righteously intrepid and pushed the movement further than it had ever been, but it has always seemed to be the obligation of the younger generation to devour the older generation in order to self-manifest. Poe made it clear that it was not the elders' movement, for good or bad, and that they needed support not speeches. Not surprisingly, the irreverent tone and sentiment of Poe's statement perturbed some elders and clergy members. Ashley Yates, who spoke just as eloquently, pleaded with the older generation to "see my humanity. See me for who I am . . . through the way people express their rage, don't judge it."[9] The Rev. Traci Blackmon, who had been on the street with some of these young people, explained to her clergy peers and others that the youth takeover may not be comfortable, but "this is what democracy looks like," which was a phrase activists regularly chanted while marching.

After making their points of view clear at Chaifetz, organizers called for demonstrators to march toward 4200 Shaw Boulevard in the neighborhood where Officer Jason Flanery had recently shot Myers, the son of an SLU employee. There they met with Myers's family members, who shared some heartfelt sentiments with the crowd of demonstrators. Organizers then mobilized the protesters toward an area called the Mangrove (the Grove), which was a mainstay for the city's most popular gay nightclubs and bars. A contingent of the marchers went a different direction, west, back toward SLU's campus. As that contingent walked, the group of protesters in the Mangrove shut down the main street and began jump-roping and playing ball to emphasize the idea that if the city played games with Black lives, then the people would play their own games, stopping traffic.

One demonstrator noted, "If we were in Ferguson, we would have already been arrested by now." [10] Having a good sense of why they were not in zip-ties or handcuffed, another disruptor stated matter-of-factly, "Girl, look who out here—it's not just us," referring to the relatively high number of white and non-Black people who had joined the march. The optics of harming white citizens, the two Black women insinuated, did not lend themselves to police's aggressively corralling the activists in the city the same way police did in Ferguson. Whatever the case, the demonstrators restarted their march after their brief stop in the Grove.

By now, organizers were as strategic as Carthage's Hannibal in the Alps when he mobilized elephants to victoriously battle Rome. As that group of protesters engaged city police in the Grove, the other contingent made its way north down Vandeventer Avenue. Police had assumed activists were going to return to the QuikTrip where a sit-in action had taken place the night before. Instead the organizers arranged for one group to act as a mobile decoy while the other group flanked the real target. Leading the groups were organizers Dhoruba Shakur, DeRay McKesson, Kayla Reed, and others.

SLU became a target, in part, because of its history of being a

IF WE DON'T GET IT 169

citadel of whiteness in a sea of Blackness but also from a need of organizers to up the ante in terms of actions. H.J. Rodgers made his way from the Ferguson Police Department to the city to meet up with fellow Tribe X members that afternoon.[11] While talking, they discussed how they had shut down the QuikTrip the day before, and they wondered how to best that action. It was Ferguson October Weekend, and there had been actions all throughout the metropolitan area; there were thousands of people in town to show solidarity with the cause. Rodgers remembered Tribe X organizers earnestly asking, "What can we do today to top what we did these last couple days? We have to do something that's going to move the train. That's all we kept thinking about."

Rodgers said a Tribe X member suggested taking over SLU, which was an idea that several members had introduced weeks earlier. Several members immediately reacted with, "Yoooo, you trippin'!" After some discussion, they talked themselves into endorsing the action. The next step was to get the collaboration of other organizations and coordinate the maneuvers of the decoy contingent and the occupying force. After studying the responses of police, Rodgers said, "We knew the police were going to combat them [the members of the decoy contingent] but not too much." The faith of young people is mystifying.

While the distraction demonstrators loudly moved northward on Vandeventer and then Grand, the occupying forces of about one thousand, according to Rodgers, "took a route through the neighborhoods, quiet as a mouse."[12] Laughing, he later said, "This is how you know it was divine intervention because how do you get a thousand people to move through a neighborhood without making a sound? This is not no trained army; this is a thousand random people all together." Perhaps they were part of Hannibal's heritage?

The groups finally converged outside the gates of SLU. The university had always enjoyed the hegemonic notion of boundaries to which the white institution and the Black neighborhood agreed.

170   STEFAN M. BRADLEY

The agreement was that there would be no transgression of the lines. That meant neighborhood people should not enter the campus, and SLU told its mostly white student body not to go into the surrounding Black neighborhoods. It was the place that poor and working-class Black people knew not to walk through for any reason, even if that meant going out of their way; SLU was the shining, colorful oasis in the midst of a gray urban landscape. Yet, here were the irreverent, nonrespectable, angry, grieving, and intrepid activists ready to breach the gates of the private, predominantly white university. In the late night of October 13, all of that was at stake, as more than 1,500 activists squared off against less than ten armed campus policemen. The sentinels made it clear that the university was private property and that if the demonstrators were not students, they could not enter.

"So here goes the hero, my boy, Jonathan," Rodgers said of his brother in arms, Jonathan Pulphus.[13] While his fellow Tribe X members marched, Pulphus had been in the library; he was a circulation clerk at the front desk. When he heard from Dhoruba Shakur and Alisha Sonnier, both members of the organization, he left. "I don't remember clocking out. I probably still owe those people money!" Pulphus recalled.[14] In his defense, how could he not answer the call to rebellion?

Pulphus and Sonnier reached out to what he called "a critical mass of students," that "believed in what we were doing in Ferguson." They instructed them to post up at every entrance to the university because they were unsure where the marchers would enter. Pulphus took post at the gate closest to Grand and West Pine Ave. When notified that marchers were coming toward campus, DPS mobilized their vehicles to block as many entrances as possible, including that at which the circulation clerk turned movement leader found himself. Shakur, who had been using a megaphone to lead chants, gave it to Pulphus.

"My name is Jonathan. I'm a SLU student. I have my ID, and I have a lot of guests," said the confident young democrat, only a

IF WE DON'T GET IT   171

year older than Mike Brown.[15] Those words that he uttered into the megaphone through a mischievous smile changed the university's modern history. Since hardly anyone in the crowd knew the campus, Pulphus and Sonnier led their "guests" down the university's main walkway and wrapped them around the Clock Tower that sits in the middle of main campus. Pulphus's friend and brother in bond, Trevor Woolfolk, was stunned with Pulphus's performance. "When I tell you big energy! He was going into battle with Goliath," Woolfolk said in amazement. Here was "literally a kid, who wasn't even drinking age," taking charge of the moment to lead the most radical people in the region. It was a remarkably bold move, and it convinced Woolfolk that Pulphus "had the biggest *cojones* in the world."

At the Clock Tower, they held a moment of silence for Mike Brown and VonDerrit Myers Jr. Once they finished honoring Brown and Myers, they celebrated themselves because, as Rodgers said, "Nigga, we made it!" No one was hurt or arrested; that was a reason for revelry. This was a significant action for the movement and SLU.

With thousands in the crowd now, SLU employee VonDerrit Myers Sr. and his family, who had marched with the protesters, spoke about his son. To an applauding audience, Myers said, "As an employee of SLU, I can pull out my badge too," placing himself in solidarity with the activists, who wanted to lift up the family.[16] "It gives my heart peace that you all are doing this for my family and in my son's name. It lets everybody know that his life meant something." Ensuring that the Myers's child and the child of Lezley McSpadden and those of so many other parents mattered, the Tribe X organizer Shakur queried the crowd as to whether they should stay, and the Ferguson October activists replied in the affirmative. Tribe X announced that they were staging a sit-in.

Along with Tribe X members, leaders like Kayla Reed, Netta Elzie, Ashley Yates, Damon Latchinson, Brittany Ferrell, Josh Williams, and even Cornel West were in the crowd. Later that morning, Reed tweeted, "#OccupySLU was amazing. Still riding that wave. Power to the people." She also remarked about the effects of trauma that plagued her and Elzie, who had a visceral reaction when the fountains around the Clock Tower shot water in the air in the very early hours of the first night of occupation. They initially thought it was tear gas, like they had inhaled in Ferguson, only to realize they were not in danger—from the fountain. Ferrell agreed with Reed's sentiment regarding the action, stating on Twitter on October 13, "#OccupySLU was brilliant." This action added great momentum to the city-based part of the movement. When it came to actually spending the night, most people left campus, and the group dwindled to perhaps fifty to sixty people, Pulphus remembered.

The protests took place at a time of transition for the university. A new president, in much the same way as Dwaun Warmack at Harris-Stowe State University was, Fred Pestello arrived at SLU to take up the presidency. He officially started in summer 2014. One of the first meetings he had with faculty told the story of what he could expect at the private institution. The president was engaging faculty members in an affable way, asking what they believed they needed to improve life at the university. One faculty member discussed the frustrating new computer operating system that the university had purchased, another mentioned the lack of respect for the humanities and social sciences in contrast to the applied sciences, and a junior faculty member from political science was deeply concerned that there was not a higher quality field for lacrosse on campus. I was the director of African American Studies at the time and brought up the fact that Black student enrollment and retention at the university was stagnant or trending downward and that the university needed to do better on both accounts. Furthermore, I said, SLU had to be a better neighbor in the city, especially in light of the racial rebellion that was happening in Ferguson. The president affirmed my commitment to diversity.

IF WE DON'T GET IT 173

Less than three months later, the issues that sparked the Ferguson Uprising came to SLU. I had taken the night to be with my family after a full weekend, so I had not attended the event at Chaifetz and was unaware of the plan to stage an action at SLU. I woke up early Monday morning to dozens of texts and missed calls from students and colleagues. I rushed to campus to see where the protesters were sitting in. At the Clock Tower, I saw several students I knew and a couple of activists I had seen in Ferguson but did not know personally. I invited Tribe X's Dhoruba Shakur and several others back to the African American Studies office to warm up and talk. While at the office, the activists and I discussed what had taken place and what their goals were. Shakur, a bright young leader exuding confidence, said he wanted an end of white supremacy. I chuckled and asked, "What is the goal for SLU?" Shakur clarified his comment by stating he wanted an end of supremacy at SLU. In addition to Shakur, there were activists from the state of New York and elsewhere who had come for Ferguson October. They let it be known that the demonstrators had their complete support and to contact them if they needed anything.

Throughout the day, the sit-in, which was being called an occupation, was the talk of every office. Between trips to check on the occupiers, the faculty in African American Studies engaged the moment. Assistant Professor Jonathan Smith was excited, explaining he was going to request supplies for the activists from his church, and Assistant Professor Chryl Laird shared her remembrances of being at the Clock Tower in the wee hours of the morning when the demonstrators decided to occupy SLU. Assistant Professors Katrina Thompson-Moore and Bukky Gbadagesin brought their classes out to meet the demonstrators. Many students had a genuine curiosity. Some, hospitably, invited the occupiers in their dorm rooms, where they got to know each other. Others bought the occupiers meals at the dining facilities while others just stood by watching.

In the virtual world, things turned dark. Pulphus recalled the traffic on an anonymous blog app called Yik Yak being quite vitriolic. "Get a bucket of chicken and head toward the Clock Tower," one post read, according to Pulphus. He remembered the post being rude and a bit comical at the time, but others were more threatening. "They called us everything but a child of God, and I was name checked plenty of times," he recollected. Others called for his resignation or termination as a resident assistant in the dormitory. He and Sonnier knew it would be risky to have a protest on campus, but the realization that so many unknown people could identify them and where they lived was extremely jarring. It made the occupation that much more dangerous for them. Further, it placed a psychological burden on their shoulders.

During the day, I received a request to meet with the president and other administrators in DeBourg Hall. When I arrived, I shook hands with President Pestello, Vice President for Student Affairs Kent Porterfield, and Associate Professor Norm White. The administrators mentioned the fact that my research focused on student activism and that White and I had great working relationships with students on campus. They asked our thoughts on the demonstration and how the university could deal with it respectfully. White, with a deep and clear voice, insisted that police and violence not be an option because the young people had not actually done anything dangerous. Pestello was sympathetic, as he had lived through the golden era of student activism. He was born and reared in the state of Ohio, where National Guardsmen gunned down activists on campus at Kent State University, which was forty miles from his home. Pestello was near the age of the occupiers when that tragedy occurred. He knew quite well the potential for fatalities.

In contrast to some of the past campus protests and the current rebellion in Ferguson, the actions of the occupiers were quite mild. I concurred with White about the need to keep police at bay and emphasized the need to actually talk to the demonstrators as equals in order to claim common ground. Moreover, I explained that I mentored at least two of the students involved and taught others, so I did not want to see them harmed in any way, including suspension or expulsion. Everyone in the room could agree that this was a trying time for the university, but that it should be viewed more as an opportunity than a crisis.

That was not the perspective of some parents of SLU students. The incoming calls overwhelmed the receptionists, so the university created a phone bank and encouraged the staff of the Cross Cultural Center, all Black or brown people, to answer the calls of the largely white middle-class students' fearful parents. Graduate assistant for the African American Males Excel initiative Josh Jones, who worked in the Cross Cultural Center, was charged with answering many of the calls. "I didn't get any calls from anybody but white parents," Jones remembered.[17] They were demanding to speak to Pestello directly. Intellectually, he understood that "there's this level of entitlement that comes with power and privilege, but to experience it in that way, was exhausting," he said. According to Jones, "they picked the right ones to be on the phone with people . . . asking obscene questions." It was shocking to the pastor's son and former college football player. For instance, he had to use a very particular set of communication skills to explain to a self-identified white caller why asking if Jones was "colored" was problematic without intimidating the caller.

The response was to close the gates to the campus and put up new video surveillance cameras focused on the area where the occupiers camped. The feed was live, and anyone could access it through the university's website. One parent called in asking, "How do I know my daughter won't get raped when she walks by the tents?" On October 16, Fox 2 News in St. Louis reported that "Occupy SLU protestors not welcomed by everyone on campus."[18] Several students and observers had complaints. Graham Tait, who happened to be white, believed that the occupiers were not being respectful. "They are just disrespecting us . . . especially turning the flag upside down is absolutely a disrespect to America and our freedom to actually do the protesting they are doing."

Escalating the potential for violence, members of the campus ROTC arrived to confront the occupiers about the flag. The ROTC students were not alone in their feelings. An October 16 tweet from Elizabeth Deutsch read, "What does dragging the American flag on the ground prove but disrespect for those who have fought for our freedom?" Another commenter, a great fan of SLU athletics, said on Twitter, "The upside down flag at #Occupy-SLU. I take offense to it." It is remarkable that in the minds of so many Americans the flag is only associated with war fighting or the military but not the Constitutional rights or civilians it is supposed to represent. Marissa Price, a student-worker in the Office of African American Studies Program, had a question of her own on Twitter: "This is the same thing the military does when there is a distress call. Why is THIS disrespectful? #occupyslu."

In a supreme contest for American citizenship, neither side backed down and both were ready for battle. The upside-down flag was taken overnight only to be replaced by two more. Latchinson, on Twitter, asked, "Like . . . really??? You care about a flag over a human life??!! #OccupySLU." Fortunately, they did not physically fight, but university officials saw what was possible.

Flying the flag upside-down is a sign of dire distress not disrespect. Still the president did receive notice that occupiers were dragging the flag on the ground and walking on it. In a meeting with White, SLU law professor Justin Hansford, myself and others, Pestello, looking exasperated, explained that the way the demonstrators treated the flag was unacceptable and angering affiliates of the university. White agreed that the acts definitely pushed the envelope, but I had a different viewpoint. I said that first, perhaps people were worried about the wrong thing, that a young Black man, who happened to be the son of SLU employee, was killed a few miles from where we sat and another teenager killed in Ferguson just months before. Second, I referred to the counsel of my

IF WE DON'T GET IT

father, who received a Purple Heart and said that he endured gunshot wounds in battle so that Americans could do whatever they wanted with their polyester flags that were likely made abroad. My position was not the most popular that day.

There was immense pressure for the president to end the occupation. In studying the reaction of institutions, I understood that the longer the demonstration went the higher the possibility of a violent confrontation with police. In 1968, after weeks and months of demonstrations, college and university officials called police to clear campuses at Columbia University and San Francisco State College. The introduction of police violence changed the trajectory of those protests, with activists being bloodied, hurt, or arrested *en masse*. Within the span of two years, law enforcement officers or National Guardsmen killed Black student protesters at South Carolina State College, North Carolina A&T University, and Jackson State College, on or near campus. With that frightening thought in mind, I, in close contact with Pulphus, Sonnier, and Chris Walter, arranged a meeting that included the president and his cabinet, Tribe X representatives and advisors, Black Student Alliance representatives, and Norm White.

Before the occupation, President Pestello and SLU had dealt with upset student-activists, but this demonstration was different. The university had always retained the bulk of power when negotiating with young people who were on scholarship or needed classes to graduate. Many of the students believed it was an honor and privilege to be enrolled and that their institution would create better life options for them. College students who protest rarely hate their institutions; rather, they protest to improve the places they love. The threat of taking a scholarship or affiliation away was enough to deter many students from taking demonstrations what universities considered "too far." Still, there are always those willing to risk it all for the cause.

That is why the occupation caught the private institution of higher education in the midst of a Black neighborhood off guard.

The occupiers, many of whom gave up everything for the movement, did not have anything for the university to take back. They had lost their jobs, some were houseless, they had been arrested, were not afraid of police, and did not think it was a privilege to be on the university's campus. Still, activists like Yates, McKesson, and Williams, who had sacrificed much, were there to support the occupation at the same university campus that their family members knew not to touch when they got off the bus. These young people, camping out at the Clock Tower, were decidedly not respectable and were willing to disrupt white supremacy and the authority figures they believed represented it to get closer to justice. Williams, as he did in Ferguson, chose to be part of the contingent that stayed at the Clock Tower for a couple of nights. Proudly, he said he "slept on the campus outside" but that it was worth it.[19] He enjoyed meeting Cornel West, whom he had only seen on TV and on social media. The most dangerous opponent is the one who has nothing to lose. The leverage of power was in favor of the rebels, but, as their advisors explained, they could not stay forever.

Into the capacious presidential suite came six members of Tribe X, some wearing their black puff vests with a purple insignia reading "organize, educate, and empower," the distinct scent of tobacco and marijuana wafting behind them. Additionally, Tribe X advisors, community activist Romona Taylor Williams and Loletta Zasaretti, who is the mother of Pulphus and was then SLU School of Medicine receptionist, accompanied them. The advisors also operated the organization Metro St. Louis Coalition for Inclusion and Equity (M-SLICE). After accepting the snacks and drinks the president's receptionist offered, the Tribe X members and advisor took seats on one side of a giant table, and the other SLU affiliates sat on the other. H.J. Rodgers recalled its being the most expensive item he had seen in his life.[20] At the lovely table, the seating arrangement was unfortunate because it set up an unnecessary "us vs. them" confrontation. The conversation was awkward in the beginning because everyone seemed guarded. Pestello

IF WE DON'T GET IT 179

eventually asked what Tribe X needed to end the occupation because the pressure on him to act was mounting. Wisely, the demonstrators said they would have to discuss the matter and get back to the administrator. Pestello insisted that they get back to him by the next day, as that would make the fifth day of occupation.[21]

Sonnier and Pulphus remember meeting in Xavier Hall around a big table with their fellow Tribe X members coming up with ideas. Some members wanted MacBooks and others wanted scholarships for themselves. Others wanted community centers and conferences about race that would educate people about what the members regularly faced as young Black people. They eventually put together a list of eleven demands to bring to the president, but some members did not believe that the university could be trusted and thought the occupation should continue. This created group conflict. Pulphus and Sonnier, the two SLU students, were willing to end the demonstration on the premise that they could hold the university accountable.

Not everyone was sympathetic to the student-activists' point of view. Shakur contended that it was precisely because Sonnier and Pulphus were students that they would want to stop the occupation, but he held no faith in the word of the university. H.J. Rodgers explained that in protesting at the Clock Tower, they, the downtrodden poor and working-class Black threats of America, became the professors, holding class outside with the students. "We're young Black activists. We're supposed to be students here, but because of the way the system is set up, we're not," they said.[22] Later, Rodgers jokingly said he never received his payroll check for the course he offered. The occupiers succeeded in charting the path from theory to praxis.

Thinking back, Rodgers felt honored to be able to share with the students and confront power because, he said, "coming from where I'm from, a lot of people I know have never seen spaces like that."[23] He did not feel the need to rush the occupation to a close. The occupiers enjoyed the support of many students who dined with them at night and engaged their ideas during the day. Trevor Woolfolk, an aerospace engineering student, was a constant dinner companion who also saw to the needs of Tribe X members whenever possible. He was shocked at just how small the worlds of many of the white students were. "This is supposed to be a university campus. I'm in engineering, and these are supposed to be the smartest people, but I have to explain the basics of my humanity to them," he remembered being exasperated.[24] The occupation stretched him because he felt as though the university leaned on Black students to do outreach to white students by offering themselves and their experiences for the educational experience of the majority student population.

For Woolfolk, there was another source of frustration and learning. There were class and cultural differences between some Tribe X members and some of the Black students. Woolfolk and some other Black students who came from households with resources knew that the occupation enhanced the university's curriculum and provided an advanced education in democracy. He was just not sure everyone took in the lessons. Woolfolk, who was not naive, said that as much as this was a transformative experience, he questioned "what exactly did the white sophomore in engineering have to do differently after all this?" Good question. For him, even as an aspiring engineer, the Uprising and occupation raised his race consciousness, which helped direct his path moving forward. As a young person from the south suburbs of Chicago, the experience was exhilarating.

Rodgers also discussed the positionality of Pulphus and Sonnier as students. Because they were both Tribe X members and students, Rodgers recalled, they could not be as vocal, and "therein lies the problem."[25] Members—at times subtly, at other times overtly—challenged Sonnier and Pulphus's loyalty to the cause because the two had other obligations to meet. Some professors, like myself, still expected them to submit assignments, and they had jobs. Both were scholarship students. They found the insinuation that they may be less loyal to the movement to be demeaning and dismissive, as they risked their freedom and lives in many of the same ways everyone else in the group did. Trying to understand their position, Rodgers said, "Yeah, they was doing their school thing. So they couldn't be, like, as vocal, and therein lies the problem." He added, "Rightfully so, they were afraid of losing scholarships or losing the opportunity for a better education because of speaking out on issues that would play them in their community." Rodgers worried that there was a trap that Black people who had the chance to excel in white spaces fell into when they tried to keep their positions but also represent those who were not in those positions.

On campus, Sonnier, Pulphus, Woolfolk, and Walter had led multiple awareness campaigns. They, along with student supporters, marched through the library, chanting. That was a particularly disruptive act, as it was midterms. Some students were furious that their study time had been disturbed and that the protesters were punishing them with their problems. The young protest leaders agreed that their campaign and the occupation in general was disruptive and inconvenient but so too were racism and police brutality. The sooner St. Louis and Ferguson resolved those issues, the sooner the activists could be quiet in the library. There were immediate calls for the suspension or expulsion of the marchers. Vice President for Student Affairs Kent Porterfield contacted me for a candid conversation about the demonstration and its leaders. We decided that it would be best to discuss the matter with a representative of the demonstrators, and so I arranged a brief meeting with Pulphus and Porterfield. We had a productive discussion.

As was the case with every other action, the members of Tribe X debated, perhaps contentiously, and came to a collective decision. The university administration, wanting to end the occupation, eagerly received the demands. The items on the list were far-reaching and thoughtful. Three of them had to do with the recruitment, retention, and education of Black SLU students. The first was an increased budget for African American Studies. The second was an "increase [in] financial aid resources for African American students." The third was "the evaluation of . . . current scholarship programs to better serve African American populations." The next three involved the development and intellectual opportunities of elementary and secondary students in Black neighborhoods. Two demands required community centers that helped with economic and other issues affecting the everyday lived experiences of Black people. For the campus, they demanded a standing university committee on race, poverty, and inequality as well as a national conference on racial equality. Perhaps the most distinct was the demand for artwork that memorialized the occupation.

Because of the direct effect these items would have on Black students at the university, I believed it was essential for the Black Student Alliance (BSA) to approve of and join in on the agreements. That was the source of some discomfort in the meeting where the demands were presented and negotiated. BSA president Chris Walter, who was present, personally agreed with the demands but needed to bring them before the larger body before officially indicating support. The members and advisors of Tribe X had not seen many Black students while occupying the campus and did not think it necessary to have any other organization's approval to move forward. Romona Williams, Lola Zasaretti, several Tribe X members, and I fervently debated the point to the extent that the university president asked if he should excuse himself to let us talk.

In a heated moment, one Tribe X member told me I did not understand what it was like to be a young Black man dealing with racism, and I smiled. The young activist then explained that there were tens of thousands of people counting on them to seal this deal. Looking back, it certainly must have appeared that the bougie, formally educated, liberal Black man in a tie was trying to prevent the young Black revolutionaries from advancing the cause.

I understood I would be viewed as a sellout. However, in much the same way that Darren Seals, Tory Russell, and others wanted those in Ferguson who would be there after the cameras and activists left to be participatory in decision-making, I wanted to ensure that the young people who had to deal with the reverberations of the occupation had the opportunity to officially endorse the demands. Perhaps it was the wrong time and place to make the stand or maybe it was paternalism, but it was important to me. Norm White intervened, stating that it seemed reasonable but that we could move forward with a conditional agreement that day, and allow BSA to endorse afterward.

Pestello returned, stating he was amenable to the demands. He wanted to add two items: the appointment of an assistant who could see to the resolution of the demands and bi-weekly meetings to stay updated on progress. Everyone shook hands to consecrate the agreement. To capture the moment, and provide evidence to their virtual followers, Tribe X members suggested the people in the room take pictures.

The next morning, Pestello called me to inform him that trucks were assisting the occupiers in packing their belongings. Tribe X was leaving, but not without a hiccup. Several members refused to vacate the Clock Tower area because they distrusted the agreement. Pestello went to assuage the anxieties of the activists. African American Studies assistant professor Jonathan Smith was there, and extended his hand to help Pestello up onto an elevated surface. When the demonstrators asked aloud how they could be sure the president would actually meet the demands, Smith responded that they could trust the president because Smith would be there to hold him accountable. That moment led to his eventual appointment as the special assistant to the president for diversity and engagement and later vice president of diversity, equity, and inclusion.

"We are proud of our achievement," a Tribe X statement released on social media read. Movement communicators like

DeRay McKesson tweeted the statement and corresponded about the demonstration, giving day-by-day updates. At the end of the occupation, the activists and institution claimed a hard-fought victory. "We fulfilled our original mission and plan to continue to work with SLU to make sure they fulfill commitments set forth in the agreement," Tribe X wrote. Members appreciated "the earnest way that President Pestello engaged us," according to the statement. Treating them as equals worked in the president's and the university's favor. In bringing the discussion of race to campus in such a dramatic fashion, Tribe X claimed to change "the dynamic" for not only the institution but also the region and beyond. It actually created a model for what was possible at higher education institutions throughout the nation. Attorney General Eric Holder offered praise to Pestello, Tribe X, M-SLICE, and others involved in bringing the occupation to a peaceful close. "Amid reports of continuing conflict, your steady hand, your respect to everyone involved, and your fidelity to the rule of law, as well as the Jesuit values that define the institution you lead have enabled you to bring about a constructive and non-violent resolution to the encampment at St. Louis University," Holder wrote to the university president.[26]

After reading about the earlier Black liberation campaigns and Occupy Wall Street, Tribe X had determined that it had to intentionally set the course of its destiny by identifying the issues that were most pressing for the community and how SLU could play a part. It was a masterful display because members demonstrated what forthright dialogue among individuals and institutional introspection could yield. No one was harmed, though some feelings were hurt among those who believed that the university should have never accommodated the protesters. Growth can be painful but necessary. With a clear conscience, Tribe X declared that it was "not on SLU's campus to further any agenda other than the people's agenda." And that it did.

Image control was important to both the activists and the

administration. Pestello, aware that the university was under a shroud of controversy, brought to campus a crisis manager and public affairs specialist, Bob Gagne, who was present in the meetings and at events. Gagne came up with the phrase *Clock Tower Accords* in reference to the thirteen agreements. In a neoliberal fashion, it was catchy and sanitized in contrast to the intensity and chaos of the demonstration. The phrase was reminiscent of the historic "95 Theses," which always seemed mild in terms of the actual protest that occurred. In any event, the introduction of the term *Clock Tower Accords* provided insight into the ways that higher education institutions could take advantage of vulnerable moments to create marketing ploys. The way that SLU currently "celebrates" the Clock Tower Accords on campus is similar to the manner in which the University of California–Berkeley has commemorated the Free Speech Movement demonstrators. The power of the protest, over time, seemed to shift back to the institutions.

For that moment, though, the victors could rely on knowing they had people power. Trust became a major factor from the start to the finish of the occupation. McKesson mentioned how things nearly derailed when the planners did not share details about where exactly they were going. The marchers had to believe that the organizers were not misleading them. They had to maintain faith that the leaders would not lightly expose them to danger or harm and that the leaders would bring them closer to justice for Brown and Myers.

12.

MIZZOU AND PRINCETON TOO

Columbia, Missouri, and Ferguson are approximately 115 miles apart, but Mike Brown brought them much closer. The University of Missouri–Columbia is the state's flagship university and an institution many aspire to attend. More than a few state politicians and leaders attained degrees from there. People all around the state enjoyed Mizzou sports teams and the resources the school offered. Furthermore, Missourians benefited from the leadership that the university developed in students. Higher education institutions like Mizzou typically like to cultivate leadership skills in the classroom and via their student affairs programming because there is an element of institutional control. Less desirable for universities is the type of leadership that grows outside of the confines of the curriculum and assessment. That kind is unpredictable and liberated in that it does not seek the validation of university or state officials. Students could only acquire that type of leadership "out the mud," as young people say. What young Black people learned from their activism in Ferguson they applied at the University of Missouri–Columbia. Their efforts eventually drew international attention.

Storm Ervin, who was president of the campus chapter of the NAACP, and other students created a coalition called MU for Mike Brown at the beginning of the 2014–2015 school year.[1] They put together actions on campus that were meant to disrupt the typical flow of college life and to bring awareness to the injustice students and their families faced in the St. Louis metropolitan area. The members demonstrated on campus and around Columbia, which was a small city of 120,000 residents. Some chalked the sidewalks and parking lots, while others led marches downtown. St. Louisan Ervin, a leader of the multiracial group, was in charge of organizing a large die-in at the MU Student Center to replicate those that Alisha Sonnier and other leaders had conducted in a popular mall and in the Delmar Loop back in St. Louis. As policing was the main theme of their protest activities in Ferguson, MU for Mike Brown met with representatives of law enforcement to discuss their practices and relationship to the Black community in Columbia. The group was largely reformist in nature and willing to work within the established system to achieve goals.

What started as an outward-facing movement grew to include an insular struggle for racial justice on campus. During the fall semester of 2014, MU for Mike Brown put together "listening sessions" to get a sense of how students were responding to the events concerning the Ferguson Uprising. There, Ervin and other leaders learned about the racial issues that greatly affected the university students where they lived on campus. It was not, they found, that Mizzou or Columbia police officers were harassing Black students, but rather some Black students' concerns were "with their professors," who made questionable remarks or behaved in ways that made Black students believe racism was at play. In the sessions, Ervin remembered Black students talking about a twisted culture where non-Black students would walk up to Black students and take their pictures because they had "never seen Black people before."[2] Ervin recollected, "The main thing that we felt burdened by was how the administration handled racism" and how "a culture of white supremacy permeated through Mizzou" in general.

Throughout the remainder of the school year (2014–2015), Ervin and her fellow student-activists exhausted their capacity for conversation and issued a set of demands to the administration in the fall of 2015. The demands included a formal apology from the chancellor; the chancellor's resignation; racial and diversity awareness training for administrators, faculty, service staff, and students; an increase of the percentage of Black faculty to 10 percent of the total by the 2017–2018 school year; funding for mental health counselors of color; and, funding for the Gaines-Oldham Black Culture Center and other social justice centers.

Ervin and several others represented a new wing of MU for Mike Brown. When searching for names they arrived at Concerned Student 1950, which was a nod to the year that Gus T. Ridgel, Mizzou's first Black attendee, began attending. They brought to the public's attention several racist incidents that included the student body president, who happened to be Black, being called "nigger" repeatedly and members of the Legions of Black Collegians also being called the slur. Later a swastika smeared in feces was found in the bathroom of a residence hall. These incidents occurred on campus, and as was the case at Saint Louis University (SLU) and Washington University, top administration officials professed the school's intolerance of racism.

Dubious of the slow bureaucratic process that unfurled, Concerned Student 1950 members took matters into their own hands by stopping the university chancellor's car during the homecoming parade. The action was a bold move that upped the ante on students' campaign.

It was "a demonstration where things went left in ways we did not anticipate," remembered Ervin. She had been on the street in Ferguson when protesters squared off against police, but the parade was even more frightful, she said. Far outnumbered, parade watchers, along with police, rushed the students who wanted answers from the chancellor. The memory still fresh, Ervin recalled, "I mean, I have been in Ferguson, and I have had guns pointed at me, but I have never had a police like actually touch me."

On West Florissant or in front of the Ferguson police station, Ervin could always feel the presence of her fellow demonstrators at her sides, but that was not the case when crowd members and police charged at her in Columbia. There were in total ten students blocking the parade, "so when their [the police officers'] hands are on you, you don't feel them [her fellow activists] there." Ervin was partly shocked because in her capacity as NAACP president she'd had what she believed were productive meetings with the Columbia police force. She wondered how the people who seemed so reasonable before could approach her so aggressively at the parade. "They were all cool," she had previously thought. "And, you know, we didn't really have much issue with them." That was until Black students attempted to check racism at a beloved cultural event of the university. The police activated to protect dear ol' Mizzou.

At that moment, neither the police nor the crowd members assisting law enforcement seemed interested in solving the issues of racism that affected students of the university. There was much at stake for both Concerned Student 1950 and the counter-protesters; the primary issue was the identity of the then 176-year-old predominantly white institution. For the members from the crowd who physically accosted the student-activists, the university was worth potentially harming someone who had already been hurt by racism. For the young people who chose to stop the parade, the university was worth enough for them to put their lives in danger from the people who just wanted a parade and not the reality of the Black experience. The counter-protesters and protesters both believed they were doing what was best for Mizzou; they just had vastly different ideas of what Mizzou should be. The Ferguson Uprising gave the students the language, model, and inspiration they needed to make such a bold and tactical demonstration. Furthermore, the Uprising encouraged the students to imagine a fundamentally new university.

Just as the actions of agitators in Ferguson escalated over the course of the Uprising, so too did the demonstrations of Concerned Student 1950. Graduate student Jonathan Butler, who was in Ferguson in the days after Wilson killed Brown, took the slow reaction of the administration and the quick reaction of the counter-protesters personally. Not unlike Alex Templeton, Josh

Williams, and Darren Seals back in Ferguson, Butler was willing to give his freedom and life to the cause of Black students at Mizzou. Historically, Black student-activists have collectively engaged in building takeovers, walkouts, boycotts, marches, sit-ins, and occasionally fistfights or property destruction to highlight their causes. The record reveals few if any hunger strikes as a form of student protest. On November 2, 2015, Butler, after trying to meet, negotiate, and courageously converse about racism, made the crucial decision to not eat until Concerned Student 1950 demands were met.

In support of Butler's hunger strike, fellow students occupied "Traditions Plaza" on campus. The story gained traction in and around Missouri. It took four days for the chancellor to issue an apology for not recognizing the impact of racism on campus and for his reaction to the parade demonstration, but he still refused to resign. Meanwhile, Butler was famished. To many, it seemed that the chancellor was content to let Butler starve. Still, others wondered if Butler was taking his demonstration too far. Even for his closest advocates, it was quite troubling to see him fading.

Ervin was shaken to her core, as she had never experienced this amount of stress at once. Between the actions, her classes, and media requests, she felt as though she was drowning. "I'm sorry. I didn't know my friend would be going on a hunger strike and rewriting his will this semester," she remembered thinking at the time.[3] She recalled, "I thought I was going to do a demonstration and go back to class." Ervin discovered that being a soldier and scholar was nearly impossible and that there were consequences. "I thought I was going to be able to do all my assignments on time," but that did not happen. She would have completed the work in time, but she was fighting racism. She hoped that she would be able to "go talk to the *New York Times* real quick and get right back to it." Her instructor was unforgiving and issued Ervin a failing grade.

While student-activists were dealing with plummeting grade point averages, Butler's organs were in threat of failing. The tides of his demonstration shifted on November 7, when members of the Mizzou football team refused to play the remainder of the season unless the chancellor resigned. By November 9, the chancellor had submitted his resignation. "I've thought and prayed about this decision. It's the right [thing] to do," he said.[4] The chancellor, once the university faced the option of losing hundreds of thousands of dollars in revenue from missed football games, recognized "this university is in pain right now[;] . . . and it needs healing." As he ended his hunger strike, Butler, whom Ferguson had taught, said that "we are worth fighting for."[5]

Students from across the nation heard Butler and saw the work of Ervin and her peers. They initiated a renaissance of student activism that had not been present on campuses since the anti-apartheid campaigns of the 1980s. The Mizzou campaign inspired thousands of students around the nation at colleges and universities to walk out of classes in solidarity. From community colleges to the Ivy League, Black students and their supporters were empathetic with the racism young people experienced in Missouri, whether it be Mizzou or Ferguson. Those student-activists were bolstered by Black alumni. Mizzou alumna Jana Williams (class of 2001) proudly stated, "I am happy that the students at Mizzou and the students around the nation are now coming together to stand united in the fight to end racism as my parents did in the '60s and '70s while they were in college."[6] The sentiment of Williams and other alumni was, "Mizzou, we know you; this is nothing new!" It was high time, members of Concerned Student 1950 believed, that Mizzou reimagine and recreate itself.

#OccupySLU, #ConcernedStudent1950, and the Ferguson Uprising deeply inspired students everywhere. The movement spread to the Ivy League. At Princeton University, St. Louisan Destiny Crockett was distraught after hearing that Darren Wilson would not be indicted. That night, she and two other peers planned an action to march through campus. Empowered, the original members and several more sought to advance life for students in the exclusive space. Although the Black students in New Jersey may not have taken up the same issues young people did in Ferguson, they adopted the ethos of fearlessly challenging white institutions and systems. In fall 2014, Crockett, who was graduating in 2017, helped establish a group called the Black Justice League, whose sole intention was to fight anti-Black racism.

On November 18, 2015, the group staged a two-day sit-in at one of the university's oldest buildings, Nassau Hall, with the goal of the Princeton president signing a list of demands it had constructed. Just as Jonathan Pulphus was quick to produce his ID and call the protesters at SLU his guests before occupying the campus, Black Justice League members were just as sharp in their demonstration. When discussing the precise timing and legitimacy of the sit-in, Crockett noted, "it was technically his [the university president's] office hours," so the protesters joined him for conversation.[7] There, they issued a set of demands.

The demands included resources for Black students, Black Studies, and Black employees. Additionally, they called for the removal of the name of Princeton alumnus and also university and U.S. president Woodrow Wilson from the school of public and international affairs as well as a residence hall. Wilson, a proud white southerner, was known for his ability to tell "darky" jokes and his maneuvers to maintain racial segregation on campus and later throughout the United States once he became president. For much of the nation Wilson was a bearer of democracy, as he ushered into existence the League of Nations. For many Black people, however, he was a racist who propagated the narrative that the Ku Klux Klan saved America by endorsing and showcasing D.W. Griffith's *Birth of Nation* at the White House. Members of the Black Justice League questioned why they should be made to respect a man and his legacy who would not have respected them.

Additionally, the students demanded a Black space on campus where they could center themselves. There were similar spaces like the Women's Center and the Carl A. Fields Center for Equality and Cultural Understanding, but nothing specifically for Black students. Then, the exclusive, mostly white eating clubs provided much of the housing and social activity for students. Historically they did not welcome or appeal to Black learners. Black Justice League members wanted a space that they and their peers could name and control. Finally, the Black Justice League demanded that Princeton faculty and staff go through diversity training and that courses based on the experiences of marginalized (Black and other) people be required of all Princeton undergraduates.

Because of the work of the Black Justice League and its supporters, many of the demands were met, but not before young people chose to confront the defenders of racism. At an institution that historically produced presidents, Supreme Court justices, and captains of industry, few believed that their traditions could be wrong or racist. In that way a university, which is ostensibly a place of universal knowledge, can become a stalwart of white supremacy.[8] The Black Justice League did not defeat racism at Princeton, but it did have the nerve to try. The young activists' fervent attempts to advance life for Black people on campus is part of the Uprising's legacy.

Ferguson taught lessons college students could have never learned in a classroom. They analyzed systems within their institutions that had been in place for centuries. In casting off their tethers of respectability, young learners were able to capture the tactical advantage over institutional officials. Students came to understand that administrators did not have a monopoly on intelligence, ethics, or justice, and that young people could also lead the way in democratizing education. Perhaps most important, they learned to create community and communicate ideas beyond their own silos. Once they transcended the concept of individual progress, they learned that they could improve the experiences of generations of Black students.

13.

HOPE BURNED: NO INDICTMENT AND DESTRUCTIVE REBELLION

"There's a difference between believing and hoping."
—Joshua Jones, 2023

There was a deafening silence before a piercing shriek, and then it felt as though Ferguson exploded. St. Louis County prosecuting attorney Robert McCulloch had announced that he would not be indicting Darren Wilson. I remember gunshots, tires screeching, and tears flowing. More than anger, hopelessness prevailed and buildings burned. Many organizers wondered if this night would be the end of a movement or the beginning of a new phase. Did the young people judge the success of their actions based on the system's response, or was the entire point to spotlight the injustice and make America answer for itself?

By November 2014, everyone's nerves were frayed. There was constant speculation as to when an announcement would be made regarding the indictment of Wilson. Protests continued in the nights, and conflicts between the police and demonstrators continued. Perhaps in an effort to maintain calm in light of the oncoming grand jury decision, Governor Jay Nixon announced the formation of the Ferguson Commission (sometimes referred to as Forward through Ferguson).[1] The co-chairs of the commission were the very well-respected Rev. Starsky Wilson of St. John's United Church of Christ in St. Louis and business leader Rich McClure, then president of UniGroup, the multi-billion-dollar-grossing owner of United Van Lines and Mayflower Transit.[2] The commission comprised community representatives that included a leader of the Young Citizens Council and Teach for America administrator, Brittany Packnett Cunningham. Other members were the Rev. Traci Blackmon, pastor of Christ the King Church; Rasheen Aldridge Jr., a local youth activist; Kevin Ahlbrand, then president of the Missouri Fraternal Order of Police; Grayling Tobias, then superintendent of the Hazelwood School District in North St. Louis County; T.R. Carr, the former mayor of Hazelwood; Rose Windmiller, then assistant vice chancellor for government and community relations at Washington University; Gabriel Gore, a former federal prosecutor and an attorney specializing in litigation; Becky James-Hatter, president of Big Brothers Big Sisters of Eastern Missouri; Dan Isom, former St. Louis City police chief and Desmond Lee Professor of Policing and the Community at University of Missouri–St. Louis; Scott Negwer, president of Negwer Materials; Felicia Pulliam, development director of FOCUS St. Louis; Byron M. Watson, a retired sergeant of the St. Louis County Police Department; and Patrick Sly, executive vice president at Emerson, the multi-billion-dollar corporation that maintains wonderfully manicured facilities several blocks from a major demonstration site.

Since the dawn of bureaucracy, people in positions of power have used committees, commissions, and task forces to slow the momentum of movements. Understandably, among activists and observers, there was skepticism about the Ferguson Commission. The presence of presidents, CEOs, superintendents, and pastors in the body contrasted with the status of demonstrators who had given up jobs or in some cases housing to engage in the movement. Even before Brown's death, they had little faith in the system, and that was not going to change because of the governor's appointed commission. Noting the timing of the commission's announcement, local rapper-activist T-Dubb-O pointed out that at the same moment Governor Nixon assured Missouri residents that he

IF WE DON'T GET IT 197

intended to find out the reasons for Brown's death and the Uprising with the commission, Nixon had also mobilized the National Guard. T-Dubb-O and his peers viewed that as a "declaration of war against the protesters," noting the militarization of police on Ferguson streets.[3]

The governor decried the potential for violence, but T-Dubb-O and others countered: "It's a complete lie that the militarization of the police has been peaceful," he said. "No police have been hurt. Our demonstrations have been peaceful, and if anybody has been hurt, it's been us." To be sure, police officials reported minor injuries that officers received from flying rocks and water bottles and from exchanges when arresting protesters. St. Louis rapper-activist Tef Poe had worked, marched, and organized with several people on the commission, but questions haunted him. For instance, he asked: "But where is the governor in all this?" Poe exclaimed: "He should be here . . . rather than tossing the ball to Traci [Blackmon] for her to figure it out." Hands Up United co-founder Rika Tyler sagely surmised: "This is not just about the Ferguson Commission," said Tyler. "It reaches and impacts every sector of the nation."

As the Ferguson Commission went about its work, various activists and organizations prepared for the blowback of a nonindictment announcement. An article in the *St. Louis American* described the efforts of Johnetta Elzie and DeRay McKesson, who distributed a newsletter, *Reform and Empowerment*. In it, they indicated that on the day of the announcement (at the time of the newsletter release that was still unknown) protesters would be meeting at the Ferguson Police Department and in the Shaw neighborhood at the memorial site of VonDerrit Myers, Jr., whom a St. Louis City police officer had shot dead in October.[4] As a reminder, the newsletter stated explicitly: "Remember, we actively advocate and profess the importance of peaceful protest. We do not support, condone, or encourage violence." The newsletter even listed a link to the rules of engagement.

In an effort to prevent further lethal violence, members of the community, including me, met with law enforcement officials at different times to discuss ways to recognize the rights of citizens to assemble and protest without being harmed by the police. As indicated in one meeting I attended, the freedoms of Black people, angry or not, could not be sacrificed for the police's desire for order.

A major point of controversy had been measures like "the five-second rule," that law enforcement conceived of in haste. It dictated that protesters could not stand in any one spot on the street or sidewalk for more than five seconds. This was clearly not constitutional, but an officer with a semi-automatic rifle and tactical gear convinced me to keep moving despite my misgivings about the viability of such an order. As was the case throughout history, the state believed it was justified in negotiating the rights of Black people. Nowhere in white America would it have been okay to treat people that way. This, however, was a primarily Black campaign about a Black boy, and authorities are given much latitude to maintain order in such cases.

For a group of people who had been restrained and civil in the face of economic, political, and physical violence, restraint was no longer an option. With that in mind, activists had to prepare for the worst. The *Reform and Restoration* newsletter listed useful items for a "Protestor Action Kit."[5] It included the jail-support number, which demonstrators wrote on their body in permanent marker; a change of warm clothes; a portable phone charger; a paper map; medications; shatterproof goggles; a liquid and antacid mix (to neutralize pepper spray and tear gas); and, a "quick reference sheet with names (first, last) and date of birth for each member of your team/cohort and any important phone numbers and addresses."

On the night of the announcement, some activists wanted to make the point clear, the city of Ferguson had to pay a price for killing an unarmed teenager and diminishing the life chances of a community. The city and law enforcement were not going to be able to extinguish life for free. At a demonstration in front of the Ferguson police station, one young man told me that he was getting tired of protesting because "it wasn't going to do anything." He did not sound hopeless but more exasperated. Talking loud enough for the officers protecting the station and everyone else around us to hear, the young citizen explained that none of this was fair. When asked why, he said that if he, a Black man, had shot an unarmed Mike Brown in broad daylight, he "would not have made it off the block." He said that we, meaning Black people, treat them (pointing at the policemen) like God. Pushed on what he meant, he said that the white man with shiny metal on his chest killed at will and walked away unscathed. The young man, now staring at a particular officer, said we need to treat them like we treat ourselves. I could not tell if the demonstrator was a provocateur or philosopher.

Graduate student and Ferguson resident Josh Jones's rational mind understood that the chances of prosecuting a police officer in St. Louis County were slim to nil, but he held out hope that all the work that young people had been doing on the ground would pay dividends in the way of an indictment. Jones's sentiments were not unique. Millennial Activist United member Alex Templeton said that they wanted to believe there would be an indictment because otherwise, "what was all the work we did out there for?" There was a need for light in what many young activists considered the darkness of oppression.

Living in parking lots, demonstrating through the night for seasons, and battling police left many activists hardened. It was difficult for them to believe in happy endings. Lost Voices leader Josh Williams remembered that he did not and could not believe that McCulloch would indict Wilson. This after Williams had protested multiple times at McCulloch's office in Clayton and even shut down the freeway to draw attention to the cause. Still, neither Wiliams's mind or heart allowed him to believe. When asked if he ever thought Wilson would be charged, Williams quickly responded "Nah, not at all! With previous killings, I never seen an officer get indicted, so" there was little possibility.[6] No matter how little faith Williams had in the legal system as it concerned officer shootings of unarmed Black boys, it still hurt deeply hearing McCulloch declare non-indictment.

For less-committed activists, motivation may have waned, but for Williams the announcement had an opposite effect. He felt he had to stay the course: "What kept me going was the youth and the people that can't fight for themselves or the poor people or the illiterate people or the mentally challenged people; they want to fight but can't." He said he stood, thinking, on West Florissant one day, and he asked himself: "Who will be there for them?" and he decided that "was where I come in." That was a powerful moment of reflection for the eighteen year old.

By the time McCulloch delivered his indictment announcement, they had been on the street for a quarter of a year. Activists like Templeton and Damon Latchinson had left their jobs to protest for justice; the movement had become their entire life. To think that one man in a suit in front of a microphone could destroy their hope was devastating. Templeton remembered being with organizer and current ActionSTL executive director Kayla Reed on the night of the non-indictment.[7] Reed, fighting through the tears, had let her fellow activists know that they had to move and keep going. I said that "it was like a kick to the gut," finding out Wilson would not be indicted. The potential for disillusionment was extremely high for young people, but to their credit, they stayed committed. Rasheen Aldridge Jr., who was a labor activist before coming to Ferguson, said that "as an organizer, you have to maintain hope" for the sake of the people alongside whom you fought, but the announcement definitely hurt morale in the moment.

In a lot in front of the police station, I saw Brown's mother and stepfather standing atop a vehicle with a bullhorn. When McCulloch finished his statement, there was a deafening silence.

Then, I heard a shrill shriek or wail I had never heard before nor since. It was Brown's mother publicly mourning. The stepfather began to speak on the bullhorn; the silence had ended. Behind him, I heard a young man say: "Get the burner, cuz." From perhaps a block away, I heard what were unmistakably gunshots ringing out. Darren Seals later said that he personally saw and took images of police taking cover while people shot into their vehicles, "Brothers was riding up, shooting up their cars, dumping choppers, handguns, whatever, not even caring."[8] Although it could not be confirmed, Seals claimed a policeman was shot through the shoulder. I was fearful someone was going to die that night.

Darren Seals, wearing his signature "Straight Outta Ferguson" T-shirt, poses with fellow activists Rev. Osagyefo Sekou, Bree Newsome (in the "People over Money shirt"), and Dr. Cornel West during the "Ferguson is Everywhere" hip-hop concert on August 9, 2015, exactly one year after Michael Brown's death. Seals was found shot dead in a burning car on September 6, 2016; he was twenty-nine years old. *Photo:* St. Louis American

With Dr. Jameca Woody-Cooper, a local psychologist who had been offering assistance in the Canfield Green apartment complex, I turned from the police station to walk to Wellspring

Church a couple blocks away; it was a refuge for protesters. Inside, there was a television playing the reactions to the decision. Angry and frustrated, I could not stop using profanity. Reared in the church, I felt extremely guilty for cursing in the "house of the Lord," so I left after making sure Woody-Cooper had a plan for a safe egress. Headed back to the police station, I felt the heat of a burning trash can on a corner. It had already been a long night, and there was more to come.

I received a call from MSNBC's *All in with Chris Hayes* about a reaction to the verdict. I agreed to make remarks. By then, I had encountered Young Citizens Council founder and nonprofit executive director Charli Cooksey near the police station. We had spent so many hours in meetings and planning sessions, and we decided to go to West Florissant in separate cars. We parked in front of the Public Storage building on West Florissant, which was across from the complex where MSNBC filmed. Typically, activists who went to West Florissant parked in the neighborhoods to keep from getting blocked in by law enforcement or their cars damaged by projectiles. Cooksey and I, not thinking about that, locked the cars, crossed the street and entered a gate that was then locked behind us. When asked why we were being locked in, the greeter said that it was for safety. Along West Florissant there was hyperactivity and noise of every fashion. As soon as we entered, someone mentioned that the beauty supply shop across the street was on fire. When I was getting situated with a microphone, I heard Hayes mention that Sam's Meat Market was up in flames as well. Cooksey and I looked at each other because the fires were moving closer to where we had parked our cars.

Finally, I went live with Hayes. The anchor asked if my students were safe and what the reaction by the police station was like. I had been in contact with several students and knew that they were in Clayton or otherwise safe. Hayes questioned me about my reaction. I explained, with sirens squealing and horns blaring in the background, that "this is what disillusionment looks like," that even though people intellectually expected a non-indictment, the idea that an armed man could shoot dead an unarmed young man based on an altercation over walking in the middle of the road was humanistically unfathomable.[9]

Then Hayes caught me off guard by asking how I was feeling. "I understand the anger, but I'm sad," I said slowly. I understood that "these people [destructive demonstrators] will seem crazy; that's the way the narrative will go." It was tragic because "worse than crazy," the people who wanted justice for Mike Brown were "hopeless," I surmised. Hayes asked what I meant, and I said that "it will never make sense in their [the general public's] minds why somebody would set afire a building or set a garbage can or police car afire. That would never make sense to them." At that moment, it occurred to me that the aggrieved people of Ferguson and those seeking justice had tried all they could to accommodate law and order, but there was nothing left to grasp. That was dangerous.

"When you're a young person and you make it to eighteen, and you see your friend get shot, and you have no where to go, that's just hopelessness. You're not going to be a police officer; you're not going to be a prosecuting attorney. It's just hopelessness." Hayes interrupted me to report that "a third fire has been started in the Public Storage" building that was across the street where Cooksey and my cars were parked.

"Okay, well, I'm gonna have to go," I said to Hayes, trying to close the interview and get to my and Cooksey's cars, which were in danger of burning. Before shaking Hayes's hand and thanking him for covering the scene, I told the anchor to "just remember: more than crazy, these people are hopeless." I took the mic off myself and met up with Cooksey, who said, "We gotta get out of here now!"

When we got back to the place we entered, the gatekeeper said he was under orders that no one could leave. Cooksey explained breathlessly that our cars were across the street and we needed to get to them. The sentry, a late-twenty-something-year-old white man, replied sincerely, "Dude, we care more about you than we do cars." Cooksey, who has always been the most sensible in every room, asked him immediately if he would get us new vehicles "if the cars exploded." The kindly liberal man thought and said "no." I asked who ordered the gates to be locked; the concerned guard said the owners of the property. I inquired further if the police had made the order, and the keyholder said "no."

Cooksey and I looked at each other and then looked down at the gate, which had about 12 inches of clearance from its bottom to the asphalt. I said "Wanna try?" and we both got on our backs and shimmied underneath the gate, much to the caring compound keeper's chagrin. I had always been self-conscious about being skinny, and said a prayer of thanks for my slight physique. We bounced up and ran into the street, which was in total chaos because the traffic lights were flashing and no one in their right mind was following the rules of the road.

After dodging death in the street, Cooksey and I made it to the Public Storage lot, where we felt the heat emanating from the flames coming out of the door of the building that was twenty feet from the cars. The door handles were extremely hot, and the vehicles were filled with smoke. We shouted goodbyes and promises to call and left the lot to enter the frenzy. We drove on the wrong side of the road to avoid burning garbage cans. There were police and National Guardsmen everywhere, but they were not acting. I was noticing a used car lot with multiple vehicles going up in flames when the phone rang.

"Now do you understand how we felt?!" a participant in the now famous 1968 rebellion at Columbia University asked me. He called to say he had caught me on TV and to see if I was safe. It was unexpected, but sweet. The Columbia alumnus told me to be careful but, more important, to not expend all my energy because there would be plenty more nights to demonstrate and many more emotionally charged issues to protest. He said that I should prepare for a protracted struggle for freedom and justice. That was sage advice.[10]

Demonstrators, dissidents, rebels, activists, protesters, and provocateurs had their way with the rest of the night. No one could stop them. For Ferguson, there was a heavy price to pay.

14.

LIFE GOES ON: WHERE ARE THEY NOW?

"We became a politically aware America because of Ferguson; we built a political education."

—*Alex Templeton*

Although life seemed to stand still in the moment that the non-indictment was announced, the world kept turning. On the night of Darren Wilson's non-indictment, Kayla Reed was determined that she and her fellow organizers had to do something to keep moving forward, and she did. Understanding the importance of local politics in the lives of Black people, Reed and many others decided to throw their support behind the son of a police officer and former Riverview Village prosecutor, Wesley Bell, who ran for the Ferguson City Council in 2015. At the time there was hardly any Black representation in any sector of Ferguson's municipal government, so there was hope that Bell could act on behalf of the people on the council. He was among those who oversaw the consent decree that the Ferguson Police Department negotiated with the U.S. Department of Justice. The election to the council, it turns out, catalyzed his political career. After serving as St. Louis County prosecuting attorney since 2018, on August 6, 2024, Bell, with substantial financial support from the American Israel Public Affairs Committee, defeated sitting Congresswoman Cori Bush.

Some activists vocalized great dismay and regret when Bell,

as a prosecutor, declined to indict Darren Wilson.[1] Templeton, not holding back, charged "Bell with using Kayla [Reed] to get elected." Templeton had been one of those prosecuted by Bell's predecessor, Bob McCulloch, and had hoped that Bell would do better by Black people. Templeton noted that Bell was a "reformer, and that he deserved to be in his position [St. Louis County prosecutor]."[2] He, however, "got there on the backs of niggas." Even if Bell knew he had, what law student Templeton called a "stinker" (a case that was not viable), Bell "let niggas' hopes ride on the review of Brown's case."

"I'm very disappointed with Wesley Bell," said attorney Justin Hansford, enthusiastically agreeing with Templeton and others.[3] To his mind, it was wrong to let people think that he would run a thorough investigation, when "he took the same evidence that McCulloch accumulated and made a decision from there." It infuriated Hansford that "there was not additional investigation." The fundamental problem was that Bell "followed McCulloch's narrative," which may have been flawed from the outset. Deeply bothered, Hansford lamented, "It seems clear to me Bell had careerist ambitions." There was nothing wrong with wanting to advance in his career; the issue was Bell's approach, according to Hansford and other activists. Still a young professor, Hansford hoped "we learned a lesson from this because that betrayal is a microcosm." In taking an anti-McCulloch position, he and other activists came to understand that they were not necessarily pro-Bell. Politics is never clean-cut, and young people during the Uprising had to learn on the fly.

The lessons were not lost on Alisha Sonnier. "Ferguson taught me what power was and who has and who doesn't have it."[4] In the movement, Sonnier said, she encountered for the first time "Black people with financial resources" and many with social resources, but "one of the resources that we really struggled with is we did not have the political capital to change some of the things that we fundamentally wanted to change." She realized then that acquiring political capital required "another level of organizing." In doing so, an organizer could determine what the people's "values are versus what their practices are" and create policy from there. Sonnier worked with Rasheen Aldridge Jr. on the Fight for $15 and campaigned for U.S. presidential candidate Bernie Sanders in 2016.

Taking the role of women in Black political power seriously, Sonnier, in 2016, campaigned for Missouri state representative candidate Cora Faith Walker and St. Louis mayoral candidate Tishaura Jones and U.S. House of Representatives candidate Cori Bush. Walker won her election, but Bush and Jones did not follow up with victories until 2020. It was Sonnier's turn to influence policy in 2021 when the newly elected Mayor Jones appointed her to the St. Louis Board of Education after Sonnier missed election by a minimal number of votes. In 2023, Sonnier won a seat as alderwoman of the seventh ward of St. Louis. The actions she had planned in Ferguson, at the St. Louis Courthouse, and at the Galleria Mall had paved a way for her political career.

Other Ferguson protesters used their organizing acumen to gain office. Bruce Franks Jr., in 2016, challenged Penny Hubbard, a member of an historic Black political family in St. Louis, for her state representative seat. Initially, Hubbard claimed victory, but employing the spirit of "If We Don't Get It!" Franks asserted there were voting irregularities and brought suit, demanding another election. He won his suit and was elected in the second election, upsetting a local family dynasty. Franks resigned from his post in 2019, citing mental health concerns. At the time, he was under investigation of campaign finance fraud.

The political futures of some other younger politicians look bright. Rasheen Aldridge Jr., the young labor organizer, took up formal politics as well after the Uprising. He first ran in 2016 for St. Louis's fifth ward committeeman and questioned the viability of the election, which led to courts deciding there needed to be a special election. Aldridge won, becoming the youngest committeeman in the city's history. In 2019, when Bruce Franks vacated his seat, Aldridge felt he could best represent the interests of the people and ran for state representative. Again, he won a seat in a special election. In 2023, Aldridge, staying committed to democracy, ran for and won alderman of St. Louis's fourteenth ward. Michael Butler was a state representative at the time of the Uprising. In 2018, he was elected St. Louis City's first Black recorder of deeds. In 2020, Butler was also elected to chair the Missouri Democratic Party. Butler has two daughters. The Uprising and the hard work of young Black citizens helped to create a leadership class that looked different and focused intently on the needs of the people.

In 2017, with the help of Hands Up United co-founder Tory Russell, John Collins-Muhammad, also a Ferguson activist, won his bid to become the first Muslim and youngest ever member of the St. Louis Board of Aldermen. He took over the seat that Antonio French had occupied before running for mayor against Tishaura Jones. Unfortunately, Muhammad, who made strong efforts to legislate on behalf of his ward, pleaded guilty to federal bribery charges in 2022 alongside two other aldermen, Lewis Reed and Jeffrey Boyd, who had also run against Jones for the office of mayor. Politics contained many pitfalls for those looking to advantage themselves. Black politicians are hyper-visible and subject to close scrutiny. There is little to no room for mistakes.

While several younger people ascended to office after the uprising, it is clear that the election of contemporary St. Louis mayor Tishaura Jones, former St. Louis City attorney Kim Gardner, former Missouri state representative Cora Walker, former Ferguson prosecutor Wesley Bell (now a duly elected U.S. congressman), and U.S. representative Cori Bush (who lost to Bell) would not have been possible without the votes of the young people who came of age on the streets of Ferguson.

Kim Gardner, a graduate of SLU School of Law, was a state representative during the Uprising and was sympathetic to the young democrats who took to the streets to protest police violence. With the backing of many in the activist community who mistrusted the bevy of white prosecutors before her, Gardner, a Black woman, ran for and won the office of circuit attorney in 2016, becoming the first Black circuit attorney. Gardner ran on a platform of ensuring accountability among police and using the circuit court's resources efficiently. Throughout her first term, she took pride in challenging the police union and in lowering the number of small and petty crimes the office prosecuted in the past.

This was an important step for many in the movement because it moved in the direction of reducing incarceration and neutralizing the effects of over-policing. Gardner also did what Wesley Bell was unwilling to do; Gardner prosecuted white St. Louis Metropolitan Police officer Jason Stockley, who had chased down a suspected drug dealer, Anthony Lamar Smith, and shot him. During the car chase, via recording, Stockley could be heard saying he was "going to kill this motherfucker, don't you know it."[5] Stockley did just that, and then, allegedly, planted a weapon in Smith's car. Gardner, who inherited and advanced the case against Stockley, made few friends in the police union. This was particularly apparent after Gardner created a list of officers whom she banned from presenting cases to her office because they had acted unethically or had posted support for harming Black protesters, flown Confederate flags, and claimed that Black History Month was racist on Facebook.[6]

Unafraid, Gardner also indicted Eric Greitens, governor of Missouri, for felony invasion of privacy. Greitens had defeated his Democratic opponent Jay Nixon on a campaign that claimed that Nixon was too soft on Ferguson protesters. Shortly after, Gardner was charged with ethics violations regarding the nondisclosure of documents during the discovery phase of the trial. In 2023, Gardner resigned under great pressure from critics who claimed her leniency led to her own undoing. Aside from the constant critique among law enforcement and campaign finance violations that she settled, Gardner had bigger problems. Members of the public claimed Gardner had abdicated her duties by allowing a man who had violated bond scores of times to once again receive bond. While out, he hit a volleyball player from Tennessee with a car. Tragically, the seventeen-year-old lived but lost both of her legs. Mayor Tishaura Jones publicly called for the circuit attorney's accountability in the matter and suggested that the prosecutor needed to do some soul searching with regard to her work. Others from both major political parties joined the chorus of critique. Gardner stepped down just weeks later. Unfortunately, inexperience and her more progressive approach to public safety contributed to Gardner's undoing as a circuit attorney in St. Louis.[7]

Jones, Hampton University alumna and daughter of St. Louis politico Virvus Jones, benefited greatly from her father's experiences in St. Louis.[8] Virvus Jones was the first Black person voted to the St. Louis Board of Alderman, so he had much insight on his daughter's bid to become the city's first Black female mayor. The Ferguson Uprising and the young democrats who led it motivated Jones to put herself in a position where she could do more for underserved and oppressed people. Rather than allowing critics and media to place her on the defensive about the actions of protesters that led to destruction, Jones leaned into the suggestions of the Ferguson Commission on which Rasheen Aldridge Jr., Brittany Packnett Cunningham, Traci Blackmon, and Starsky Wilson worked. Although she had amassed a strong constituency as a state representative and treasurer, Jones appealed to and received the support of the activist community. Kayla Reed and Alisha Sonnier organized passionate young citizens to vote for Jones in the 2017 election. Jones lost in a very full primary race by less than nine hundred votes.

When the announcement came that she did not win, it was not the candidate with tears in her eyes, but rather her politically savvy father. In that election she confirmed what she had already learned about the power of young people who demanded change. Once young people are committed and aware, they are as unstoppable as the tide. For the next election, in 2021, Jones emphasized a candidacy with a "social justice lens" and considered progressive young voters who had been turned on to politics in Ferguson to be one of her campaign's "key demographics."[9] Further, she courted the Movement for Black Lives and vowed to use her resources to "uproot racism," if elected. She learned that action is requisite from her observations of politicians who curried the favor of Black voters but were quiet when it was time to challenge the system that exploited them. Taking in the wisdom that her father imparted on her, Jones understood that if she received progressive youth support, then she would need to be responsive to their needs. She believed in them, and apparently they did her, as Jones was elected the city's first Black female mayor in 2021. Jones joined a cadre of Black women mayors of major cities, such as Baltimore, Atlanta, New Orleans, and San Francisco.

Almost a decade from the beginning of the Uprising, Mayor Jones is proud of the work that the people who came of age during the Uprising have pushed her to do. In their fight against the prison–industrial complex, Jones, in collaboration with Gardner, prison abolitionists, OBS, leaders of the activist community like Kayla Reed, and others, pressured city officials to announce the closure of the "Workhouse," a notoriously neglected and violent medium security penitentiary in St. Louis City that housed a highly disproportionate number of Black offenders. Making it clear that representation was not enough, activists organized town halls to ensure that they were holding Jones to her word that she would close the Workhouse. The movement won on that issue, and the Workhouse is no longer.[10]

Although proud of the victory, Jones worried that in the movement's push to garner political power and representation steps were missed among the activists who pursued electoral offices. She believed that if some of the legislators who resigned early or were convicted of charges would have had stronger mentoring, they would have stood a better chance of furthering their success in office. She admits that she had the benefit of her father and other elders in St. Louis's political history. Jones's father had been convicted of federal tax evasion, and so it was important that Jones pay close attention to matters of money and finance.

Conservative news outlets, in an effort to neutralize those who ascended in politics through the movement, painted scandal on legislators like Cori Bush, who in 2020 successfully won a bid for the U.S. House of Representatives. Fox News and the *Washington Times* outdid themselves claiming that Bush was involved with a scandal when it was revealed that she paid her U.S. Army veteran husband to head her security team.[11] It was ironic that the conservative sites would be so distraught, as the president of the United States from 2017 to 2021 had appointed more than a few family members to key governmental posts and had paid them directly from the businesses he owned. Bush ignored the accusations of impropriety and continued to agitate on behalf of constituents with the spirit of Ferguson. The media refers to her as part of "The Squad," a group of congresswomen of color who take progressive stances and are vocal about social justice. Bush learned from Ferguson that if she has the audacity to challenge the way that things have always operated and the will to place Black and marginalized people at the center of her platform of justice, then there will always be those who seek to undermine her efforts. This became especially true when Bush loudly opposed Israel's war in Gaza that led to the deaths of tens of thousands of Palestinians. In response, the American Israel Public Affairs Committee (AIPAC) mobilized millions of dollars against Bush in her congressional race.

Most of the nonprofit organizations and leaders have remained. Jamala Rogers continues to work faithfully with OBS and Coalition against Police Crimes and Repression. She learned lessons about the need for infrastructure and leadership training. Some of the conflicts and infighting that occurred during the Uprising could have been avoided with prior planning and strategy design. That also meant strengthening networks within and outside of

St. Louis. Providing Black and other progressive youth with opportunities is still central to Rogers's work. Charli Cooksey also remains in her beloved St. Louis and is the founder and CEO of We Power, whose vision is "a future where systems are accountable to powerful communities that have been historically oppressed, and nurture our freedom, well-being, dreams, and joy." Her organization is attempting to empower the high-poverty Black community in terms of wealth, education, housing, and health.

The Urban League of St. Louis provided resources on the ground during the Uprising and afterward. As one of the largest nonprofits in the metro area that works primarily with Black people, it has taken seriously the charge to provide infrastructure in Ferguson and St. Louis. In January 2015, the Urban League launched its "Save Our Sons" skills development and jobs placement program based in North County, which was where Brown was educated and lived. The program attracted more than $1.25 million in donations from St. Louis City and County corporations that had benefited from the Black community and taken advantage of major tax breaks. Realizing that if there were more steady employment available in North County, there likely would be less need for rebellion, companies chose to invest, at the urging of McMillan, in the cultivation of five hundred unemployed Black men who were out of school. McMillan said in an interview with St. Louis Public Radio, "We went out onto the street and we went to young people and all of them, to a one, said, 'We need jobs in this community; we need economic opportunity.' "[12] The Urban League, seizing the moment, sought to provide that opportunity with the program. There were, of course, critiques from those who emphasized that it was not only men in need of development and job opportunities. Subsequently, the Urban League established "Save our Sisters" to service young women.

Not stopping there, in July 2015, the Urban League of St. Louis announced its plans to break ground on the Ferguson Community Empowerment Center. At the opening ceremony in July 2017, the president of the National Urban League, Marc Morial, stood with McMillan at the site on West Florissant where the QuikTrip once stood before it was burned to the ground. The owners of the QuikTrip chose not to rebuild but instead donated the land to the Urban League of St. Louis. They both referred to the new $3 million Ferguson Community Empowerment Center as a phoenix rising from the ashes to offer something new and better to the people. The center shares space with the Salvation Army and became the headquarters of the Save Our Sons program. More than that, it has become a physical symbol of what is possible to residents. Aesthetically, the Urban League St. Louis and others realized how demoralizing it was to have abandoned lots and properties along West Florissant, so it orchestrated the investment of $25 million to repurpose buildings on the Ferguson street that the world watched in 2014–2015. Funded in part by donations from the Centene and Emerson corporations, which had facilities in Ferguson and North County, one of the new buildings would be a forty-four-unit housing facility for senior citizens. The Urban League development coincided with the creation of a new "city plaza" that would feature restaurants, banks, and other businesses.[13]

Some nonprofit leaders moved away but are still advancing the cause. Dwaun Warmack left Harris-Stowe State University to take the helm of Claflin University in South Carolina, where he shapes minds and shares the resources of the HBCU. Reena Hajat Carroll and her husband, David Carroll, moved to Los Angeles, where she is the executive director of the California Equal Justice Initiative and he is Los Angeles County director of youth development. They have a son and daughter.

On the one-year anniversary of Mike Brown's death, Kira Van Niel and I met up in Ferguson to reflect. As we sat on the curb across the street from the McDonald's on West Florissant, discussing how different and calm everything was in contrast to the previous year, a young man sprinted from the McDonald's side of the street in our direction. His hand was raised and we heard pops and bullets lodging into the building behind us. Van Niel and I quickly took cover behind a parked car. As we looked up, we saw another young man bleeding on the ground. We did not have much time to check on the injured young person because police came running to his aid, asking if we saw which direction the shooter went. We did not see where the assailant ran because we were attempting to avoid the fate of the young man on the ground. Van Niel and I left expeditiously. Once we got far enough away, we chided each other for speaking too soon of peace and jinxing the night. Van Niel is still at Boeing and focuses on corporate philanthropy. She acknowledges the irony of companies' recording record profits by the billions and then donating the money while receiving tax benefits, but while capitalism reigns, Van Niel is hoping to use the corporation's resources to help her community. One way she does this is by recruiting and mentoring young Black women, which is her favorite project.

"When we fight we win!" activists from the twentieth and twenty-first centuries confidently declared. It is the phrase that former presidential candidate Kamala Harris frequently employs. The pressure that politicians and organizers placed on legislators during and after the Uprising bore fruit. In St. Louis City and North County, including Ferguson, there was change of seven police chiefs in five years, according to Forward through Ferguson, which grew out of the Ferguson Commission. Additionally, in 2015 protesters achieved the longtime goal of establishing a civilian oversight board in St. Louis City. In 2017, legislators approved the Ferguson Civilian Review Board as well.[14] Had it not been for the Uprising, the level of police accountability would have been even further out of the reach of civilians.

There were more victories in Ferguson, such as the appointment of a Black man, Donald McCullins, as the city's municipal judge. To restore faith in the system that so recklessly exploited its residents, Judge McCullins withdrew all arrest warrants that had been issued prior to December 2014. The violators would still have to pay their fines, but they were not under threat of arrest. This was no small gesture in that many of the warrants were for minor traffic infractions and if executed would have landed working people in jail, where they would have taken up more resources and accrued more fines. Under the judge's order, there would be a reduction in fines, payment options, as well as options for community service. In North County, where Ferguson sits, judges and lawyers pushed for unification of fine and fee schedules. The Missouri Supreme Court made a requirement that judges take into account the ability of the violator to actually pay the fines. If they could not, then judges could place them on payment plans or reduce or waive the fines altogether. The evaluation of traffic fines and fees spread to cities and towns all throughout the United States. America found that justice did not have to mean repression or racial capitalism.[15] The Ground Zero activists fought and won for the people.

In addition to politics, organizers pushed forward in every way possible. Brittany Packnett Cunningham, using her new White House network and education connections, arranged a visit by the U.S. secretary of education, Arne Duncan, to St. Louis City and County in December 2014. While there, he met with students at Clyde C. Miller Career Academy, a mostly Black magnet school in the city, and Riverview Gardens High School in North County, which was a predominantly Black public school. Duncan brought with him the president of the American Federation of Teachers, Randi Weingarten, and then U.S. representative Lacy Clay. The students with whom the officials met, in the spirit of the Uprising, spoke truth to power, leaving the appointees and administrators emotional.[16]

Later, Packnett Cunningham arranged a meeting of those officials and young educators, as well as activists, at Greater St. Mark's Missionary Baptist Church. Similar to the students, the educators, which included McKesson, me, and others, were candid. Packnett Cunningham eloquently linked education to violence and life chances. I asked about the nation's seemingly wavering commitment to public education at the federal level. McKesson put it plainly to the officials, stating, "Kids can't learn if they can't live." Duncan and Weingarten did their best to reaffirm their investment in the lives of all American children, but especially those who were attempting to be educated under these terribly stressful circumstances. I liberated (stole) Duncan's pen to mark the occasion.

"Ferguson Protester who set fire at Berkeley QuikTrip sentenced to 8 years in prison," read a December 10, 2015, headline. The previous December, two days before Christmas, Lost Voices member Josh Williams attended a protest against the Berkeley police killing of eighteen-year-old Antonio Martin. The Berkeley municipality is five minutes from Ferguson by car. The thirty-four-year-old white police officer was answering a larceny call at the Mobil On the Run gas station on North Hanley Road. The policeman observed two young Black men matching the description of the suspected larcenists. Not wearing his assigned body camera, the officer claimed to see one of the young men draw a firearm, and the policeman discharged his service weapon, as he ran and fell backward. He killed Martin.[17]

As police investigators taped off the scene at the Mobil station, a crowd of angry and distraught demonstrators gathered in the parking lot of the QuikTrip, which was directly across the street. Remembering Mike Brown, Kejieme Powell, and VonDerrit Myers, the protest became destructive, with people breaking the glass front of the convenience store. Once inside, looters took items and smashed displays. Josh Williams, still nineteen years old, took a bag of chips and set fires inside and outside the store with a lighter while leaving. He was arrested and jailed on Christmas Eve, 2014.

Tribe X member H.J. Rodgers, another unlikely activist, currently lives in Florida. Over the past ten years, he moved around frequently, doing construction work in states as far away as Hawaii. He is very proud of his journey into the movement, but he laughed when he considered some of the decisions he made back then. Regarding his choice to quit his job, Rodgers said, "I didn't make a logical decision." He admits that if he had it to do all over again, he would not have stopped working, as that was the only way he had to make money. The uneasiness of life during that period was incredibly stressful for him, but he has no major regrets. If anything, he is happy he learned to step out on faith. Rodgers said the experience taught him that "if you really want something and change gon' come from it, then you gon' step your best foot forward."

Going back over all the time and energy he put into organizing, Hands Up United co-founder Tory Russell said, "I wanted to hold up my end of that social contract."[18] That contract, based on the unalienable rights of American citizenship, entailed service to community for freedom. He saw how Trayvon Martin was demonized after his death and how the law worked to protect killers of Black boys. Russell did not want to be complicit in a system that worked toward the destruction of young people like his son, so he worked feverishly to achieve justice in spite of the law.

Russell, who is still quite active in Ferguson, has been somewhat disappointed in the lack of devotion people seemingly had to the movement in the years since 2014–2015. Russell has not wavered in his commitment to community since the Uprising. The weekend program that he started in 2014, Books and Breakfast, still operates regularly and is a model of revolutionary education and community care.

Books and Breakfast is very much in the tradition of the Black Panther Party for Self-Defense Free Breakfast Program that fed children in urban areas throughout the United States during the 1960s and 1970s. Russell has not run for office and still resides in St. Louis County. He is unafraid to criticize police, politicians, or the protesters who have moved on from Ferguson. An organizer with the International Black Freedom Alliance, Russell remains a strong advocate of democracy from the bottom up.

IF WE DON'T GET IT 221

Kayla Reed has continued to seek political power for Black people. She is co-founder and executive director of Action St. Louis, which has worked tirelessly and strategically to elect progressive candidates to public office in the St. Louis metropolitan area. Reed scaled her vision out to create the Equal Justice Initiative under the auspices of the Movement for Black Lives. The initiative is attempting to check Black voter-suppression tactics, educate the Black electorate, and to support Black organizations interested in advancing freedom through policy and politics. Reed and Russell admirably model citizenship.

"A lot of the St. Louis Black student intake is due to us," revealed Damon Latchinson.[19] Several organizers pursued education at Washington University, the institution once called the Harvard of the Midwest. The "Delmar Loop [near Washington University's campus] was always a place that we were told not to go into . . . so I never even thought about Washington University." The pressure that activists put on white institutions in the area forced officials to reflect on their roles in perpetuating racism. Washington University, the university with the largest endowment in the state, committed to diversity and inclusion and funded the education of multiple organizers and a larger number of students from St. Louis.

Kayla Reed, who started at SLU, finished her bachelor's degree at Washington University in 2020. Assistant Professor Jonathan Fenderson, after the Uprising, finished his first book and earned tenure and promotion at Washington University. His mentees, Danielle Blocker and Rueben Riggs-Bookman, were consummate scholar-activists who graduated with their bachelor's degrees. Riggs-Bookman was accepted into a Ph.D. program in anthropology at the University of Michigan, where he analyzes the synergies between scholarship and activism. Blocker worked with the Poor People's Campaign and then founded a nonprofit, Young People for Progress, based in the Washington, D.C., metropolitan area. Damon Latchinson, who was known as Diamond during the Uprising, also finished a bachelor's degree. Each of the young democrats continue to use the privilege of education to liberate those who could not attend institutions like Washington University.

"If Wash U Alex was in Ferguson, we got a problem! We got a fucking problem, brother," Washington University School of Law student Alex Templeton confidently stated.[20] Looking back over the decade, Templeton surmised that if the Uprising had occurred under the current lax Missouri gun laws, "things would have looked a lot differently." If more street activists and organizers had armed themselves, Templeton indicated, police would have approached them with much less aggression. Police consistently maintained the power because the majority of protesters arrived unarmed and raised their hands in the air to shout "Hands Up, Don't Shoot!" There were some armed agitators, but law enforcement had the advantage in terms of weaponry.

If young Black people had taken advantage of the Second Amendment rights and gun laws that scholar Carol E. Anderson described in *The Second: Race and Guns in a Fatally Unequal America* (2021), law enforcement would have had to respect the efforts of protesters in the same way it does Proud Boys demonstrations, opined Templeton. In principle, that may have worked, but history shows that white authority fears armed Black rebellion in such a way that it will unabashedly employ repressive tactics (including fatal methods) to maintain order.

There was more, however, to Templeton's idea about Black armament. Templeton, implicitly, understood the prospect of mass casualties or even fatalities, but Templeton also learned about the psychological evolution necessary to feel equal and valued in the face of authority. If the fear of firearms is what controlled the people, then what happens when the people acquire legal firearms too? Symbolically, with firearms, Black people could be both safe and dangerous (physically and mentally) at once. That is an

IF WE DON'T GET IT   223

invaluable lesson. As Templeton put it, "Oh, okay, we can get with these muthafuckas a little bit."[21]

By "getting with" or resisting the people who controlled and exploited poor Black neighborhoods, Black St. Louisans were able to create a space for themselves that remains. Because the eyes of the nation turned to the inequitable racial capitalism that manifested in the form of traffic stops in North St. Louis County, law enforcement had to refrain from employing such tactics. That allowed Black people to move around the city and county with more freedom. Templeton believes that the actions of protesters on the street during the Uprising and the work of activists in the political and policy arena exposed the weakness in the police force.

The Ferguson Uprising is what catalyzed the movement to "defund" police departments, and it greatly advanced the push for abolishing prisons and policing as the nation now knows it. The killing of George Floyd in 2020 in Minneapolis added great fuel to the campaign. Attorney Derecka Purnell, who at one point lived in Ferguson and who graduated from Harvard Law School, made the decision to become an abolitionist in large part because of what she saw in her home city and around the nation. She was not originally in favor of abolitionism because she thought the idea "was created by white activists who did not know the violence that I know, that I have felt."[22] She "feared letting go." In 2014, she still believed that the enterprise of policing could be reformed in the way of training, diversification, and with body cameras. By 2021, Purnell, after seeing the inability of law enforcement to police itself, the refusal of the court system to hold abusive police accountable, and the unwillingness of legislators to challenge the authority of police unions, concluded that it was best to extirpate altogether the system of policing. "In Ferguson, I started to understand why we need police abolition rather than reform," Purnell wrote. She was not alone.

Abolitionism was not a particular demand in Ferguson, but young activists began to question why police deserve pay raises and additional resources even if they are cited for patterns and practices of discrimination toward poor Black people. By leaning into the reports of the Ferguson Commission and Department of Justice, young activists who were not formally educated or trained in the law understood that their suspicions about abuse of power were well founded. Templeton, who is finishing law school, asserted that the police and all the people defending the biased system were lucky that they caught Templeton in 2014 and not later in life. "If Wash U.-Alex was on the street, it would've been over" because they much better understood the networks of oppression. Because "a crack was shown in the system, . . . a lot shifted after Ferguson," observed Templeton.

Not everything, however, shifted for the better. In reflection, Templeton admitted: "There is no Trump without Ferguson." Politicians from the municipal to the federal level ran on campaigns to prevent or contend with the next "Ferguson." That meant the rise of "All Lives Matter" and "Blue Lives Matter" in reaction and contradistinction to the work that so many organizers and activists did in Ferguson. As was the case with crack and gang violence in the 1980s and 1990s, politicians in either of the two major parties did not want to be seen as unsupportive of policing. The pressure to "Back the Blue" was so great that some lawmakers who regularly recited King's "March on Washington" speech every January could not form their mouths to say Black Lives Matter for fear that their conservative and moderate constituencies might castigate them.[23]

The Republican Party became particularly adept at using the Defund the Police campaign as a bludgeon to beat down equivocating Democrats who wanted to discuss the nuances of police reform. Progressives from the left also attacked mainstream Democrats, which created opportunity for the followers of Trump's Make America Great Again campaign to prevail. Trump and so many other conservatives won office because of the inability of progressive and moderate Democrats to close ranks in the way

IF WE DON'T GET IT

that ultraconservative and moderate Republicans did. Still, progressives, like those activists on the street of Ferguson, pulled the Democratic Party leftward in ways that at least acknowledged that the penal system and policing are deeply flawed and corrupted with institutional racism.

In the American past, there have been patterns concerning Black protest. It begins with the overbearing white repression that leads to Black contestation, which yields white concessions before giving way to some form of regression. An example in history is the Voting Rights Act of 1965. Dozens and potentially hundreds of Black people like Jimmie Lee Jackson of Selma died as a result of protest when Alabama disrespectfully denied the freedom rights of citizens. When local organizations, bolstered by well-known organizers like the Rev. Martin Luther King Jr., brought the issue to national attention, the insular towns of the former slave state had no choice but to concede voting rights, which allowed Black people access in ways they had not seen since Reconstruction.

There was a moment of celebration before realizing the movement to disenfranchise Black people is relentless. To neutralize the Black political power that was taking hold, local and state legislatures with the help of federal lawmakers created policies that allowed for the regression of Black rights in the form of gerrymandering and redistricting. As soon as practicable, white lawmakers sued to do away with the preclearance clause of the Voting Rights Amendment. The U.S. Supreme Court, *Shelby v. Holder* (2013) overturned the federal oversight for states seeking to change voting requirements for citizens.

In Ferguson and St. Louis, after Black citizens resisted repression the power structure offered concessions. Some were symbolic, like Governor Jay Nixon's placing the Black state highway patrol captain Ron Johnson in charge of security operations in Ferguson after a disastrous response from white law enforcement officials. It did not take long, however, before law enforcement revealed its nature and resumed the tear gas, arrests, and other tactics.

Student-activists have stayed in the struggle. Clifton Kinnie, with the support of organizers like Brittany Packnett Cunningham, Justin Hansford, and Charli Cooksey, graduated from Lutheran North High School and Howard University, where he pledged Alpha Phi Alpha Fraternity, Inc. At Howard, the young man majored in political science and Afro-American Studies. Kinnie carried Ferguson to the U.S. Congress, where he testified, sharing tales of what he saw on the streets, and also into his burgeoning career as an educator. He took a position as a special education teacher at Gateway High School STEM. Focusing on the passing of a universal gun-safety bill, Kinnie is still a leader of progressive-minded young people, upholding the spirit of the movement.

Similar to Kinnie, Storm Ervin and Destiny Crockett have stayed committed to community in their respective journeys. Ervin works for a think tank, Urban Institute, where she used the academic training she got from Mizzou to research justice projects. Her title is Technical Assistance Manager, and she works for the Justice Policy Center in the institute, where she is seeking strategies to interrupt intimate partner violence. Destiny Crockett chose to pursue advanced education. She graduated from Princeton University, where she majored in English with certificates in African American Studies and Gender and Sexuality Studies. Then she graduated with a Ph.D. in English with certificates in Africana Studies and Women, Gender, and Sexuality Studies from the University of Pennsylvania. She was awarded a Mellon Humanities Postdoctoral Fellowship at Rutgers University in the Department of Childhood Studies. Focusing on Black youth in literature, Crockett is a rising scholar in multiple disciplines. Trevor Woolfolk finished SLU with a degree in aerospace engineering and is currently working for HCL Technologies, where he is an embedded systems engineer. He also pledged Alpha Phi Alpha Fraternity, Inc., to maintain ties to the community by registering voters and mentoring high school students.

IF WE DON'T GET IT 227

In 2020, following the horrific death of George Floyd in Minneapolis, hundreds of former student leaders sent a letter with a set of demands to Fred Pestello and the upper administration of SLU. Chief among the demands was the university's recommitment to the thirteen agreements (which it refers to as the Clock Tower Accords) it made during #OccupySLU in 2014. The letter read in part, "Our respective experiences at SLU were marked by a culture of casual yet institutionalized white supremacy, anti-Blackness, racism, and ahistorical approaches to understanding the present."[24] It continued, "Many . . . watched with dismay as the University's administration again ignored and even actively undercut the potential for real progress along these agreed upon terms. We were and remain continuously disappointed in the lack of funding, resources, and priority given to the Clock Tower Accords, as well as most actions related to equity and inclusion for marginalized communities on campus." To be sure, by then the operating budget of the African American Studies Program had increased to $20,000 annually and Assistant Professor Jonathan Smith had been appointed vice president for diversity and community engagement, but some of the outward-facing agreements had not been met. Smith, sadly, passed away in 2021.

SLU's inability or unwillingness to live up to the agreements, while also celebrating and commemorating the Clock Tower Accords, drew the ire of some activists and community members who had occupied the campus. H.J. Rodgers, nearly a decade after demonstrating on campus, said, "I think the school [SLU] did it to save face and not to be viewed with a certain lens, but I don't really think they had intention of having healthy dialogue with us and to come with positive resolutions." The university still maintains a webpage dedicated to the agreements that shows which agreements it believes it has adequately fulfilled. The ultimate arbiter of whether the predominantly white institution in the majority Black city satisfied the agreements is the community that surrounds SLU and the members of Tribe X, M-SLICE, and BSA.

Joshua Jones, who was a graduate student at SLU during the occupation, is deeply concerned about the holdover trauma associated with Brown's shooting death and the reaction of police to community action.[25] When the tanks and protesters and cameras left, the residents and activists were seemingly expected to move on with life as though all was well, but how could it be? Jones, who is now a licensed counselor of social work employed as a staff therapist at Washington University School of Medicine, wondered about the long-term effects associated with post-traumatic stress syndrome.

Jones's friend and schoolmate Jonathan Pulphus experienced residual psychological effects of the trauma that occurred during and after the Uprising. The untimely and mysterious deaths of activists pushed Pulphus to the mental brink. In October 2019, NBC News reported, "Two young men were found dead inside torched cars. Three others died in apparent suicides. Another collapsed on a bus, his death ruled an overdose."[26] That was too much coincidence, bad timing, and death for Pulphus's sane mind to contain because he knew and worked with these activists. Activists Deandre Joshua first and then Darren Seals were found shot and burned inside of their cars in 2014 and 2016, respectively. No arrests have been made in those gruesome deaths. MarShawn McCarrel shot himself in Ohio in 2016. A year later, Pulphus's inspiration, Ed Crawford, who threw back the tear-gas canister, shot himself to death. That same year, Danye Jones was found dead, hanging in a tree. Danye Jones's mother, Melissa McKinnies, had been a regular Ferguson protester with the group Lost Voices. In 2019, Bassem Masri fell dead on a bus of a Fentanyl overdose.

This was all too much for Pulphus, who knew or knew of the dead protesters. His mind swam, as he wondered if he were next. As did many soldiers who saw battle, Pulphus picked up habits that helped him cope but were not healthy. For instance, he smoked cigarettes and marijuana to find relief from the constant stress of confrontation. A young man in college, he also tried other recreational drugs. Once the everyday protesting and demonstrating faded, Pulphus, like some others, experienced something of an identity crisis. Who would he be if he were not courageously challenging the police, shutting down malls, or occupying campuses? Famous athletes and entertainers often feel that loss of self when they leave the field or stage. The violent and tragic deaths, combined with the crisis of identity, overwhelmed him, resulting in a frightening breakdown of mental health. Once again Sonnier was there to help carry Pulphus through the danger, but this time he had to struggle without the assistance of their other protest family. Pulphus and Sonnier individually sought healing by working with therapists.

Looking to escape the emotional and mental trauma that she felt at SLU, Sonnier transferred to the University of Missouri–St. Louis (UMSL) and graduated in 2019 with a degree in psychology. Although she left SLU behind, she continued her relationship with her mentor, Associate Professor Kira Hudson Banks. From UMSL, she completed a post-baccalaureate program at Washington University of St. Louis. She knew intimately the importance of mental health to the community. Tribe X's Sonnier was not the only organizer to graduate from UMSL.

Christopher Walter, like Sonnier, started at SLU and transferred to UMSL when SLU became unaffordable and stressful for him. With the assistance of mentors like Etefia Umana, UMSL dean of admissions Alan Byrd, and institutional support from the Scholarship Foundation of St. Louis, Walter graduated with a degree in business administration. Staying committed to community wellness, Walter eventually became a manager of policy and community engagement at the nonprofit Alive and Well STL, which is supported by the Missouri Foundation for Health and the St. Louis Mental Health Board.

Brittany Ferrell also finished her bachelor's degree and earned a master's degree in public health to become a registered nurse. She became the chairperson of Jamaa Birth Village in Ferguson and treasurer of Action STL. Ferrell is pursuing a Ph.D. in nursing science from Washington University. She, too, remains a local and national voice of freedom.

Some of the attorneys continue to contribute to the movement. The director of the Thurgood Marshall Civil Rights Center at Howard University, Justin Hansford, regularly writes briefs and participates on cases regarding Black freedom. He, along with myself and others, testified to the U.S. Civil Rights Commission about the injustices in Ferguson. With delegates representing Hands Up United, OBS, and MORE, Hansford appealed to the United Nations in Geneva to sanction the United States because of the mistreatment of protesters. Hansford received a prestigious Democracy Fellowship from Harvard University's Charles Warren Center, and he still maintains regular contact with Mike Brown's family. Derecka Purnell finished her studies at Harvard Law School and intensified her work in the movement. She wrote *Becoming Abolitionist: Police, Protests, and the Pursuit of Freedom* and in 2022 was selected as the Marguerite Casey Foundation Freedom Scholar. Purnell helped construct the Justice Project for the Advancement Project in Washington, D.C. In 2023, she was scholar in residence at Columbia University Law School's Center for Contemporary Critical Thought. She is rearing two sons.

Black Studies scholars have carried forward as well. Washington University associate professor Jonathan Fenderson received tenure and a promotion and teaches a course on the Uprising. He continues to work with organizations such as OBS. I, like Hansford, left SLU. My family moved to Los Angeles in 2017, where I chaired the Department of African American Studies at Loyola Marymount University. In Los Angeles, I had the opportunity to work with and expose students to community engagement with several local organizations. In 2021, my family moved to

Massachusetts, where I took a position as the Charles Hamilton Houston '15 Professor of Black Studies and History at Amherst College. The Ferguson Uprising remains a consistent part of this educator's coursework, counsel to students, and scholarship.

After Darren Wilson was not indicted in 2014, MAU co-founder Ashley Yates needed to change her life. "I needed some space to heal and grow," she said in 2015, about her decision to move to Oakland, California.[27] It was the city in which the Black Panther Party for Self-Defense was born; she thought she could benefit from the spirit of what was. After the non-indictment, Yates found herself slipping into a depression even as she went to work for the Black Lives Matter organization. She was deeply sensitive to always having to respond to Black death and to solve problems caused by anti-Black racism. Then, of course, when one draws attention to the flaws of the nation, one does not always get to be the most beloved, especially when one is an outspoken Black woman. Seeing how life ended for Eric Garner's daughter, Erica, who was also an activist, scared Yates. Like Pulphus, Yates wondered if she would be next to die. Coming to terms with a potential death was difficult, but living was not easy either, especially when she moved to one of the most expensive areas to live in the nation. Yates needed and found help to heal.

Her decision to move changed her life and worldview. Living elsewhere helped her see how injustice affects poor, Black, and marginalized people everywhere. Yates, as a co-founder of Millennial Activists United, taught St. Louis, Ferguson, and the world that women and queer people have always been at the forefront of Black liberation. MAU's work cleared the path for the #metoo movement, as well as the trans and queer rights campaigns that gained steam during and in the years after the Uprising.

Johnetta "Netta" Elzie, who is authoring a book on the movement, understood well the strain of maintaining sanity inside and outside the movement. "I'm just really trying to get over this feeling of extreme loneliness that comes with it. It's really scary, and it's just me. I definitely have an amazing group of friends, like my friends from before the movement, and my friends I've made through being a protester and being in the movement, [but it's still] lonely because the people I want to be close to me aren't anymore," admitted Netta Elzie.[28] There is a price exacted from those who are dedicated to the movement. Of course, there are the legal prices and the potential for economic insecurity, but the real cost to bear comes in the form of emotional isolation. Elzie, who is now the mother of a toddler, had to take a break from social media to gather her peace and come to terms with herself. She, like Packnett Cunningham and McKesson, was one of the most recognizable representatives of the movement. Each under forty years old, they gained their acclaim from being excellent communicators and effective organizers.

They reached heights unimaginable for many. Elzie and McKesson were named to *Fortune* magazine's "World's Greatest Leaders" list, and both were awarded PEN's Howard Zinn Freedom to Write Award. With their beautiful smiles, they graced the covers of the most popular periodicals, and a portrait of McKesson was created and sits in the Smithsonian National Portrait Gallery. They, along with Packnett Cunningham, have also done important work to shine a light on police violence, putting together the "Mapping Police Violence" database and traveling to protest in cities like Charleston, Baton Rouge, Minneapolis, and Baltimore where law enforcement brazenly killed Black people. Some accused them of being professional protesters because of their presence in areas where there is unrest. McKesson wrote a memoir, *On the Other Side of Freedom: The Case for Hope* (2018) and is the subject of a 2024 Hulu documentary, *Making of an Activist*. In regular contact with Brown's mother, Lezley McSpadden, McKesson said that they are in the process of planning a summer camp for Ferguson children.[29]

IF WE DON'T GET IT 233

Brittany Packnett Cunningham has lived a full life since 2015. She was named to several leading magazines' top 100 lists. She did vital work on the Ferguson Commission and President Barack Obama's White House Taskforce on 21st Century Policing. Along with Elzie and McKesson, she started Campaign Zero. Additionally, she ascended in Teach for America to become vice president of national community alliances. She, like Hansford and Poe, spent time creating knowledge at Harvard University, where she was a resident fellow of the Kennedy School's Institute of Politics. She even traced her genealogy on the popular PBS show, *Finding Your Roots*.[30] In 2020, Packnett Cunningham established Love and Power, which, according to her website, is "an umbrella for her social justice projects, consultation, and advisory work."

Perhaps most notable, Packnett Cunningham started a family, marrying organizer Reggie Cunningham and giving birth to a beautiful but premature boy. With the birth of her son, all of the activism, organizing, demonstrating, and leading finally made sense because, as she said on her podcast, *Undistracted*, "I want to raise a free Black child." Over the past decade, Packnett Cunningham received much attention in news media and in other outlets, but she has always placed youth at the center of her purpose.[31] Blessedly, Packnett Cunningham is expecting another son.

Tef Poe has shared a stage with Stevie Wonder! That fact alone makes his life worthy of the history books, but that is not what Poe wants to be remembered for. He along with his fellow revolutionaries took Ferguson everywhere, as he continued his rap and organizing journey. At the White House, he met with President Obama. He, along with Mike Brown's parents and other organizers like Justin Hansford, went to Geneva to appeal to the United Nations, but that was just the beginning for Poe, who also visited Palestine with Phil Agnew and the Dream Defenders

234 STEFAN M. BRADLEY

delegation. He is currently a cultural ambassador to the country of Jordan.[32]

Ferguson gave him the opportunity to make music with some of the most well-regarded hip-hop artists in the world, including Kendrick Lamar, Mos Def, Talib Kweli, Big KRIT, and Dead Prez. Poe even released an album with renowned scholar—and at one point presidential candidate—Cornel West as the narrator. The most notable artist with whom Poe's name is now associated is that of Nasir "Nas" Jones. In 2016–2017, Poe was awarded the highly coveted Nasir Jones Hip Hop Fellowship at Harvard University's prestigious W.E.B. Du Bois Research Institute. Additionally, he was appropriately named an American Democracy Fellow at Harvard University's Charles Warren Center for American Studies, which is only a dream for so many scholars. Poe's dream since August 9, 2014, is justice for Mike Brown, and he will not stop organizing and protesting until he realizes that dream.

Poe, always good with words, encapsulated the grit of the Ferguson Uprising: "We went to jail a lot, we stayed in court fighting different cases and whatnot. We had friends who died, and we know people in prison behind the Ferguson Uprising." That is not to say there was no happiness or joy, but the movement he and the other young democrats made was dangerous and required sacrifice. There were not always happy endings that involved traveling to new places or winning awards. They chose to engage history, so it was ugly and beautiful, right and wrong. In his view, "The real story wasn't made for TV."

In 2024, Josh Williams remains in prison in Potosi, Missouri. Time was added to his sentence for a weapons charge he received while inside the facility. To be sure, the slightly built Williams, in the eyes of the law, had barely become a man when entered the system. To pass time, he listens to artists like Kevin Gates and Lil Durk but also tries to read about different cultures. For exercise,

IF WE DON'T GET IT 235

he jogs around the yard. He has a job cleaning the facility that keeps him occupied as well. Just as he said about the movement, Williams's current living situation is dangerous, but there is little refuge. "The hardest part of this time is being around dudes you don't know everyday," he said.

Williams regularly engaged strangers protesting on the outside, but at least in that capacity there was an assumption that everyone was supportive of the cause. There were thrill seekers and provocateurs, but, by and large, people could rally around justice for Mike Brown. While inside, the only cause for most is survival, and that is not an easy task. "You got to deal with a lot of fake dudes" inside, Williams revealed. In 2014, when he was an activist with Lost Voices, he could avoid people with what he believed were ill or disingenuous intentions. That is definitely not the case for him while he is incarcerated.

"People are not who they say they are," Williams said of some other inmates. The same could be said about free people on the outside. He is, unfortunately, learning life lessons in a potentially deadly environment, which has led the once optimistic youth activist toward skepticism. Rightfully, Williams still views himself as a freedom fighter and even as a political prisoner; his sentence and stay have been woefully incongruent with the actual crime. He explained that "I feel like it [his sentence] was unfair because, before this, I never been in trouble [and] never had a rap sheet or nothing." It was clear that Missouri attempted to make an example of Williams and to chill protest in general.

Scholars have ably shown that over-sentencing has long been a tactic of the legal system as it concerns Black offenders. There is no doubt that Williams committed an offense, but keeping a young man who could have cared for his family and community, worked, paid taxes, and generally contributed to society behind bars is illogical. The historical message, whether it was members of the Black Panthers or SNCC, is that those who resist loudly and those who threaten the status quo have to be neutralized at all costs, even if that means sacrificing the life of Black boys like Williams or Mike Brown.

Life, Williams admits, has been hard. He does not regret his journey, but when asked if he would do it all over again, he responded resoundingly: "Hell nah!" Still, he believes of his overall experience that "it was worth it for me personally because it allowed me to get a peek at the inside of the system rather than looking in from the outside."

Williams's story is very much in line with so many segments of the Black American experience; however, it could easily be categorized as a Greek tragedy. There are three elements consistent within the Greek tragedy: hamartia, anagnorisis, and peripeteia.[33] Hamartia is the main character's flaw that leads to his or her downfall. Often, the flaw is what propelled the character to power or prominence, but that characteristic could also prove tragic. In the case of Williams, it was the recklessness that came along with his youth that seemed to tip the scales toward tragedy. The second element is anagnorisis, which is when the main character actualizes. For Williams, that was the moment on West Florissant when he reflected and asked himself if he would be willing to defend the defenseless and whether he was willing to be a leader in the movement even though he had never been political before the Uprising. The struggle to achieve justice for Mike Brown gave Williams purpose, and he finally recognized his role. Then, the third element of the Greek tragedy is peripeteia, the dramatic shift in the main character's trajectory that changes his or her life forever. Williams's imprisonment was just that life-altering departure from the course he was on as a leader in the movement.

By any measurement, Williams's story is tragic because if circumstances were different for him and similar young people, places like St. Louis, Ferguson, and many other American cities would thrive. Williams contends his experience with the prison–industrial complex will help him advance the movement when he eventually finishes his sentence. Once out, he plans to work with youth artists and to create "Elevation Studios" for talented "at-risk" young people so that they may stay far away from prison. The thought of helping people in the way that he needed makes him happy and gives him hope.

In addition to his studio, Williams hopes to get back together with some of the people from the movement because, as he noted, "people are still being killed out here." He worries that some of his peers have "forgot[ten] about what happened," but for "those who was out there for real, you can't forget about it because it's stained in our memory; it's stained on our brain."

While the tanks and sirens are difficult to get beyond mentally, Williams revealed that some have seemingly found a way to forget him. When asked if any politicians had checked on him, he said that former Missouri state representative Bruce Franks Jr. was the only one to reach out to him since the Uprising. Some of the organizers, like Jonathan Pulphus, Jamala Rogers, and others, periodically do fundraisers for him, but Williams has not been able to hear back from others who became internationally known. It is the nature of life for people to move on, but for Williams, who is trapped in the system he fought when he was free, he cannot move.

Inside the facility, Williams struggles. He, of course, still needs money. Then, he has to deal with the realities of prison life, which include confrontations with individuals over material goods and plays for power. When last in contact with me, Williams revealed that he is having trouble remaining positive in his thinking and that it was difficult to elevate beyond the reality of his current circumstances. In hopes of providing some positivity, I wrote to him, "Do what you have to, but understand you're made for something bigger than this. They are going to test you in there because you are meant for something great. The most important of our leaders have to face adversity to make them strong."

Williams, despite his detention, still tries to inspire others. In 2022 he wrote, "Thank you for your fight, thank you for your strength that you show each and every day. I sit in prison and think of ways to fight harder for you all every day and when I get out." Williams declared: "I'm going to take the fight directly to the streets again. It's no brakes on this fight, just gas. Love y'all."[34] At the end of 2023, he maintained the spirit of community and collective resistance. To all those who are still interested in freedom but are deterred or disappointed, Williams sends this message, "Stay strong! Stay in this fight! If you can't fight small [battles], how can we fight a war? Keep standing[;] Rome wasn't built in one day."[35]

Josh Williams, a member of Lost Voices and day-one activist during the Ferguson Uprising, served more than ten years in prison for an arson conviction and subsequent offenses. *Photo: Mariah Stewart*/St. Louis American

Freedom fighters not only risk their freedom but also confront the threat of erasure when the state finally captures them. That concerns Williams. The Uprising of 2014–2015 was such a transformational period in his life that he cannot help but think about it daily, he said. For his deep sacrifice, he deserves to be remembered. Most of all, Williams deserves hope.

CONCLUSION
AMERICA, YOU'RE WELCOME

"We're supposed to do the work the elders couldn't finish."
—Missouri State Representative Rasheen Aldridge Jr.

Perhaps Tory Russell said it best: "I tasted freedom and ain't nothin' taste like it since."[1] Proudly, he declared, "if you wasn't in Ferguson when it was poppin' and live, . . . you missed freedom." There was something spiritual about fighting against odds and believing in the improbable that is indescribable. The young democrats went up against the empire and made their mark. Of course, the empire strikes back, but this time no one can prevent the people who had the least, the ones who were unheard, or the folks who were deprived of rights from holding space in the history books.

Movements are microcosms of society, and from these young people America learned what it takes to birth a moment with the tensions and conflicts, both external and internal, that arise. As many of the Ground Zero activists and organizers in this book have not been publicly highlighted, beyond local praise, they are owed thanks for challenging Americans to reconcile who and what they really are. The complex and amazing people in this book rescued the remnants of American democracy. This section offers lessons for youth activists based on the observations made from their experiences on the ground and conversations with participants in the Uprising. Although the reader may find inspiration in the struggle, this conclusion will not represent a happy ending in terms of Black freedom in St. Louis and the nation.

Darren Wilson lives. Although he does so anonymously and not as a police officer, he still draws breath. He should be thankful for life, but he has landed on the wrong side of history. Right-wing extremists will hold him up as a hero, but sensible people understand that Mike Brown should be alive. Mike Brown's parents continue to fight against injustice and have never backed down from the moment. I had the opportunity to shake hands with and thank Michael Brown Sr. in the Canfield Green apartment complex in August 2023. Brown Sr., in honor of his fallen son, established a foundation called Chosen for Change with some of the settlement money he received from his son's death. Lezley McSpadden is also founder and president of the Michael O.D. Brown Foundation. Both parents miss their child terribly, so they stay in community with other parents who have lost their children to

On August 17, 2014, just over a week after Ferguson police officer Darren Wilson killed their unarmed son, Michael Brown Jr., parents Michael Brown Sr. and Lezley McSpadden fight back tears at Greater Grace Church in Ferguson. Today, they keep their son's legacy alive with the Chosen for Change Foundation and the Michael O.D. Brown Foundation. *Photo: Scott Olson/Getty Images*

police violence. Incidentally, Brown's parents wonder where the money raised in their son's name has gone.

Young people in the St. Louis metropolitan area, without previous political experience, succeeded in changing the national political narrative. Political candidates, for the first time in decades, were forced to address topics that they typically dodged in the past. Ferguson protesters pressed officials like presidential candidate and former U.S. Secretary of State Hilary Clinton to speak to issues like institutional racism, sexism, poverty, militarized policing, education, and housing segregation. The political Right, as was the case in the past, demonized the courageous young people as terrorists and anti-American. Liberals and moderates, not unlike those in the past, expressed sympathy with the causes of the youth but anguished over their tactics, which included highway shutdowns, die-ins, and disruptive marches. Ferguson activists retaught what those who study the history of Black freedom have always known: there is no nice way for one to demand one's rights, that fighting for justice is unpopular, and above all that young Black people have most often stood at the forefront of social change. They will continue to do so.

The tentacles of the Ferguson Uprising touched all aspects of American culture. For instance, Yates popularized the phrase "Assata Taught Me" on T-shirts after coming up with the idea in MoKaBe's Coffeehouse. When activists wore the shirt in Ferguson, others donned similar shirts elsewhere. Those T-shirts can be seen all around the world on activists and those who enjoy fashion alike. McKesson, during an interview with a news network, coined the phrase "he should be alive today," which is now ubiquitous in the tragedies of unnecessary Black deaths at the hands of police or vigilantes. Tef Poe said that the Uprising was not a story made for TV, but in 2022, Black Entertainment Television (BET) ran a College Hill Celebrity series. It featured an episode in which the celebrities, attending Texas Southern University in Houston, Texas, participated in a mock trial based on the facts of Darren Wilson and Mike Brown's fateful encounter on August 9, 2014. The date, the claim that the teenager attempted to take the officer's gun, the cruelty of the shooting, and the aftermath of the incident are forever part of the cultural memory of Black people worldwide.

The grassroots reaction to the deaths of George Floyd, Brianna Taylor, Ahmaud Arberry, and others in 2020 mirrored that of the Ferguson Uprising. The policy gains in St. Louis and Ferguson paved the way for concessions throughout the nation. In the five years after Wilson shot Brown, police departments around the nation invested in body cameras, tasers, and other non-lethal weapons, but police shootings did not significantly slow. For that reason, civilians have become adept at recording with their devices. Some policy progress is evident. Departments reexamined and in some cases revised the use of force protocols. Penalties for violating protocols remain light, with slight reprimands and reassignments. Even when relieved of duty, misbehaving officers can be rehired in different departments. Fearing that the movement's calls to "Defund the Police" could manifest, *Politico* reported that "states passed 243 policing bills."[2] Also, significantly, it is costing municipalities more money to kill unarmed and legally armed Black people. Scholar Treva Lindsey, who visited Ferguson several times during the Uprising, put it succinctly in her book, *America Goddam: Violence, Black Women, and the Struggle for Justice* (2022), "Police violence has not only cost billions of dollars in settlements . . . It's also cost us billions of dollars in rebuilding in the aftermath of these fatal encounters with government-paid and protected employees."[3] The Ferguson Uprising illustrated the point that extinguishing Black life costs municipalities dearly.

The legislative action did not prevent further Black death at the hands of law enforcement.

Cameras and new policies have not ended the mistreatment of Black citizens, and that is in large part due to the intransigence of police unions in the wake of the Ferguson Uprising. Even when police chiefs tout "community policing efforts" and release video clips of their officers line dancing with residents, police union representatives intensify their claims that officers are increasingly under attack. Still, even unions could not protect the policemen who killed Walter Scott, George Floyd, Tyre Nichols, and twenty-three-year-old Elijah McClain. The recordings of civilians turned the tides in each of those cases.

Millions of Americans took to the streets during and after the summer of 2020 with the same chants that Ferguson Uprising protesters used. As my family and I marched through the streets of Los Angeles, it seemed familiar when organizers shouted "SAY HER NAME!" or "THE WHOLE DAMN SYSTEM IS GUILTY AS HELL." By and large, the demonstrations seemed much more peaceful than in Ferguson; I thought that perhaps police had learned not to antagonize people who needed to mourn. Not long after that thought entered my mind, the police cut off the march line and began aggressively using batons to move the crowd off the streets. I gathered my family and ran to safety. Many of the celebrities and entertainers who protested that summer used their fame to bring attention to the injustice that plagued Ferguson and all municipalities where Black people were policed differently than other Americans.

The cadence and tactics of the Uprising reappeared in the demonstrations for a ceasefire in the Israel–Gaza war that started in October 2023. In much the same way that Ferguson demonstrators organized and executed airport actions in 2014 and 2015, in major cities around the nation, ceasefire activists shut down roads leading into the airports, disrupting traffic and causing delays in 2023.[4] The ceasefire activists took to heart the chant that constantly went up during the Ferguson Uprising, "If We Don't Get It, Shut It Down!"

St. Louis seventh ward alderwoman Alisha Sonnier calls the Ferguson Uprising a "crash course in life." Death, humanity, oppression, and liberation were the class's major themes. The young learners in the class completed assignments in the fields of leadership dynamics, organizational behavior, interpersonal relations, rhetoric, communication, artivism, criminal justice, chemical warfare, tactical evasion, and financial development. Not everyone passed, but those who did have become super-citizens. In interviewing these American leaders, some key lessons for aspiring organizers and activists arose.

Regarding leadership, they explained not everyone needs to be a leader; good and intelligent followers are necessary for the movement to work. It is imperative to learn the difference between tree shakers and jelly makers; the former unsettles and disturbs, while the latter reaches out, refines, reconciles, and negotiates sustainable concessions. Some are meant for physical action and others are meant to strategize; some can do both, but not every circumstance requires the same leader. Sometimes there is a demand for crisis leadership, but at other times visionary leadership or facilitation works best; then again, a figurehead may be appropriate at times. The function of the leader will determine the form of leadership. Typically, however, a viable leader needs the participation, consultation, and consent of the group. Although it seems obvious, the Ground Zero demonstrators showed that leaders may not look like or have the experience of what is typically presented in the media. Judge the leader by ideas, courage, and execution.

Another lesson is the need for political education and awareness of the power points that affect the lives of activists and the people on whose behalf people are activating. This requires reading widely for an understanding of how people have handled similar situations before and what people are doing now. Never underestimate the importance of knowing how people live, eat, move, and acquire knowledge. Ferguson organizers learned that political education requires engagement in the democracy and having a clear-eyed awareness of those who can do immense harm or offer tremendous help to the most vulnerable in the community. In light of incumbent Congresswoman Cori Bush's recent

IF WE DON'T GET IT

and surprising congressional primary loss to the exorbitantly well-funded St. Louis county prosecutor Wesley Bell, it is clearer than ever that money matters in politics and that external money seemingly turns tides. Organizers and activists alike learned that, fundamentally, voting is important, but so too is running for office. Best of all, Ferguson taught, is having enough influence with policy-makers to immediately and efficiently exact accountability. With that said, patience is a must if sustainable political change is the goal. That which is built hastily falls quickly.

Perhaps the most paramount lessons have to do with expectations of self. Maintaining physical, psychological, and emotional health are requisite. Missing an action or taking a break will not keep one from contributing to the movement. Along those lines, romanticizing struggle can be detrimental to self and others. That means understanding personal limits so that one can be optimally productive for the movement. The young mobilizers taught that one should be careful that extreme passion does not overtake relationships that are intended to last. The Uprising drove activists and organizers to say and do things to people they would never even consider doing under normal circumstances. Thinking twice before unleashing hell may save a vital relationship. On a different note, whenever possible, one should know how one will acquire financial resources. So many activists in the movement had an added element of stress because they left their source of income without having a sense of how they would live. They survived, but not without an extreme cost. That led to controversies over what activists believed the movement was supposed to provide. If it is unlikely for one to raise enough funds for self-upkeep, then there should be a strategy for collectivizing.

The case of youth organizers in the Ferguson Uprising teaches would-be activists and protesters to figure out the balance between following instincts and impulse control. Human beings have survived for millennia because of their ability to react to danger without thinking. That is a crucial function, but so too is the ability to not always respond to urges. This is no less important on the street when confronting police or counter-protesters than it is when negotiating changes in policies with decision-makers. Young activists should bear in mind that what is good for those who are activating right now might not be good for the community in the near future. Tearing down or destroying an existing system may be very necessary, but not having something to take its place could be as harmful. The question must always be, "For what? For what are we doing this action? For what are we sacrificing and risking? For what, in the end, is victory for our people?" Those were the questions that organizers arrived at once they passed through the fog of street war.

The Black youth of the Ferguson Uprising were the vanguard of the last true American democrats. For a brief moment in history, they, by way of their protests, demonstrations, and organizing, saved the republic. America's most vulnerable youth risked life and limb to protect whatever semblance of constitutional freedoms existed. In the end, those flawed heroes rescued democracy, if only for a while. Because the nation will likely not ever thank the young citizens who frightened the beneficiaries of the status quo those leaders have every right to say, "America, you're welcome."

ACKNOWLEDGMENTS

Lezley McSpadden and Mike Brown Sr. endured great and unrelenting pain to create space for a modern justice movement during a period they should have been mourning. I thank God for the Black youth in Ferguson who smelled like weed, sported tattoos, cursed profusely, and were crazy enough to confront the system when so many respectable people thought change impossible. They jolted others into action. Together, with students and concerned citizens, they made me a believer. I feel abundantly blessed to have witnessed the collective courage and leadership of young people. They gave their time, energy, health, wealth, and lives to uplift the voices of the most oppressed. For that I am thankful.

Sharing thoughts is natural, but writing a book is not. It requires the assistance of so many. The patience, fearlessness, steadiness, and innovation of my editor, Marc Favreau, is unparalleled. He along with the noble staff of The New Press have done everything possible to bring this "people's history" to light. There is so much more to say and write, but they allowed me to make a start with this book. I do not know much about the business end of bookselling, but I do know about the ethics of storytelling and sharing knowledge. Marc and the staff modeled the morality that is necessary for this moment.

Putting together this book required extended periods of time, which was not always conducive to my being a good family man. I am so appreciative of my Weezie, who endured the process and cheered for me. I send a big shoutout to my beautifully bright

250 ACKNOWLEDGMENTS

Bae-Guhl, who was an excellent assistant. They both allowed me the space to work on the manuscript. I also acknowledge my dearly departed mother-in-law, Elaine, who in the midst of a gallant battle with cancer, still checked in to see how the project was coming. May peace be upon her always. My father, Alphonso Bradley, after observing the early Uprising in person, greatly encouraged the effort. He, along with the supportive family I have gathered throughout the years, sustained me. Thanks to the Mizzou Crew and the Brotherhood of the Escargot Room. There are also dozens of historians and scholars who inspired me and helped me think through my thoughts. Great thanks to those who read and commented on the manuscript in its various forms. I must recognize specifically Philip J. Gibson Professor of Education Derrick Alridge for his generous operational assistance and guidance regarding oral history.

There is no contest; my students, contemporary and former, are the best. They have offered love and leadership on the street and on campus. They encouraged me and made this book possible. Thanks especially to Alderwoman Alisha Sonnier for her early assistance with planning and interviewing. Proudly, I have learned a great deal from Jonathan Pulphus, who contributed his moving words and critique to this book. My current student, Ms. Avery Cook, with dedication and efficiency, worked diligently as my research assistant. Her inquisitiveness is only matched by her dogged work ethic. I deeply love and cherish my students from SIUE, SLU, LMU, and now Amherst College.

I was blessed to have the opportunity to interview so many people who participated in and led the movement. Great thanks to Damon Latchinson, Alex Templeton, Mayor Tishaura Jones, Alderman Rasheen Aldridge, Jonathan Pulphus, Josh Jones, Trevor Woolfolk, Danielle Blocker, Charlie Cooksey, Kira Van Niel, Dr. Marva Robinson, Dr. Traice Webb-Bradley, Professor Justin Hansford, Chris King, Rebecca Rivas, DeRay McKesson, H.J.

ACKNOWLEDGMENTS

Rodgers, and Josh Williams, as well as others who anonymously offered insight and good will.

I am very thankful for institutional support. At Amherst College, I received bountiful help from Provost Catherine Epstein as well as a timely sabbatical that allowed me the chance to write. It was such a pleasure to present my work at the Faculty Colloquium and to hear the comments of colleagues. I am so humbled and honored to be part of the departments of Black Studies and History. Colleagues like Olufemi Vaughan, Rhonda Cobham Sanders, Rowland Abiodun, Hilary Moss, Carol Bailey, Cheikh Thiam, Elizabeth Herbin-Triant, Russell Lohse, Solsiree Del Moral, Khari Polk, Jalicia Jolly, Jared Loggins, and Robyn Rogers in Black Studies never denied me the opportunity to talk about the young people in Ferguson. They consistently showed love. So, too, did good colleagues like Nellie Boucher, Frank Couvares, Sergey Glebov, Mekhola Gomes, Adi Gordon, Rick Lopez, Jen Manion, Trent Maxey, Ted Melillo, Christine Peralta, George Qiao, Sean Redding, Vanessa Walker, Kristen Luschen, Carey Aubert, and Eva Diaz of the history department. I am deeply appreciative and happy to receive the support of University of Massachusetts–Amherst Center for Racial Justice and Youth Engaged Research and the W.E.B. Du Bois Afro-American Studies Department by way of the John H. Bracey-Demetria Shabazz Fellowship. UMass colleagues like Almicar Shabazz, Keisha Green, Toussaint Losier, Whitney Baptiste, and Yolanda Covington-Ward have been particularly collegial. Forgive my heart if I forgot someone.

In the end, the St. Louis metropolitan area, and, Ferguson especially, help me grow and actualize as a man and scholar. For that I am forever grateful. Black youth, onward toward freedom.

NOTES

Foreword

1 Emphasis added. The quotation was taken from an article published after Hampton's death. Fred Hampton, "I Believe I'm Going to Die," *New York Times,* July 21, 1971, p. 35.

2 "STLAM Video: Tribe X's Black Friday Protest Shuts Down Galleria Mall for Mike Brown," *St. Louis American,* November 29, 2014; "Ferguson Protesters Take to Lambert Airport on Busy Travel Day," Fox 2 Now, December 26, 2014, fox2now.com/news/ferguson-protesters-take-to-lambert-airport-on-busy-travel-day; "Protesters Stage 'Die-In' in the Delmar Loop," stltoday.com, November 16, 2014; "Protesters Storm St. Louis Police Headquarters with Eviction Notice," *HuffPost,* December 31, 2014.

3 Taylor Ardrey, "Michael Brown's Father and Ferguson Activists Want a Chunk of the $90 Million that BLM Raised During the Racial Reckoning of 2020," *Business Insider,* March 6, 2021; Alisa Chang, Jason Fuller, and Kathryn Fox, "Secret $6 Million Home Has Allies and Critics Skeptical of BLM Foundation's Finances," *NPR,* April 7, 2022.

4 Sarah Kendzior, "Meet Darren Seals. Then Tell Me Black Death Is Not a Business," de Correspondent, October 1, 2016, thecorrespondent.com/5349/meet-darren-seals-then-tell-me-black-death-is-not-a-business/1512965275833-fe73c5b1.

5 "Protesters Pay Early Morning Visit to Steve Stenger's Home," stltoday.com, February 23, 2015.

Author's Note

1 Tory Russell, "Notes on an Uprising: Reflections of a Ferguson Organizer 5 Years After the State-Sanctioned Killing of Mike Brown," *Essence,* August 9, 2019.

2 Ibid.

3 Quoted in Jerome Brooks, "The Art of Fiction No. 139," *Paris Review,* November 9, 2020.

254 NOTES

Introduction

1 Ferguson Voices: A Moral Courage Project, "Darren Seals, Community Leader," www.fergusonvoices.org/voices/darren-seals.

2 "Ferguson Police Release the Name of Officer Involved in Michael Brown Shooting," *PBS Newshour,* August 15, 2014, www.youtube.com/watch?v=6XJ1Kh1CTB8.

3 "Chief Defends Release of Robbery Surveillance Video," *MSNBC,* August 15, 2014.

4 Ibid.

5 Devlin Barrett, "Obama Calls for Understanding in Ferguson; Attorney General Holder Faults Officials for 'Selective' Leaks About Case," *Wall Street Journal,* August 18, 2014.

6 Talia Lavin, "Behind the 'Thin Blue Line' Flag: America's History of Police Violence," *MSNBC,* April 22, 2021; India Thusi, "Blue Lives & the Permanence of Racism," *Cornell Law Review* 105 (March 2020), www.cornelllawreview.org/2020/03/03/blue-lives-the-permanence-of-racism.

1. Red's Ribz and Racial Capitalism in Ferguson

1 Charli Cooksey, interview by author, Zoom meeting, September 5, 2023.

2 Joshua Jones, interview by author and Alisha Sonnier, St. Louis, Missouri, August 9, 2023.

3 Mama Lisa Gage, "Tutoring Michael Brown," *St. Louis American,* September 18, 2014.

4 Ibid.

5 Cori Bush, *Forerunner: A Story of Pain and Perseverance in America* (New York: Alfred Knopf, 2022), 162.

6 Quoted in Jennifer E. Cobbina, *Hands Up Don't Shoot: Why the Protests in Ferguson and Baltimore Matter, and How They Changed America* (New York: New York University Press, 2019), 27.

7 H.J. Rodgers, interview by author, telephone, September 26, 2023.

8 Ibid.

9 For wider contemporary discussions of racial capitalism, see Donna Murch, *Assata Taught Me: State Violence, Racial Capitalism, and the Movement for Black Lives* (Chicago: Haymarket Books, 2022) and Jared A. Loggins and Andrew J. Douglas, *Prophet of Discontent: Martin Luther King Jr. and the Critique of Racial Capitalism* (Athens: University of Georgia Press, 2021).

NOTES

10 United States Department of Justice, "Ferguson: The Department of Justice Investigation of the Ferguson, Missouri, Police Department," United States, 2015. https://www.justice.gov/sites/default/files/opa/press-releases/attachments/2015/03/04/ferguson_police_department_report.pdf

11 Jamala Rogers interview, September 7, 2023.

12 German Lopez, "Why Ferguson's Government Is So White," *Vox*, August 14, 2014.

2. Today *Was* a Good Day: Michael Brown Encounters Darren Wilson

1 Kelly Moffitt, " 'We Are in the Middle of a Social Movement:' College Professors Reflect on the 'Lessons of Ferguson,' " St. Louis Public Radio, August 9, 2016, www.stlpr.org/show/st-louis-on-the-air/2016-08-09/we-are-in-the-middle-of-a-social-movement-college-professors-reflect-on-the-lessons-of-ferguson.

2 "Words of John Lewis," Office of Human Rights, Washington, D.C., ohr.dc.gov/marchforward#:~:text=Words%20of%20John%20Lewis&text=We%20want%20our%20freedom%20and,that%20is%20sweeping%20this%20nation.

3 Ibid.; Kristin Braswell, "#FergusonFridays: Not All of the Black Freedom Fighters Are Men: An Interview with Black Women on the Front Lines in Ferguson," *Feminist Wire*, October 3, 2014, thefeministwire.com/2014/fergusonfridays-black-freedom-fighters-men-interview-black-women-front-line-ferguson.

4 Ibid.

5 Charli Cooksey, interview by author, Zoom meeting, September 5, 2023.

6 Joshua Williams, interview by author, telephone, September 28, 2023.

7 Ibid.

8 Trymaine Lee, "Portrait of a Protester in Ferguson, Missouri," *MSNBC*, September 11, 2014.

9 Quoted in Wesley Lowrie, *They Can't Kill Us All* (New York: Little Brown and Company, 2016), 196.

10 Ferguson Voices: A Moral Courage Project, "Darren Seals: Community Leader," www.fergusonvoices.org/voices/darren-seals.

11 Ibid.

12 Joshua Williams interview, September 28, 2023.

13 Alex Altman, "Nobody Is Winning in Ferguson," *Time*, August 20, 2014, https://time.com/3146684/ferguson-michael-brown/.

14 Ibid.

NOTES

15 Braswell, "#FergusonFridays."

16 Ferguson Voices, "Darren Seals: Community Leader."

17 Joshua Williams, interview by author, email, September 26, 2023.

18 Yamiche Alcindor, "Amid Weekend of Protests, 'World Is Watching' Ferguson," *USA Today*, October 11, 2014.

19 H.J. Rodgers interview.

20 Ibid.

21 Derecka Purnell, interview by author, Zoom meeting, October 5, 2023.

22 Lezley McSpadden, *Tell the Truth & Shame the Devil: The Life, Legacy, and Love of My Son Michael Brown* (New York, Regan Arts), 12–14.

23 Daniel Kreps, "Ferguson Police Chief Apologizes to Michael Brown's Family," *Rolling Stone*, September 25, 2014.

3. Who Let the Dogs Out?: Repressive Police Action

1 #TeamEbony, " 'When I Close My Eyes at Night, I See People Running from Tear Gas,' " *Ebony*, September 14, 2014.

2 Reported on in Aura Bogado, "Police Officer Calls Ferguson Protestors 'Animals,' " *Colorlines*, August 11, 2014.

3 #TeamEbony, " 'When I Close My Eyes at Night.' "

4 Alex Altman, "Nobody Is Winning in Ferguson," *Time*, August 20, 2014.

5 John Stossel, "The Truth about Libertarians, Police and Ferguson's Fury," *Fox News*, August 20, 2014.

6 "Attorney General Holder in Ferguson, Missouri," *CSpan*, August 20, 2014.

7 Colleen McCain Nelson, "White House to Review Programs that Supply Military Gear to Local Police; Assessment Follows the Police Response to Protests in Ferguson, Mo.," *Wall Street Journal*, August 24, 2014.

8 Simon Vozick-Levinson, "Watch Ferguson Freedom Fighters Share Stories from Frontlines," *Rolling Stone*, December 16, 2014.

9 Trymaine Lee, "Portrait of a Protester in Ferguson, Missouri," *MSNBC*, September 11, 2014.

10 Alex Templeton, interview by author and Alisha Sonnier, St. Louis, August 7, 2023.

11 Ibid.

12 Ferguson Voices: A Moral Courage Project, "Darren Seals, Community Leader," www.fergusonvoices.org/voices/darren-seals, October 9, 2023.

NOTES

13 Damon Latchinson, interview by author and Alisha Sonnier, St. Louis, August 7, 2023.

14 "Ferguson Could Spark a New Civil Rights Movement," KSDK 5 On Your Side, November 29, 2014, www.ksdk.com/article/news/local/ferguson/ferguson-could-spark-a-new-civil-rights-movement/63-211180779.

15 Moni Basu, "Our Ferguson, 'After MB,' " CNN, August 9, 2015.

16 Amy Hunter, "To Heal Our Communities, We Must Treat Each Other as Family," YWCA, August 15, 2014, www.ywca.org/blog/2014/08/15/to-heal-our-communities-we-must-treat-each-other-as-family.

17 Tishaura Jones, interview by author, Zoom meeting, November 20, 2023.

18 LaTanya Buck, "Protecting All of Our Sons," *St. Louis American,* March 25, 2015, accessed November 20, 2023.

19 Cori Bush, *The Forerunner: A Story of Pain and Perseverance in America* (New York: Alfred Knopf, 2022), 169.

20 Ibid., 168.

21 Alvin Reid, "Kwame Building Group CEO Tony Thompson Takes a Bold Stance Following Police Shooting of Michael Brown," *St. Louis Magazine,* August 19, 2014.

22 Ibid.

23 Ibid.

24 Gene Demby, "In Ferguson, Mo., a City Meets the Spotlight," *NPR,* August 19, 2014.

25 Ibid.

26 Ibid.

27 Mike Jones, "The Political Negligence of Black Leadership," *St. Louis American,* August 14, 2014.

28 Ibid.

29 Tishaura Jones, interview by author, Zoom meeting, November 20, 2023.

30 Quoted in Demby, "In Ferguson, Mo., a City Meets the Spotlight."

31 Justice for Mike Brown, "Darren Seals on Deray McKesson, Black Lives Matter Movement, and Mike Brown Protests," Facebook, September 15, 2016, https://www.facebook.com/watch/?v=1336082946409738.

32 "Ferguson Activists Call Out Black Celebrities for 'Saying Nothing,' " *Rolling Stone,* December 22, 2014.

33 Lamont Lilly, "Ferguson Activist Says: 'We Need More Than Change, We Need Revolution,' " *Truthout,* August 22, 2018.

4. Democracy Is in the Streets: Mothers, Thugs, and the Dispossessed

1 "Ted Nugent Slams 'Ferguson Thugs' & The 'Plague of Black Violence,'" *HuffPost,* October 2, 2014; "Huckabee: Michael Brown Acted Like a 'Thug,'" *CNN,* December 3, 2014. On racialized media depictions in Ferguson, see Bryan Adamson, "Thugs, Crooks, and Rebellious Negroes: Racist and Racialized Media Coverage of Michael Brown and the Ferguson Demonstrations," *Harvard Journal on Racial and Ethnic Justice,* Vol. 32 (2016): 189–278.

2 Jonathan Pulphus, interview by Alisha Sonnier and author, St. Louis, August 8, 2023.

5. Moment or a Movement?: Youth Organizing for Freedom

1 "Ferguson Activists Ashley Yates & Tory Russell: The System Wasn't Made to Protect Us," GlobalGrindTV, October 15, 2014, www.youtube.com/watch?v=rBPM1el37GQ.

2 Quoted from the *Combahee River Collective Statement (1977).* "(1977) Combahee River Collective Statement," BlackPast.org, www.blackpast.org/african-american-history/combahee-river-collective-statement-1977.

3 H.J. Rodgers, interview by author, telephone, September 26, 2023.

4 Storm Ervin, interview by author, telephone, November 13, 2023.

5 Antonio French, "Faces of Ferguson: Five Years Later," *St. Louis Post-Dispatch,* July 28, 2019.

6 Kristin Baswell, "#FergusonFridays: Not all of the Black freedom fighters are men: An Interview with Black Women on the Front line in Ferguson," *Feminist Wire,* October 3, 2014, thefeministwire.com/2014/10/fergusonfridays-black-freedom-fighters-men-interview-black-women-front-line-ferguson.

7 Ibid.

8 Quoted in Wesley Lowrie, *They Can't Kill Us All* (New York: Little Brown and Company, 2016), 197.

9 Ibid., 197–99.

10 Lowery, *They Can't Kill Us All,* 198.

11 Ferguson Voices: A Moral Courage Project, "Darren Seals, Community Leader," www.fergusonvoices.org/voices/darren-seals.

12 Ibid.

13 "On Movement Theory, Institutional Activism, and Cultural Change," *Harvard Journal of African American Public Policy,* 2015–16.

NOTES 259

14 Makayla Gathers and Angelo Vidal, "Lessons from the Frontlines of Ferguson: Q&A with Mother and Activist Kris Hendrix," September 15, 2023, https://www.archcitydefenders.org/lessons-from-the-front lines-of-ferguson.

15 Justin Hansford, interview with author, Zoom meeting, October 4, 2023; Justin Hansford, "I Went to Ferguson to Protect the Protesters. I Got Arrested Instead," *Vox,* October 24, 2014.

16 Jeff Ordower and Tory Russell, "Lessons from the Ferguson Uprisings," *The Forge: Organizing Strategy and Practice,* July 20, 2020, forgeorganizing.org/article /lessons-ferguson-uprisings.

6. Bring Toilet Paper: Police Repression and Young Professionals

1 Cori Bush, *The Forerunner: A Story of Pain and Perseverance in America* (New York: Alfred Knopf, 2022), 162–65.

2 Danny Wicentowski, "Police Thwart I-70 Blockade by Blocking I-70, Arrest 32 Ferguson Protesters," *Riverfront Times,* September 11, 2014.

3 Molly Knefel, "Ferguson's Kids Go Back to School," *Rolling Stone,* August 26, 2014.

4 Cori Bush, *Forerunner: A Story of Pain and Perseverance in America* (New York: Alfred Knopf, 2022), 164.

5 Rory Carroll, " In the Ferguson Tempest, Fury and Resentment Fuel Protesters' Fire," *The Guardian,* August 17, 2014.

6 Danielle Blocker, interview by author, Zoom meeting, October 5, 2023.

7 Ibid.

8 Quoted in Yasmine Hafiz, "Greater St. Mark Family Church, Shelter for Ferguson Protestors, Reportedly Raided By St. Louis County Police," *HuffPost,* August 20, 2014.

9 Hafiz, "Greater St. Mark Family Church."

10 Joia Williamson, "Friendly Temple Celebrates New Sanctuary," *St. Louis American,* February 4, 2010.

11 "Kevin Powell Hosts Ferguson Townhall at Missouri History Museum Tonight," *St. Louis American,* August 25, 2014; Wayne C. Harvey, General Counsel of Alpha Phi Alpha Fraternity, Inc. to Austin A. Layne Mortuary, Inc., August 14, 2014, in News One Staff, "Alpha Phi Alpha Fraternity to Pay Full Cost of Michael Brown's Memorial and Funeral Services," News One, August 17, 2014,

thelightnc.com/9484397/alpha-phi-alpha-fraternity-to-pay-full-cost-of-michael
-browns-memorial-and-funeral-services.

7. Thug Life: Representation of Black Youth in Local and National Media

1 Robert T. Starks, " 'The Ferguson Effect'—Myth and the Reality," *Chicago Defender,* November 4, 2015, www.proquest.com/newspapers/ferguson-effect -myth-reality/docview/1737977123/se-2.

2 Chris King, interview by author, telephone, November 3, 2023.

3 Rebecca Rivas, interview by author, telephone, November 19, 2023.

4 Ibid.

5 Earl Ofari Hutchinson, "The Second Slaying of Michael Brown," *Chicago Defender,* August 20, 2014, amherst.idwww.proquest.com/newspapers/second -slaying-michael-brown/docview/1562001725/se-2.

6 "All in with Chris Hayes," *MSNBC,* August 19, 2014.

7 Ibid.

8 Ibid.

9 Betsey Bruce, "MHP Captain Ron Johnson takes charge in Ferguson: 'I Got a Big Dog in This Fight,' " Fox 2 News, August 14, 2014. The captain wrote about his experiences in Ron Johnson with Alan Eisenstock, *13 Days in Ferguson: Captain Ronald Johnson* (Carol Stream, IL: Tyndale Momentum, 2018).

10 Justin Hansford, interview with author, Zoom meeting, October 4, 2023.

11 Lee Rowland, "There Is No 5-Second Rule for the First Amendment, Ferguson," ACLU, October 6, 2014.

8. Whose Movement and Whose Streets?

1 Josh Williams interview, September 28, 2023.

2 Alex Templeton, interview by author and Alisha Sonnier, St. Louis, August 7, 2023.

3 Jonathan Pulphus, interview by Alisha Sonnier and author, St. Louis, August 8, 2023.

4 Justice for Mike Brown, "Darren Seals on Deray McKesson, Black Lives Matter Movement, and Mike Brown Protests," Facebook, September 15, 2016, www.facebook.com/watch/?v=1336082946409738.

5 DeRay McKesson, interview by author, Zoom meeting, December 6, 2023.

NOTES   261

6 Damon Latchinson, interview by author and Alisha Sonnier, St. Louis, August 7, 2023.

7 Justice for Mike Brown, "Darren Seals on Deray McKesson."

8 Templeton interview.

9 Ibid.

10 Ibid.

11 Patrisse Cullors, "Black Lives Matter Began after Trayvon Martin's Death. Ferguson Showed Its Staying Power," Think, *NBC News,* January 1, 2020.

12 Latchinson interview.

13 Justin Hansford, interview with author, Zoom meeting, October 4, 2023.

14 Templeton interview.

15 Latchinson interview.

16 Ibid.

17 Cullors, "Black Lives Matter Began after Trayvon Martin's Death."

9. Leadership and Money in Movement Making

1 Charli Cooksey, interview by author, Zoom meeting, September 5, 2023.

2 Jonathan Pulphus, interview by Alisha Sonnier and author, St. Louis, August 8, 2023.

3 Charli Cooksey interview.

4 DeRay McKesson, interview by author, Zoom meeting, December 6, 2023.

5 Damon Latchinson, interview by author and Alisha Sonnier, St. Louis, August 7, 2023.

6 Alex Templeton, interview by author and Alisha Sonnier, St. Louis, August 7, 2023.

7 Ibid.

8 Ibid.

9 Ibid.

10 "Ferguson Activists Ashley Yates & Tory Russell: The System Wasn't Made To Protect Us," GlobalGrindTV, October 15, 2014, www.youtube.com /watch?v=rBPM1el37GQ.

11 Rasheen Aldridge, interview by Alisha Sonnier and author, St. Louis, August 8, 2023.

12 Arlene Stein, "Between Organization and Movement: ACORN and the Alinsky Model of Community Organizing," *Berkeley Journal of Sociology* 31 (1986): 93–115.

262 NOTES

13 "Jeff Ordower," The Forge, forgeorganizing.org/author/jeff-ordower.

14 "George Soros Funds Ferguson Protests, Hopes to Spur Civil Action," *Washington Times;* Lynette Holloway, "Report: George Soros Spent $33,000,000 to Bankroll Ferguson Protests," *The Root,* January 18, 2015.

15 Pulphus interview, August 8, 2023.

16 Danielle Blocker, interview by author, Zoom meeting, October 5, 2023.

17 Jamala Rogers, interview by author, Zoom meeting, September 14, 2023.

18 Aldridge interview.

19 Jamala Rogers interview.

20 Statement transcribed in Kristinn Taylor, " 'We gonna just **** you up'; Black #Ferguson Activists Threaten White Liberals for Protest Pay," Gateway Pundit, May 15, 2015, www.thegatewaypundit.com/2015/05/we-gonna-just-you-up-black-ferguson-activists-threaten-white-liberals-for-protest-pay.

21 Jamala Rogers, "#Cutthecheck Is Not a Movement," *St. Louis American,* May 28, 2015.

22 Rogers interview.

23 Rogers, "#Cutthecheck Is Not a Movement."

24 Templeton interview.

25 Pulphus interview.

10. Fun in the Frenzy: Comedy in the Chaos

1 Jonathan Pulphus, interview by author, telephone, December 9, 2023.

2 H.J. Rodgers, interview by author, telephone, September 26, 2023.

3 Danielle Blocker, interview by author, Zoom meeting, October 5, 2023.

4 Pulphus interview, December 9, 2023.

5 Danny Wicentowski, "St. Louis Police Chief Says Tear-Gassing of MoKaBe's Was Unintentional [See Update]," *Riverfront Times,* December 3, 2014.

6 Storm Ervin, interview by author, telephone, November 13, 2023.

7 Pulphus interview, December 9, 2023.

8 Rebecca Rivas, "Revolutionary Love: Ferguson Protest Leaders Get Engaged at City Hall," *St. Louis American,* December 16, 2014.

9 Ibid.

10 Kory Grow, "J. Cole Mourns Michael Brown in Somber New Song 'Be Free,' " *Rolling Stone,* August 15, 2014.

11 Josh Levs, "Michael Brown's Parents Address U.N.: 'We Need the World to Know,' " *CNN,* November 12, 2014.

NOTES 263

12 Ibid; Justin Hansford, interview with author, Zoom meeting, October 4, 2023.

13 Rick Hampson, "King's Legacy Respected, Reinterpreted by New Activists," *USA Today*, January 7, 2015.

14 Rebecca Rivas, "Brittany Packnett Cunningham to Serve on White House Taskforce on Policing," *St. Louis American*, December 24, 2014.

15 DeRay McKesson, interview by author, Zoom meeting, December 6, 2023.

11. Soldiers and Scholars: Ferguson Comes to SLU

1 Khorri Atkinson, "College Students Nationwide Show Solidarity with Michael Brown," *New York Amsterdam News*, August 28, 2014.

2 Rebecca Rivas, "Vonderrit Myers' Family Releases Autopsy, Findings Contradict with Police Reports," *St. Louis American*, October 23, 2014.

3 Yamiche Alcindor and Doug Stanglin, "Protests Resume in St. Louis over Police Shooting, *USA Today*, October 9, 2014.

4 Quoted in Terrance Pitts, "Montgomery to Ferguson: A New Movement for Democracy," Funders for Justice, October 14, 2014, https://fundersforjustice .org/montgomery-to-ferguson-a-new-movement-for-democracy/.

5 In St. Louis Project, "The Mirror Casket," September 13, 2019, instlouis .wustl.edu/mirror-casket.

6 Ibid.

7 Matt Pearce, "Ferguson October Rally Shows Divide over Civil Rights," *Detroit Free Press*, October 13, 2014.

8 Ibid.

9 Ibid.

10 Kenya Vaughn, "#FergusonOctober Protesters Peacefully 'Occupy' SLU, University President Responds," *St. Louis American*, October 13, 2014.

11 H.J. Rodgers, interview by author, telephone, September 26, 2023.

12 Ibid.

13 Rodgers interview.

14 Pulphus interview, August 8, 2023.

15 Ibid.

16 Vaughn, "#FergusonOctober Protesters Peacefully 'Occupy' SLU."

17 Joshua Jones interview.

18 Betsy Bruce, "Occupy SLU Protestors Not Welcomed by Everyone

on Campus," Fox 2 News, October 16, 2014, fox2now.com/news/ferguson
-protesters-still-camping-out-on-saint-louis-university-campus.

19 Josh Williams, interview by author, email, December 5, 2023.

20 Rodgers interview.

21 Pulphus interview.

22 Rodgers interview.

23 Ibid.

24 Trevor Woolfolk, interviewed by the author, telephone, December 5, 2023.

25 Ibid.

26 Koran Addo, "Digest," *St. Louis Post-Dispatch,* November 7, 2014.

12. Mizzou and Princeton Too

1 Storm Ervin, interview by author, telephone, November 13, 2023.

2 Ibid.

3 Ibid.

4 Daniel Arkin, Alex Johnson, and Jon Schuppe, "University of Missouri President Tim Wolfe Resigns Amid Racial Unrest," *NBC News,* November 9, 2015.

5 Ibid.

6 Robert Starks, "Today and Yesterday, Black College Students Fight for Equality," *Chicago Defender,* November 25, 2015, www.proquest.com/newspapers /today-yesterday-black-college-students-fight/docview/1755076749/se-2.

7 Ellen Li and Omar Farah, " 'PART II | 'Resurfacing History': A Look Back at the Black Justice League's Campus Activism," *Daily Princetonian,* July 30, 2020; Ellen Li and Omar Farah, "PART I | 'Resurfacing History': A Look Back at the Black Justice League's Campus Activism," *Daily Princetonian,* July 30, 2020.

8 For more on the history of Black student activism at Princeton, see Stefan M. Bradley, *Upending the Ivory Tower: Civil Rights, Black Power, and the Ivy League* (New York: New York University Press, 2018).

13. Hope Burned: No Indictment and Destructive Rebellion

1 "Ferguson Commission to Hold First Public Meeting on Monday," *St. Louis American,* November 28, 2014.

2 "Get to Know the WWT Board: Rich McClure," World Wide Technology, www.wwt.com/get-to-know-the-wwt-board-rich-mcclure.

3 Herb Boyd, "Activists Respond to Ferguson Commission." *New York Amsterdam News,* November 20, 2014.

NOTES

4 "Many Plan for No-Indictment Grand Jury Decision," *St. Louis American,* November 17, 2014.

5 Ibid.

6 Josh Williams interview, telephone, September 28, 2023.

7 Alex Templeton, interview by author and Alisha Sonnier, St. Louis, August 7, 2023.

8 Justice for Mike Brown, "Darren Seals on Deray McKesson, Black Lives Matter Movement, and Mike Brown Protests," Facebook, September 15, 2016, www.facebook.com/watch/?v=1336082946409738.

9 "Hopelessness in Ferguson," *All in with Chris Hayes,* MSNBC, November 24, 2014.

10 Excerpts taken from Stefan M. Bradley, "Ferguson, USA: A Historian's Collision with History, Part One," OAH Process: A Blog for American History, June 23, 2015, www.processhistory.org/ferguson-usa-an-historians-collision-with-history.

14. Life Goes On: Where Are They

1 Justin Hansford, interview with author, Zoom meeting, October 4, 2023.

2 Alex Templeton, interview by author and Alisha Sonnier, St. Louis, August 7, 2023.

3 Hansford interview.

4 Templeton interview.

5 "Tensions Simmer in St Louis after White Officer Acquitted of Killing Black Motorist," *The Guardian,* September 15, 2017.

6 Jim Salter, "Prosecutor Adds 22 St. Louis Officers to Exclusion List," AP, June 19, 2019.

7 "Eric Greitens Case at Center of Scrutiny for St. Louis Prosecutor," *CBS News,* April 11, 2022; Rachel Lipmann, "St. Louis Circuit Attorney Gardner Has 'Lost the Trust of the People,' Mayor Jones Says," St. Louis Public Radio, February 22, 2023, www.stlpr.org/government-politics-issues/2023-02-22/st -louis-circuit-attorney-gardner-has-lost-the-trust-of-the-people-mayor-jones-says.

8 Tishaura Jones, interview by author, Zoom meeting, November 20, 2023.

9 Tishaura Jones interview.

10 Skyler Aikerson, "St. Louis's Movement-Backed Mayor Promised to Close an Infamous Jail. What's the Hold Up?" *In These Times,* March 16, 2022.

11 Joe Schoffstall, "Cori Bush's Campaign Paid Her Husband for Security Services—But He Doesn't Have a Private Security License," *Fox News,* February 28,

NOTES

2023; Haris Alic, "Rep. Cori Bush Accused of Ethics Violations after Paying New Husband $62K for Security," *Washington Times*, March 3, 2023.

12 Maria Altman, "Urban League Starts Jobs Program in North St. Louis County," St. Louis Public Radio, NPR, January 13, 2015, www.stlpr.org/economy -business/2015-01-13/urban-league-starts-jobs-program-in-north-st-louis-county.

13 Rebecca Rivas, "Ferguson Community Empowerment Center Opens," *St. Louis American*, July 26, 2017; Pepper Baker, "Urban League to Develop 3 Properties on West Florissant Avenue," 5 On Your Side, KSDK News, January 30, 2022, www.ksdk.com/article/news/local/urban-league-develop-three-properties -west-florissant-avenue/63-6b0f991c-7f29-46c3-9510-4cc968f34707.

14 "The State of Police Reform: What Has and Hasn't Changed in St. Louis Policing?" Forward through Ferguson, forwardthroughferguson.org /stateofpolicereform.

15 "Donald McCullin, Beloved Judge: April 14, 1941–October 6, 2016," *St. Louis American*, October 11, 2016; Jennifer S. Mann and Jeremy Kohler, "Municipal Courts: A Progress Report on Reforms," *St. Louis Post-Dispatch*, June 20, 2015.

16 Elisa Crouch, "U.S. Education Chief Visits to Talk with Local Students about Ferguson," *St. Louis Post-Dispatch*, December 16, 2014.

17 Denise Hollinshed, "Ferguson Protester Who Set Fire at Berkeley Quik-Trip Sentenced to 8 Years in Prison," *St. Louis Post-Dispatch*, December 10, 2015; "Video Shows Moments Before Police Shooting Near Ferguson, Missouri," *ABC News*, December 24, 2014.

18 Jeff Ordower and Tory Russell, "Lessons from the Ferguson Uprisings," *The Forge: Organizing Strategy and Practice*, July 20, 2020, forgeorganizing.org/article /lessons-ferguson-uprisings.

19 Damon Latchinson, interview by author and Alisha Sonnier, St. Louis, August 7, 2023.

20 Templeton interview.

21 Ibid.

22 See Derecka Purnell, *Becoming Abolitionists: Police, Protests, and the Pursuit of Freedom* (New York: Astra House, 2021), 3–4.

23 Monica Anderson, "The Hashtag #BlackLivesMatter Emerges: Social Activism on Twitter," Pew Research Center, August 15, 2016; Joshua Paul, " 'Not Black and White, but Black and Red': Anti-identity Identity Politics and #AllLivesMatter," *Ethnicities* 19, no. 1 (2019): 3–19.

NOTES

267

24 Student Leaders of SLU to Fred Pestello, Ph.D., President of Saint Louis University, July 23, 2020, https://medium.com/@betterslu/former-current-slu-student-leaders-we-demand-the-university-do-better-for-black-students-and-aad4320d68b2.

25 Joshua Jones, interview by author and Alisha Sonnier, St. Louis, Missouri, August 9, 2023.

26 "Deaths of Six Men Tied to Ferguson Protests Alarm Activists," *NBC News,* March 17, 2019.

27 Lamont Lilly, "Ferguson Activist Ashley Yates Talks Oakland, Assata Shakur and Black Woman Leadership," Workers World, July 2017, www.workers.org/2017/07/32308; John Eligon, "They Push. They Protest. And Many Activists, Privately, Suffer as a Result," *New York Times,* March 26, 2018.

28 Bene' Viera, "How Activist (and ESSENCE Cover Star) Johnetta 'Netta' Elzie Speaks Her Truth and What It's Like Fighting for Yours," *Essence,* October 27, 2020.

29 DeRay McKesson, interview by author, Zoom meeting, December 6, 2023.

30 "Brittany Packnett Cunningham," *Finding Your Roots,* PBS.

31 " 'I Want To Raise a Free Black Child': Brittany Packnett Cunningham and Reginald Cunningham On Parenthood," Undistracted with Brittany Packnett Cunningham, Apple Podcasts, podcasts.apple.com/ca/podcast/i-want-to-raise-a-free-black-child-brittany/id1534591370?i=1000557582935.

32 Leslie D. Rose, "Tef Poe: 'That Makes Me the Only Emcee in the World with This Combination of Academic Accolades,' " *Medium,* July 9, 2021.

33 "The Importance of Tragedy," Oxbridge Applications, oxbridgeapplications.com/blog/the-importance-of-tragedy.

34 Joshua Lamar Williams, "Cries of the Lost: Ferguson Political Prisoner Speaks," *San Francisco Bay View,* May 14, 2022, https://sfbayview.com/2022/05/cries-of-the-lost-ferguson-political-prisoner-speaks.

35 Joshua Williams to Stefan Bradley, email, December 27, 2023.

CONCLUSION: America, You're Welcome

1 Ferguson Voices: A Moral Courage Project, "Tory Russell, Organizer," www.fergusonvoices.org/voices/tory-russell.

2 Liz Crampton, "States Passed 243 Policing Bills—and Left Activists Wanting," *Politico,* May 26, 2021.

3 Treva B. Lindsey, *America, Goddam: Violence, Black Women, and the Struggle for Justice* (Berkeley: University of California Press, 2022), 38.

4 Jesse Zanger, "Pro-Palestinian Demonstrators Block Traffic on Van Wyck Expressway Near JFK Airport," *CBS News,* December 27, 2023; Nathan Solis, "Protesters Calling for Cease-fire in Gaza Arrested after Briefly Blocking Traffic Near LAX," *Los Angeles Times,* December 27, 2023.

INDEX

abolitionism, police, 223–24

Action St. Louis, 221

African American Studies program, SLU, 75, 80–81, 172, 173, 182, 227

Agnew, Phil, 98–99, 109, 233

Ahlbrand, Kevin, 196

Aldridge, Rasheen, Jr., 7

  distribution of funds raised, 136, 139, 141–42

  Ferguson Commission, 196

  on non-indictment announcement, 200

  queer activists, 119

  after the Uprising, 8, 209–10

  White House visits, 155

Alinsky, Saul, 137

All In with Chris Hayes, 59–60, 108, 202–3

Allen, Aleidra, 81

Alpha Phi Alpha Fraternity, 100, 226

alumni, Black, 192

American Civil Liberties Union, 111

American Israel Public Affairs Committee (AIPAC), 207, 214

Amnesty International, 99

Arch-City Defenders, 84–85

arrests

  Black rebellion history, 21–22

  legal and bail services, 84–85

  perception of, 62–63, 93, 115

  racial capitalism, 16–18

  as West's mission, 166

Association of Black Psychologists (ABPsi), 90, 92, 93

Association of Community Organizations for Reform Now (ACORN), 137

attorney activists, 84–86, 230

August, significance of, 20–21

bail relief, 62, 84, 85

Banks, Kira Hudson, 81, 90, 229

Banner, David, 101

Baruti, Haki, 72

Behavioral Health Response, 91–92

Bell, Wesley, 207–8, 210, 247

Belmar, Jon, 32–33

Better Family Life (BFL), 89, 90

Black alumni, 192

Black armament, 222–23

Black clergy, 95–100

Black elders

  at Chaifetz Arena event, 166–68

  frustrations with, 49–52

INDEX

Black elders (*cont.*)
  Seals's critique of, 119–20
  at the *St. Louis American* meeting,
    57–58
  support of, 43–49, 72
  See also Black clergy
Black Entertainment Television
  (BET), 243–44
Black Freedom Movement activists,
  85, 99, 140. *See also* civil rights
  movement
Black Justice League, 104, 193–94
Black Lives Matter (BLM), 6, 113,
  118–19, 120–25
Black middle class, 11–12
Black Panther Party, 22
Black Power Movement, 167
Black professionals, 89–95
Black protest cycles, 225
Black rebellion, significance of August
  in, 20–21
Black Student Alliance (BSA),
  182
Black youth, media's representation of,
  103–11
Blackmon, Traci, 61, 96, 97, 166, 167,
  196
Blocker, Danielle, 87, 96, 138, 144,
  145, 221
Boeing, 93–94, 217
Books and Breakfast program,
  220
Bosley, Freeman, Jr., 101
Boyd, Jeffrey, 210
Boyd, L. Jared, 59
Brooks, Cornell William, 166

Brown, Michael
  delay in covering body of, 22–23,
    32–33, 54
  escalation of encounter with
    Wilson, 19
  funeral of, 100–102
  image of body of, on social media,
    23–24
  news media's representation of,
    107–8
  as Normandy High School student,
    12–13
Brown, Michael, Sr., *242,* 242–43
Buck, LaTanya, 44, 45, 60, 81
Bush, Cori
  activists' support of, 210
  Bell's defeat of, 207
  conservative media's coverage of, 214
  on Ferguson Uprising, 13, 45–46
  loss of, to Bell, 246–47
  and the need for mental health
    services, 89–90, 91
  Sonnier's campaigning for, 209
Butler, Jonathan, 96–97, 190–92
Butler, Mark, 58
Butler, Michael, 8, 58, 64, 210

Campaign Zero initiative, 156–57
Canfield Green
  initial protests, 25–26, 30, 68
  police blockades, 32
  police military tactics, 36–38
  rappers at, 143
  residents, 23, 48, 89–92
Carr, T.R., 196
Carroll, David, 216

INDEX

Carroll, Reena Hajat, 59, 94, 216
Centene corporation, 216
Chaifetz Arena event, 165–67
Chappell-Nadal, Maria, 72–73
Chicago Defender, 106–7, 111
children's mental health, 91–92
Christ the King Church, 97, 98
civil rights, police infringement of,
110–11
civil rights movement, 20–21, 167. *See
also* Black elders; Black Freedom
Movement activists
civilian oversight boards, 58, 217
class divisions, 87, 88, 180
Clay, Lacy, 218
Clayton, Missouri, 30, 85, 199, 202
clergy, 95–100. *See also* specific
ministers
Cleveland "Black Lives Matter
National Convening," 122–24
Clock Tower Accords, 185, 227–28
CNN, 37, 105–6, 152–54
Cobb, Jelani, 98
Cole, J., 143, 152
college faculty, 80–81, 173
college students. *See* student activists
Collins-Muhammad, John, 210
Columbia (Missouri) police, 189–90
Combahee River Collective, 68
community mental health services,
90–91
Concerned Student 1950
(#ConcernedStudent1950),
189–92
Congress of Racial Equality, 167
consent decree, 207

conservative media, 51, 107, 137, 141,
214
Cooksey, Charli
at initial protest, 24
on leadership styles, 128–29, 131
McCaskill's meeting with, 64, 65
night of non-indictment
announcement, 202, 203–4
on North County, 11, 12
St. Louis American meeting, 55, 58
after the Uprising, 215
corporate philanthropy, 93–94, 217
counseling. *See* mental health issues
Crawford, Edward, 145–46, 228
Crestwood, Missouri, 15
Crockett, Destiny, 104, 192–93,
226
Crump, Benjamin, 101, 107–8
Cullors, Patrisse, 121–22, 124
Cunningham, Reggie, 233
#cutthecheck campaign, 139–42

Daniels, Cathy "Mama Cat," 43–44,
143, 147
Deaconess Foundation, 138–39
"Defund the Police" campaign, 223,
224
Democratic Party, 224–25
Department of Public Safety (DPS),
170
Diversity Awareness Partnership
(DAP), 94
diversity of protesters, 60–61
dogs, police use of, 35–36
donations. *See* funds, raising and
distribution of

272   INDEX

driving while Black. *See* racial
    capitalism
Duncan, Arne, 218–19

economic and financial issues
    class divisions, 87, 88, 180
    cost of police violence, 244
    racial capitalism, 16–18, 217–18
    raising and distributing funds,
        136–42
education, meetings on, 218–19
Elzie, Johnetta "Netta," 50
    Campaign Zero initiative, 156
    meeting with NAACP leaders,
        49–50
    narrative leadership, 129–30
    on news media coverage, 105,
        106
    on police response, 36, 37
    Reform and Empowerment
        newsletter, 197
    Saint Louis University occupation,
        171, 172
    social media posts, 23, 109
    after the Uprising, 231–32
    White House visits, 155
Emerson corporation, 196, 216
Equal Justice Initiative, 221
Ervin, Storm, 74, 147, 187–92,
    226

Facebook. *See* social media
faculty, college, 80–81, 173
faith leaders, 95–100
Falconer, Jameca, 90
family issues, 78, 83–84

Fenderson, Jonathan, 81, 221, 230
Ferguson, Missouri
    Black middle class of, 11–12
    Black residents' relationship with
        police in, 13–18, 62
    Blacks' lack of political power in, 49
    victories in, 217–18
    See also Canfield Green
Ferguson, Rodney, 98
Ferguson City Council, 207
Ferguson Civilian Review Board, 217
Ferguson Commission, 155, 195–97,
    212, 217
Ferguson Community Empowerment
    Center, 215–16
Ferguson Market video, 2–4, 19
"Ferguson October," 162–64, 165,
    169–85
Ferguson Police Department
    apology regarding, 33–34
    changes in chiefs, 217
    consent decree, 207
    as "gang," 28
    initial protests at, 24, 30–32, 71
    military tactics, 35–38
    press conferences, 2–4
    relationship with Black residents,
        13–18, 62
"Ferguson town hall" event, 100
Ferrell, Brittany, 77
    activism, 77–78
    bail relief services, 85
    Cooksey on, 131
    founding of Millennial Activists
        United, 68
    queer activism, 118, 119

INDEX

romantic relationship with
Templeton, 148–49
Saint Louis University occupation,
171
after the Uprising, 229–30
Fight for $15, 209
financial issues. *See* economic and
financial issues
fines and fees, traffic, 16–18, 217–18
firearms, 222–23
Flanery, Jason, 30, 160, 168
Forward through Ferguson. *See*
Ferguson Commission
Fox News, 19, 39, 106, 107–8, 214
Francis, Leah Gunning, 98
Francis, Rodney, 96
Franks, Bruce, Jr., 209, 237
free speech rights, 110–11
French, Antonio, 72, 210
Friendly Temple Missionary Baptist
Church, 98, 100–101
Frye, Marquette, 21
funds, raising and distribution of,
136–42

Gage, Mama Lisa, 12–13
Gagne, Bob, 185
Galleria Mall event, 116, 117
Gammon, Ashley, 91
gang members at initial protests, 27–28
Gardner, Kim, 210–12, 213
Garner, Erica, 231
Garvey, Marcus, 20
Gbadagesin, Bukky, 81, 140, 173
Givens, Henry, 95
Gore, Gabriel, 196

Gray, Anthony, 101
Gray, Ashley, 81
Greater St. Mark's Family Church,
98–99, 218–19
Green, Percy, 9
Greitens, Eric, 211
Grills, Cheryl, 92
Grove demonstration, 168
guns and gun laws, 222–23

Hampton, Fred, 20, 28–29
Hands Up United, 40, 68, 132, 154,
230
Hansford, Justin
arrest of, 122
on Bell, 208
on Black Lives Matter, 124
effects of street action experience, 82
on Johnson's arrival, 109–10
as legal observer, 85–86, 111
McCaskill's meeting with, 64, 65
meeting with White, 176
at the *St. Louis American* meeting,
58
at United Nations Committee
against Torture meeting, 154–55
after the Uprising, 230
Harlem uprising, 20
Harris-Stowe State University, 47, 95,
173, 216
Harvard University Black Law Student
Association, 159–60
Harvey, Thomas, 84–85
Hayes, Chris, 59–60, 108, 110, 202–3
Hendrix, Kris, 84–85
Henry, Ron, 37

274 INDEX

high school student activists, 79–80

Hill, Marc Lamont, 95

Holder, Eric, 5, 39–40, 159–60, 184

homecoming parade demonstration, 189–90

housing issues, 60

Howard University, 159

Hubbard, Penny, 209

hunger strike, 97, 191–92

Hunter, Amy, 44–45

Hutchinson, Earl Ofari, 107

incarceration. *See* arrests

initial protests
  at Canfield Green, 25–26, 30, 68
  challenges for young organizers at, 71–73
  diversity of protesters, 60–61
  at Ferguson Police Department, 24, 30, 31
  gang members at, 27–28
  and the need for "grown-man energy," 62–63
  police military tactics, 36–38
  tenor of, 61–62

Instagram. *See* social media

inter-organizational relations, 70, 113–25

interpersonal relationships, 147, 148–50

intersectional identities, 128

Isom, Dan, 196

Jackson, George, 21–22

Jackson, Jesse, 51–52, 96–97, 101

Jackson, Jonathan, 21–22

Jackson, Kareem. *See* Poe, Tef (Kareem Jackson)

Jackson, Tom, 2–4, 33–34

jailing of protestors. *See* arrests

James-Hatter, Becky, 196

job skills development and jobs placement initiative, 215

Johns, Barbara, 55

Johnson, Amber, 81

Johnson, Dorian, 19, 101

Johnson, Ron, 109–10, 111, 225

Johnson, Willis, 25, 90, 99

Jones, Danye, 228

Jones, Joshua, 11–12, 59–60, 100–101, 175, 199, 228

Jones, Michael F., Sr., 96, 98, 100, 101–2

Jones, Mike, 48–49, 51, 60

Jones, Tishaura
  on Black elders, 51
  McCaskill's meeting with, 64
  mothers as protectors, 44, 45
  at *St. Louis American* meeting, 58
  after the Uprising, 209, 210, 212–14

Jones, Van, 152–53

Jones, Virvus, 58, 212, 214

Joshua, Deandre, 228

joy and fun, 143–46

Khiyyam, Jihad, 89–90

King, Chris, 103, 105

King, Martin Luther, Jr., 21, 85, 167

Kinnie, Clifton, 12, 26, 79–80, *80*, 226

Knowles, James, 37

Krauss, Evan, 58

INDEX

275

Kwame Building Group, 46, 47

Kweli, Talib, 143, 152–53

Laird, Chryl, 81, 173

Lamkin, Renita, 99

Latchinson, Damon

    on Black Lives Matter, 120, 122–24

    on family's reaction to Brown
        killing, 43

    intersectional identities, 128

    on leaders' media appearances, 117–18

    queer activists, 119

    role in movement, 131

    Saint Louis University occupation,
        171, 176

    after the Uprising, 221–22

Lawyers Guild legal observers, 86

leadership, 6, 119, 127–33, 246. *See
also* specific leaders

Lee, Trymaine, 25

legal observers, 86, 111

legal services, 84–86, 230

Lemon, Don, 105–6, 152–54

lessons learned, 241–48

Lewis, John, 21, *156*

Lindsey, Treva, 244

local versus outsider activists, 113–25

Los Angeles rebellion, 21

Lost Voices, 30, 117, 132, 139

lumpen proletariat, 42–43, 88

Lutheran North High School, 11, 12, 79

Malcolm X, 20

"Mama Cat," 43–44, 143, 147

Mangrove demonstration, 168

Martin, Antonio, 219

Masri, Bassem, 228

Mays, Jennifer, 91

McCarrel, MarShawn, 228

McCaskill, Claire, 63–65

McClure, Rich, 195–96

McCullins, Donald, 217–18

McCulloch, Robert, 30, 64–65,
    144–45, 164. *See also* non-
    indictment of Wilson

McCune, Jeffrey, 81

McKesson, DeRay, *50*

    on Brown, in interview, 243

    Campaign Zero initiative, 156–57

    at Ferrell-Templeton betrothal, 148

    leadership style, 129–31

    media attention, 115–19

    Reform and Empowerment
        newsletter, 197

    relationships with fellow activists,
        146–47

    Saint Louis University occupation,
        178, 184

    social media use, 109

    on trust in leaders, 185

    after the Uprising, 218–19, 232

    White House visits, 155

McKinnies, Melissa, 228

McMillan, Michael, 90, 101, 215, 216

McSpadden, Lezley, *242*

    comparison of Till's mother to, 102

    on reception in Switzerland, 154

    Sharpton's interactions with, 120

    treatment of, by police, 33

    after the Uprising, 232, 242–43

    Williams on reaction of, 25

medical assistance, 98

mental health issues, 90–92, 228

mentoring, 60, 68, 72, 80–81, 213–14

Metro St. Louis Coalition for Inclusion and Equity (M-SLICE), 178

militarization of police, 21, 35–40, 197

Millennial Activists United (MAU), 68–69, 77, 132, 139, 231

ministers, 95–100

mirrored casket, 164–65

misogyny, 127, 133–34

Missouri History Museum, 100

Missourians Organizing for Reform and Empowerment (MORE), 136, 137–40, 230

Mizzou. *See* University of Missouri—Columbia

mock trials, 144, 243–44

MoKaBe's coffeehouse, 146

Montgomery Bus Boycott, 63

Morial, Marc, 106–7, 216

"mothers" as protectors, 43–45

MU for Mike Brown, 187–89

Muhammad, John, 8, 210

Murch, Donna, 101

Myers, VonDerrit, Jr., 30, 160–61, 168

Myers, VonDerrit, Sr., 161, 171

NAACP, 49–51, 166, 167, 190

narrative leadership, 6, 129–31

Nash, Sarah, 73–74

National Guard mobilization, 21, 39, 177, 197

National Urban League, 167

Negwer, Scott, 196

New York Amsterdam News, 38

news media

attention to certain activists, 117–18

conservative media, 51, 107, 137, 141, 214

convenience store footage of Brown, 19

early coverage by, 37

on funding conflicts, 141

Kweli interview, 152–53

on police tactics, 39

representation of Black youth in, 103–11

See also specific news outlets

Newsome, Bree, *201*

Nichols, De, 164–65

Nixon, Jay, 109, 195, 196–97, 211, 225

non-indictment of Wilson, 195, 198–205, 207–8

non-resident police in Ferguson, 14–15

nonprofit organizations. *See* specific organizations

Normandy High School, 12–13

North County

Black middle class of, 11–12

businesses, 13

faith institutions, 98

post-Uprising changes in, 217, 218

"Save Our Sons" program, 215

Obama, Barack, 38, 39, 40, 155, *156,* 233

O'Keefe, James, 137

Olson, Walter, 39

op-ed pieces, 38, 41, 59, 107, 140

operational leadership, 129, 131

INDEX

277

Ordower, Jeff, 137–38, 139–40, 141

Organization for Black Struggle
(OBS), 68, 136, 137–40, 154, 230

organizing
churches as spaces for, 97–98
family issues, 83–84
for political capital, 208–9
protesting as distinct from, 82–83
Russell on, 71, 86, 220
tension between activism and,
86–88

Our Destiny STL, 79–80

outcomes of Ferguson Uprising, 6, 225,
243–44

Packnett Cunningham, Brittany,
156
Campaign Zero initiative, 156–57
Ferguson Commission, 196
at initial protests, 24
McCaskill's meeting with, 64
McKesson's association with, 116
meeting with Holder, 40
meeting with Obama, 155–56
mentorship by, 104
narrative leadership, 129–30
Purnell's association with, 32
social media use, 109
at the *St. Louis American* meeting,
58
after the Uprising, 218–19, 232–33

performative activism, 114–15

Perry, Ivory, 9

Pestello, Fred, 144, 174–79, 183–85,
227

Pierson, Tommie, Sr., 96, 98, 99

Poe, Tef (Kareem Jackson), *163*
arrest of, 122
at Chaifetz Arena event, 166–67
and challenges of initial protests,
72–73
on the Ferguson Commission, 197
at Ferguson October event, 164
founding of Hands Up United, 68
on need for "grown-man energy," 63
operational leadership, 131
on police response, 36, 37–38
Rogers's advice for, 23–24
social media posts, 84
at United Nations Committee
against Torture meeting, 154
after the Uprising, 233–34
on the Uprising, 243
at Young Citizens Council meeting,
62

police
abolitionism, 223–24
free speech compromises requested
by, 110–11
as a gang, 28
militarization, 21, 35–40, 197
reform policies, 244–45
See also specific police departments

politics and policies
Black leadership and, 49
Equal Justice Initiative, 221
lessons learned, 246–47
political aspirations of activists,
207–14
post-Ferguson Uprising, 6–8,
224–25, 244–45
See also specific politicians

Porterfield, Kent, 174, 181

Powell, Kajieme, 160

Powell, Kevin, 100

press conferences of August 15, 2014, 2–4

Price, Wiley, III, 105

Princeton University, 104, 192–94

professionals, young, 24, 59, 89–95

Progressive politics, post-Ferguson, 213, 214, 221, 224–25

protests, initial. *See* initial protests

public policy. *See* politics and policies

Pulliam, Felicia, 196

Pulphus, Jonathan
   All In with Chris Hayes appearance, 108
   disruption of McCulloch lecture, 145
   as early Tribe X member, 31
   on funding conflicts, 139, 142
   on joy and fun, 143, 145
   on leadership styles, 129
   on McKesson, 116
   on Ordower, 138
   pepper spraying of, 56–57
   relationship with Sonnier, 149–50
   relationships with fellow activists, 146–47
   Saint Louis University occupation, 170–71, 172, 174, 177, 179, 180–81
   as student and activist, 74–75
   tear gas exposure, 76–77
   Umana's association with, 47, 48
   after the Uprising, 228–29

Purnell, Derecka, 32, 59, 164, 223, 230

queer activists, 42, 69–70, 118–19, 121, 127–28, 133

QuikTrip, 35, 38, 59, 168–69, 216, 219

racial capitalism, 14, 16–18, 217–18

rappers, 150–53. *See also* individual artists

Red's Ribz, 13

Reeb, James, 99

Reed, Kayla, *123*
   at "Black Lives Matter National Convening," 122–23
   on non-indictment announcement, 200
   as operational leader, 131
   political support for Jones, 212
   queer activists, 119
   Saint Louis University occupation, 171–72
   support of Bell, 207–8
   after the Uprising, 221

Reed, Lewis, 210

Reform and Empowerment newsletter, 197

Republican Party, 224–25

Revolutionary Action Movement, 28, 167

Riggs-Bookman, Rueben, 221

Rivas, Rebecca, 105, 148

Roberts, Cassandra, 57

Robinson, Derrick "D-Rob," 13

Robinson, Marva, 90, 91, 92–93

Rodgers, H.J.
   on encounters with police, 15–16
   at initial protests, 30–32
   on Interstate 44 shutdown, 143

INDEX

on organizing, 69–70

Saint Louis University occupation, 169, 170, 171, 178–79, 180–81

after the Uprising, 219–20, 227

Roediger, Brendan, 85–86

Rogers, Jamala

on distribution of funds, 138, 139, 140–41

leadership of, 9

mentoring by, 68, 72

Poe's contacting of, 23–24

on racial capitalism, 17–18

after the Uprising, 214–15

romantic relationships, 148–50

ROTC students, 176

Russell, Tory

arrest of, 84

on the Ferguson Uprising, 241

founding of Hands Up United, 68

on his experience as an organizer, 86, 87

mentors and, 72

organizing by, 71

on politics, 52

on protesting/organizing distinction, 82–83

support of Muhammad, 210

Templeton and, 135

after the Uprising, 220

Rustin, Bayard, 63, 85

Saint Louis University

Chaifetz Arena event, 165–67

mentorship by faculty and staff, 80–81

mock trial held at, 144

occupation of, 168–85

student-activists, 74–78

students' connection to Myers, 161

Tribe X's request for McBooks, 148

after the Uprising, 227–28

Sanders, Bernie, 209

"Save Our Sons" initiative, 215, 216

schools, counseling in, 91–92

Seals, Darren, *201*

on bond among protesters, 81–82

critique of older civil rights leaders, 119–20

death of, 228

at initial protests, 26–27, 28

on Jackson, 52

and the lumpen proletariat, 42–43, 88

on McKesson, 116–17, 118–19

on night of non-indictment announcement, 201

as operational leader, 131

Sekou, Osagyefo, 99, *201*

Shahid, Anthony, 72, 90

Shakur, Assata, 77

Shakur, Dhoruba, 147, 170, 171, 173, 179

Sharpton, Al, 51, 101, 120

Shaw neighborhood, 161–62, 165, 168

Shelby v. Holder, 225

Simmons, Montague, 68, 162–63

Sinyangwe, Samuel, 156

Sly, Patrick, 196

Smith, Anthony Lamar, 211

Smith, Jonathan, 81, 173, 183, 227

280 INDEX

social media
    activists' use of, 6, 84, 109
    image of Brown's body on, 23–24
    McKesson's use of, 117
    narrative leadership through, 6,
        130–31
    performative activism, 114
    Saint Louis University occupation,
        174, 183–84
Sonnier, Alisha
    All In with Chris Hayes appearance,
        108–9
    and Black lives matter/Black Lives
        Matter, 120, 122, 123, 124
    disruption of McCulloch lecture,
        145
    as early Tribe X member, 31
    on heteronormative ideas of
        leadership, 119, 133–34
    at initial protests, 56, 57
    political support for Jones, 212
    relationship with Pulphus,
        149–50
    Saint Louis University occupation,
        170, 171, 174, 177, 179, 180–81
    as student-activist, 74–75
    on Templeton, 42
    Umana's association with, 47, 48
    after the Uprising, 8, 208–9, 229
    on the Uprising, 245–46
Spann, Jamell, 148–49
speeding tickets. *See* traffic fines and
    fees
St. John's United Church of Christ
    (the Beloved Community),
    97

St. Louis American
    Buck's poem in, 45
    coverage of the Uprising by, 103–5,
        111
    Jones's critique of black elders in, 49
    meeting at, 57–59
    preparation for non-indictment
        announcement, 197
    Rogers's op-ed in, 140
St. Louis area
    faith institutions, 98
    "Ferguson October," 162
    politics, 221, 243
St. Louis County Children's Service
    Fund, 92
St. Louis Metropolitan Police, 146,
    160
St. Louis Students in Solidarity, 144
Stockley, Jason, 211
student-activists
    high school students, 79–80
    Princeton University, 192–94
    Saint Louis University, 74–77,
        80–81
    St. Louis American's coverage of,
        104
    University of Missouri—Columbia,
        74, 187–92
    University of Missouri—St. Louis,
        77–78
    after the Uprising, 221–22,
        226–30
    Washington University, 81
    See also specific activists
Student Non-Violent Coordinating
    Committee (SNCC), 140, 167

INDEX

Suggs, Donald M., 58, 100, 101, 103–4

Sweetie Pie's restaurant, 13

T-Dubb-O, 40, 196–97

Tait, Graham, 175

Taskforce on 21st Century Policing, 155, 233

Teach for America program, 104, 115–16

Templeton, Alex, 77
  on arrest and authenticity, 115
  on Bell, 208
  on Black lives matter/Black Lives Matter, 120, 121, 122
  founding of Millennial Activists United, 68
  on funding conflicts, 142
  on hope for Wilson's indictment, 199
  leadership, 41–42, 131, 132–33, 134–36
  and the lumpen proletariat, 88
  on non-indictment announcement, 200
  queer activism, 119
  relationships with fellow activists, 146–47
  romantic relationship with Ferrell, 118, 148–49
  after the Uprising, 222–23, 224

1033 Program, Department of Defense, 38

Thompson, Tony, 46–47

Thompson-Moore, Katrina, 81, 173

Till, Emmett, 20–21, 102

Till, Mamie, 20–21

Tillman, Mark, 100

Tobias, Grayling, 196

traffic fines and fees, 14, 16–18, 217–18

Tribe X
  die-in held by, 116
  leadership style of, 132
  mock trial held by, 144
  operating procedures, 69–71
  relationships among activists, 147
  Rodgers on, 31–32
  Saint Louis University occupation, 169–73, 177–85
  shut down of Interstate 44, 143

Trump, Donald, 224

Turner, Nat, 20, 35–36

2020 protests, 227, 244, 245

Twitter. See social media

Tyler, Rika, 197

Umana, Etefia, 47–48, 57

United Nations Committee against Torture, 154

United Way of Greater St. Louis, 91–92, 94

University of Missouri—Columbia, 74, 187–92

University of Missouri—St. Louis, 77–78, 229

Urban League of St. Louis, 90, 101, 215–16

U.S. Department of Defense 1033 Program, 38

U.S. Department of Justice, 16–17

282 INDEX

Van Niel, Kira, 58, 93–94, 216–17
Vaughn, Kenya, 105
Vega, Elizabeth, 147, 162, 164
video of Brown at the Ferguson
    Market, 2–4, 19
Voting Rights Act of 1965, 225

Wade, Charles, 147
Walker, Cora Faith, 209, 210
Walter, Christopher, 56–57, 75–77,
    177, 181, 182, 229
Wanzo, Rebecca, 81
Warmack, Dwaun, 47, 94–95, 97,
    216
Washington Metropolitan African
    Methodist Episcopal Zion
    Church, 98
Washington Tabernacle Missionary
    Baptist Church, 53–54, 98
Washington Times, 214
Washington University, 81, 221–22,
    230
Watson, Byron M., 196
Watts neighborhood, Los Angeles,
    21
We Power, 215
Webb-Bradley, Traice, 90–91
Weingarten, Randi, 218–19
Wellspring Church, 98, 99, 201–2
West, Cornel, 166, 171, 178, *201,*
    234
White, Norm, 166, 174, 176, 177,
    183
White House visits, 155–56
Wilkins, Roy, 167
Williams, Eugene, 20

Williams, Jana, 192
Williams, Josh, *238*
    incarceration, 119, 219
    at initial protests, 24–26, 27
    leadership, 29–30
    lessons learned, 40–41
    on non-indictment, 199–200
    on performative activism, 114–15
    Saint Louis University occupation,
        171, 178
    after the Uprising, 82, 234–39
Williams, Robert L., 90, 92
Williams, Romona, 178, 182
Wilson, Darren
    account of encounter with Brown,
        19
    McCaskill's doubts about
        indictment of, 64–65
    naming of, in initial press
        conferences, 2–3
    non-indictment of, 195, 198–205,
        207–8
    as non-resident of Ferguson, 15
    after the Uprising, 242
Wilson, Starsky, 96, 97–98, 138–39,
    166, 195
Wilson, Woodrow, 193
Windmiller, Rose, 196
Witherspoon, Anthony, 98
Wolff, Michael, 144
women leaders, experiences of, 68, 127,
    133–34. *See also* specific women
Woody-Cooper, Jameca, 201, 202
Woolfolk, Trevor, 75–77, 108, 171,
    180, 181, 226
Workhouse closure, 213

INDEX

Yates, Ashley, *77, 163*
  "Assata Taught Me" T-shirts, 243
  to Black elders, 167
  on the commitment of leaders,
    78–79
  founding of Millennial Activists
    United, 68
  on gang metaphor for police, 28
  on motivation, 52
  on reaction of Black elders, 43

  Saint Louis University occupation,
    171, 178
  on social media use, 23
  after the Uprising, 231
Young, Whitney, 167
Young Citizens Council, 59, 62,
    64–65, 93, 95
young professionals, 89–95

Zasaretti, Loletta, 178, 182

ABOUT THE AUTHOR

Stefan M. Bradley is the Charles Hamilton Houston '15 Professor of Black Studies and History at Amherst College. He has appeared on C-SPAN Book TV, NPR, PRI, as well as in documentaries on the Oprah Winfrey Network and the History Channel. The author of several prizewinning books, including *Upending the Ivory Tower* and *Harlem vs. Columbia University* as well as *If We Don't Get It: A People's History of Ferguson* (The New Press), he lives in Amherst, Massachusetts.

PUBLISHING IN THE PUBLIC INTEREST

Thank you for reading this book published by The New Press; we hope you enjoyed it. New Press books and authors play a crucial role in sparking conversations about the key political and social issues of our day.

We hope that you will stay in touch with us. Here are a few ways to keep up to date with our books, events, and the issues we cover:

- Sign up at www.thenewpress.com/subscribe to receive updates on New Press authors and issues and to be notified about local events
- www.facebook.com/newpressbooks
- www.x.com/thenewpress
- www.instagram.com/thenewpress

Please consider buying New Press books not only for yourself, but also for friends and family and to donate to schools, libraries, community centers, prison libraries, and other organizations involved with the issues our authors write about.

The New Press is a 501(c)(3) nonprofit organization; if you wish to support our work with a tax-deductible gift please visit www.thenewpress.com/donate or use the QR code below.